The Assistant Principal

Essentials for Effective School Leadership

L. David Weller   Sylvia J. Weller

CORWIN PRESS, INC.
A Sage Publications Company
Thousand Oaks, California

For information:

Corwin Press, Inc.
A Sage Publications Company
2455 Teller Road
Thousand Oaks, California 91320
E-mail: order@corwinpress.com

Sage Publications Ltd.
6 Bonhill Street
London EC2A 4PU
United Kingdom

Sage Publications India Pvt. Ltd.
M-32 Market
Greater Kailash I
New Delhi 110 048 India

Printed in the United States of America

Library of Congress Cataloging-in-Publication Data

Weller, L. David.
   The assistant principal: Essentials for effective school leadership
/ by L. David Weller and Sylvia J. Weller.
      p. cm.
   Includes bibliographical references and index.
   ISBN 0-7619-7793-7 (c) — ISBN 0-7619-7794-5 (p)
   1. Assistant school principals—United States. 2. School management
and organization—United States. 3. Educational leadership—United
States.   I. Weller, Sylvia. II. Title.
   LB2831.92 .W46 2001
   371.2'012—dc21

                         2001002196

This book is printed on acid-free paper.

01 02 03 04 05 06 07 7 6 5 4 3 2 1

Acquiring Editor:	Robb Clouse
Associate Editor:	Kylee Liegl
Corwin Editorial Assistant:	Erin Buchanan
Production Editor:	Olivia Weber
Editorial Assistant:	Ester Marcelino
Typesetter/Designer:	Denyse Dunn
Cover Designer:	Sandra Ng
Cover Photo:	PhotoDisc™ Images © 2000 PhotoDisc, Inc.

Contents

Introduction

The role of the assistant principal is one of the *least researched* and *least discussed* topics in professional journals and books focusing on educational leadership. No universal definition of the role or clearly defined job description of the position of assistant principal exists. The role thus is open to interpretation by principals and central office personnel alike, and it often becomes one that fulfills the common contractual phrase of "performing any and all duties assigned by a superior."

The ambiguity in the role of assistant principal allows for the ineffective use of this position, which should be a vital link between the principal and teachers, parents and students, and an extension of the principalship in promoting effective, quality-oriented outcomes. In no other position does one walk such a fine line between the maintenance and survival needs of the school and the needs and demands of the students, teachers, and principal. In addition, the position of assistant principal is between that of teachers and principal, and this "between" position makes the leadership role of the assistant principal a difficult one. The effectiveness of those in this position depends on their ability to master and apply salient leadership knowledge and skills.

This book's contents and format are unique, representing several firsts in a publication and addressing the multiple needs of students, instructors, and practitioners alike. The need for the text originated with the concerns and frustrations of our students and colleagues who, as assistant principals, lacked a clear role definition and purpose for the position of assistant principal. These assistant principals also wanted guidance on developing the skills they needed to move up the leadership ladder to the principalship or other leadership positions. These concerns led us to an extensive review of the literature and, in conjunction with interviews with practicing assistant principals, formed the basis for the questionnaire we devised. This questionnaire was administered to 100 assistant principals to assess the knowledge and skills they needed for effective leadership, their actual roles and responsibilities, and their ideas about the essential components of a text that would help them perform their duties more effectively and gain the skills they need for advancement. This book thus represents the first book on assistant principals based on field-based research findings. As such, the book focuses on the actual needs of practitioners rather than the perceived needs of theorists.

This book is also a first in that it can be used as a self-contained staff development program for those preparing teachers for the role of assistant principal and for assistant principals preparing for the principalship or other leadership positions. Theory, experimental research, and field-based research are combined in one volume, complete with case studies, exercises, and examples based on real-life situations and the actual requirements of those in the assistant principalship. This unique blend makes the work practitioner-friendly and allows for the immediate application and reinforcement of newly learned content.

This text can also be used as a reference guide for practicing assistant principals. It contains the most current information on "best" leadership practices; practical examples that work, provided by practitioners in the field; and examples of surveys, evaluation instruments, and so on, designed for immediate application and easy use.

Each chapter of this book contains survey results from 100 practicing assistant principals and addresses the specific needs, concerns, and issues confronting practicing professionals. Chapter 1 focuses on the knowledge and skills essential to effective leadership, and discusses the nature of leadership, formal and informal power, the manager-versus-leader debate, and the practice of leadership through influence and persuasion. Effective leadership characteristics are presented along with the findings of effective schools research; this information provides the reader with the current research on student learning and leadership-effectiveness indicators.

The transition from manager to leader is the focus of Chapter 2. Research on the roles played by both managers and leaders is presented and related to the responsibilities of the assistant principal. Moving from manager to leader requires commitment, time, and a "personal plan" that includes core leadership competencies and self-made opportunities to practice effective leadership. The chapter also discusses the importance of conducting action research, ways to increase teachers' job satisfaction, and a model for developing the teacher-as-leader concept in the classroom and school.

Chapter 3 examines informal groups and their leaders as sources of power that compete with the formal leadership for control and resources within an organization. Tactics of informal leaders for achieving power are discussed through the topics of "power games," communication networks existing in informal groups, and the use of grapevine and rumor. Practical, proven methods are presented for dealing effectively with both the overt and covert political activities of informal groups that can undermine the achievement of the school's goals and the authority of school administrators.

Public relations and community power agents are the focus of Chapter 4. The chapter explores the nature of power, the school as a political organization within the overall political structure of the community, and the importance of having comprehensive public relations programs to foster community confidence and support for education. Central to this chapter are three research methods that can be easily applied to identify community power structures and their power agents. Models are presented to deal effectively with special interest groups that seek to impose their goals or use their power to influence decision makers to advance their own objectives or favor their own cause. This chapter concludes with practical examples on how to build community confidence in the school, techniques for handling criticism, and instruments for measuring public opinion.

Chapter 5 addresses the topic of effective communication and listening. Research on effective oral and written communication is presented in the context of building positive working relationships and developing effective leadership characteristics. Barriers to effective communication and listening are presented as well as methods to improve listening and communication skills. The chapter presents examples on how to conduct effective meetings, prepare meeting agendas, and maximize human potential in group situations.

Leadership for instructional improvement is the focus of Chapter 6. The chapter presents the characteristics of effective instructional leaders and the essential variables associated with leadership for instructional effectiveness. The significance of leadership in curriculum development is presented along with curriculum development models found in effective schools. Models are also presented for building an instructional climate, coordinating action research projects, preparing teacher-made tests with built-in validity and reliability, assessing teacher performance, supervising instruction, and remediating teacher weaknesses.

The final chapter focuses on leadership for staff development. Emphasis is placed on models that provide both a continuous and a personalized approach to staff development. Techniques are presented to identify and meet the individual and professional growth needs of teachers and to develop holistic staff development programs. Also provided are examples of assessment instruments that assistant principals can use to determine the effectiveness of staff development programs and to develop specific strategies to help teachers master newly acquired knowledge and skills.

Acknowledgments

The authors pay special recognition to Linda Taylor for her valuable assistance in manuscript preparation. Her dedication to this book is deeply appreciated. Special recognition also goes to LaNelle Davis, Linda Edwards, and Donna Bell for their valuable assistance in manuscript preparation. The authors are appreciative of the assistance and professional courtesy extended by practicing assistant principals and their candor and willingness to share freely with the authors their personal experiences in the "real world" of leadership.

The authors are grateful to the school systems of Douglas County, Madison County, and Carroll County, Georgia, and to Northeast Georgia Regional Educational Service Agency for providing examples for use in this book.

The contributions of the following reviewers are also gratefully acknowledged:

Lawrence Leonard
Proctor
University of Saskatchewan
Saskatchewan, Canada

Bill Grobe
Junior Division Teacher
Mother Teresa Catholic School
Cambridge, Ontario

Sylvia Roberts
Associate Professor
City College of New York
New York, NY

Bob Savidge
Principal
St. Joseph School
Camp Hill, PA

About the Authors

L. David Weller, Jr., earned his PhD in educational administration from Iowa State University. Currently, he is Professor in the Department of Educational Leadership at the University of Georgia. He has been a high school teacher, a middle school principal, a marketing representative for Xerox Corporation, and Department Head of Middle School Education at the University of Georgia. He serves as a consultant to public and private schools and universities in the areas of organizational development and Total Quality Management. He has been a visiting lecturer at several British universities, teaching in the areas of leadership and organizational theory.

Sylvia J. Weller earned her EdD in educational administration from the University of Georgia. Currently, she is Assistant Superintendent for Curriculum and Instruction for Barrow County Schools in Barrow County, Georgia. She has been a high school teacher of gifted and advanced placement English, assistant principal, personnel director, and director of secondary curriculum and gifted. She has won many awards for her teaching and leadership skills. She would welcome comments or questions from her readers. Her e-mail address is sweller@barrow.k12.ga.us.

*To Ginger, whose quiet and loving support
provides the motivation and strength to endure and excel*

1

Leadership Knowledge and Skills: The Essentials for Effectiveness

In This Chapter

What is leadership? The survey responses of 100 practicing assistant principals indicate that most accepted the position with only a general knowledge of leadership theory and a rudimentary understanding of the traits of effective leaders. What these assistant principals believe they lacked when they entered the ranks of administrators is an ability to apply theory to practice and to use positional authority "to get things done."

This chapter summarizes the research on effective leadership and the knowledge and skills essential to persuading and influencing subordinates to be effective in performing their tasks. Included is an exploration of the practical applications of theories of leadership and sources of power.

The Nature of Leadership

Leadership is an enigma. Researchers have studied it, philosophers have engaged in long discussions and written treatises about it, and practitioners have tried mightily to target exactly what is meant when we use the term *leadership*. These various perspectives on leadership have led us to examine variables such as the concept and use of power, traits of effective leaders, environmental and personal contingencies, leadership styles, and leadership theories and models. Yet in the 3,000+ empirical articles on the topic and the 350 definitions provided by a variety of experts (Lunenburg & Ornstein, 1996), no conclusive findings exist as to what constitutes effective leadership.

Historically, definitions of leadership focused on behaviors of leaders. For example, in Plutarch's *Parallel Lives,* written in the first century of the current era, the behaviors, conduct, and values of famous ancient Romans and Greeks were described, and during this time, their behaviors were emulated as part of leadership training (Bonner, 1977). In the 16th century, Machiavelli's *The Prince* provided Lorenzo de Medici with political prescriptions on how to be a successful leader in an Italian city-state, and in the 20th century, James MacGregor Burns's *Leadership* (1978) examined the dynamics of the leader-follower relationship in the context of conflict and power.

Traits of leaders have been studied to identify the work and personal characteristics of leaders and the skill traits associated with leader effectiveness. *Work* traits include persistence, willingness to assume responsibility, decisiveness, dependability, and tolerance of stress; *personality* traits include dominance, decisiveness, cooperation, self-confidence, and energy; and *skill* traits include intelligence, creativity, diplomacy, persuasiveness, and organizational ability.

Historical theorists, such as Thomas Carlyle, have described the "Great Man" theory of leadership, which states that leaders are born, not made. Karl Marx and Georg Hegel maintained that leaders are a product of the social and economic forces of their time. Gardner (1990), combining these views of leadership, states that both historical and environmental forces create conditions that allow leaders to emerge. Gardner's example is the charismatic Martin Luther, who emerged in the early beginnings of the social and political upheaval of the Reformation, and whose 95 theses nailed to a church door made him a historical force.

In this historical and research-based context, definitions of leadership abound. However varied these definitions may be, what is clear and undisputed is that leaders have *loyal* and *committed* followers and that leaders do not exist in isolation. Leaders, as we argue elsewhere (Weller & Weller, 2000), are products of their times, their environments, their offices, their followers, their values, their personality traits, and their conceptualizations of leadership. Leaders are *prime movers* who allow others to achieve common goals and who unite others for a common purpose. They command yet they serve their followers. They allow their followers choices but provide direction on how ends should be achieved.

What is it then that these definitions and insights can provide the assistant principal? First, they suggest that one definition of leadership is as valid as another. There is no right or wrong answer to the question, "What is leadership?" Second, these definitions reflect fads, wishes, academic trends, political influences, and reality as known to those who have attempted to define the term. Third, existing definitions "provide a sliver of insight with each remaining an incomplete and wholly inadequate explanation" (Bennis & Nanus, 1985, p. 4) of the phenomenon called leadership.

On Leaders and Leadership

Every man of action has a strong dose of egotism, pride, hardness, and cunning. But all of these things will be forgiven him, indeed, they will be regarded as high qualities if he can make them the means to achieve great ends.

Charles de Gaulle

A leader is a dealer in hope.

Napoleon I

An automobile goes nowhere efficiently unless it has a quick, hot spark to ignite things, to set the cogs of the machine in motion. So I try to make every player on my team feel he's the spark keeping our machine in motion.

Knute Rockne

What a man dislikes in his superiors, let him not display in the treatment of his inferiors.

Tsang Sin

When Pack meets with Pack in the jungle,
    and neither will go from the trail,
Lie down till the leaders have spoken
    —it may be fair words shall prevail.

Rudyard Kipling

Nearly all men can stand adversity, but if you want to test a man's character, give him power.

Abraham Lincoln

Never tell people *how* to do things. Tell them *what* to do and they will surprise you with their ingenuity.

George Smith Patton

The question, "Who ought to be boss?" is like asking, "Who ought to be tenor in the quartet?" Obviously the man who can sing tenor.

Henry Ford

If you don't know where you want to go, it doesn't matter how you get there.

paraphrased from Lewis Carroll

The man who commands efficiently must have obeyed others in the past and the man who obeys dutifully is worthy of being some day a commander.

Cicero

On Leaders and Leadership (*continued*)

The genius of a good leader is to leave behind him a situation which common sense, without the grace of genius, can deal with successfully.

Walter Lippman

I sit here all day trying to persuade people to do the things they ought to have sense enough to do without my persuading them.

Harry S. Truman

The Manager-Versus-Leader Debate

The manager-versus-leader debate is an ongoing discussion about which of the two roles effective leaders play. The terms *leader* and *manager* tend to be used interchangeably, but major differences exist. Managers, in general, are "nuts and bolts" oriented whereas leaders are visionaries, conceptualizers, and catalysts. Those who excel as leaders may excel as managers, but those who excel as managers infrequently excel as leaders. The best schools can hope for is having competent leaders *and* managers in the administrative ranks.

Leaders plan, delegate, coordinate, and motivate. They focus on developing human potential and on influencing and persuading others to accomplish organizational goals. Leaders seek to "bond" with subordinates and to align the goals of subordinates with those of the organization. Authority vested in leaders through the organization's line staff chart is used only as a last resort when influence and persuasion fail.

The ability to influence and persuade others is a primary characteristic of leaders that sets them apart from managers, who achieve results by directing the work of others. Leaders inspire and motivate others to action. Leaders rely more on their cognitive and human relations skills to attain their objectives than on their authority to tell others what to do. Leaders have "mature wisdom," according to Gardner (1990), which allows them to provide clear direction and purpose to their followers; know the needs, concerns, and expectations of their followers; and develop a "social compact" with their followers. When social compacts are formed, followers willingly entrust their future welfare to the leader, who in turn willingly entrusts the welfare of the organization to the followers.

In schools, principals often assume the role of leader, whereas assistant principals—due to the types of job responsibilities generally delegated by the principal, such as discipline and student supervision—are more often viewed as managers. One of the purposes of this book is to help those in the assistant principalship acquire the skills and knowledge necessary to transition to the leadership role of the principalship. Even if the principalship is not the assistant principal's ultimate goal, leadership knowledge and skills can give the assistant principal the edge that is needed to move to other leadership positions. If the *assistant* principalship is the goal, the application of such knowledge and skills while aspiring to or holding the position of assistant principal can elevate the person, and whatever position the person holds, to a much higher plateau in the organization. In other words, a person does not have to be in a leadership position to be a leader, as will be discussed in other sections throughout this book. Such a person should not be surprised, however, when he or she is approached and recruited by those in formal leadership positions. A more accurate way of placing the manager-versus-leader debate in perspective, then, is to understand that a leader can have managerial responsibilities—in other words, a person doesn't have to be one or the other. Rather, it may help to distinguish between leaders and nonleaders.

Some factors help differentiate leaders from nonleaders. Newstrom and Davis (1997) found that a high level of personal drive, the desire to lead, personal integrity, self-confidence, flexibility, analytical ability, creativity, and personal warmth are the attributes of leaders in the most current research findings. Caution should be taken, because these leadership characteristics do not *guarantee* successful leadership. They can best be viewed as *competencies* to be developed.

It seems clear that leadership is more personally demanding than managership because leadership requires a voluntary commitment to promote one's goals through influence and persuasion; to be fair, trustworthy, and honest; and to use authority and power wisely and sparingly. Leaders who are successful and who do rely on their power and authority to accomplish their goals are students of power. That is, they study the various power sources, presented in the next section, and then use these sources when situations exist that require the exercise of power and authority.

Sources of Formal and Informal Power

Power in organizations can be accrued and used by individuals and groups. Leaders have power to *influence* the behavior of others both through their personal attributes and as legitimate representatives of the organization. *Formal* power is defined as that power that is legally vested in a position and sanctioned by the organization; *informal* power stems from personal attributes, outside of formal power, that attract allegiance and support from peers. French and Raven (1968), who pioneered the analysis of power in organizations, identified five major sources of power leaders use to influence the behavior of individuals:

1. *Reward Power:* Rewards are provided by virtue of the leader's position or influence over others. Reward power depends on the kind of reward the leader can provide and on the attractiveness of the reward to others. Examples of extrinsic rewards include salary increases, promotions, and good work assignments; intrinsic rewards include praise.

2. *Expert Power:* Expert power is derived from special abilities or knowledge possessed by the leader and desired by the followers. Examples are education, experience, and special training.

3. *Referent Power:* Referent power stems from the ability of the leader to acquire a following through charisma. The leader's personality traits command respect and attract others to the leader's presence. Referent power may also be derived from a leader's association with powerful people, with the leader influencing the behavior of others through actual or perceived contacts with others.

4. *Legitimate Power:* Legitimate power, or formal authority, is vested in the leader by the position held in the organization. Legitimate power allows the leader to direct others to achieve organizational goals. Power also comes from followers' belief that legitimate power will be used rationally and in the followers' best interests.

5. *Coercive Power:* Coercive power is used to threaten and punish, to make people conform, and to achieve the leader's goals. Coercive power is the opposite of reward power. Examples of coercive power include demotions, threats of punishment, undesirable work assignments, and a lack of pay increases.

Legitimate, reward, and *coercive* power are organization based and are part of an assistant principal's power derived through the position. *Expert* and *referent* power are personal powers and come from the personality of the leader. We have stated (Weller & Weller, 2000) that early school administrators relied on coercive and legitimate power whereas their contemporary counterparts tend to use reward, referent, and expert power. The decline of coercive power is attributed to changing social norms, court rulings, teacher unions, and research on effective leader-follower relations. Coercive behavior is discouraged because it violates the concept of empowerment and can lead to hostility, aggression, covert action, and high absenteeism on the part of subordinates. Research has shown expert and referent power to be positively correlated with subordinates' job satisfaction and work performance; legitimate, reward, and coercive power have not been shown to be so correlated.

The results of using legitimate power are mixed. Legitimate power is effective when requests are reasonable, when the requested tasks are part of the job assignment, and when compliance is desired. Legitimate power alone does not correlate with task commitment, but work commitment increases when expert or reward power is coupled with legitimate power. Hoy and Miskel (1996) note that school leaders who use the threat of coercive power and then reward teachers for performance produce a positive effect on work commitment. We have found (Weller, 1999; Weller & Weller, 2000) that principals and assistant principals who are authoritarian and who use coercive power or legitimate power as a means to control teachers end up reducing teacher loyalty and work performance and lowering morale.

Using Too Much or Too Little Power: Is There a Balance?

Lord Acton's famous statement "Power corrupts and absolute power corrupts absolutely" certainly seems to be an accurate assessment of the way power influences many people. But some power is needed to promote effective and efficient organizational outcomes. The question is, how much power should one use? For leaders, the answer depends on their personal attributes and their knowledge and skill levels. Most research agrees that a balance in the application of the power sources (excluding coercive power) is best. Following are some guidelines that can help a leader find that balance.

Less legitimate power is needed when leaders personally know the needs, dispositions, and aspirations of their followers and can apply other power sources. The key to applying legitimate power is to maintain favorable relationships so followers retain respect and goodwill toward the leader. When other sources of power such as expert, reward, and referent are lacking, however, the greater exercise of legitimate power is a better alternative than coercive power. On the other hand, too little use of legitimate power may be perceived as weakness and can result in poor outcomes, confusion, and frustration, leading to chaos among subordinates.

Coercive power, always an option, is discouraged due to its numerous negative effects. Using coercive power is appropriate, states Yukl (1994), when discipline is required to deter behavior detrimental to other individuals or the organization. For example, when leaders must thwart potential rebellion or deal with people who refuse to obey directives, coercive power is appropriate. But the excessive use of coercive power diminishes the effectiveness of informal authority and referent power, and leads to hostility, alienation, and covert action. Coercive power is most effective when subordinates have a clear understanding of the rules and policies of the organization and when coercive power is administered swiftly, fairly, and consistently. The need for coercive power can be reduced when *requests*, not orders, are given to obey directives; when the requests are clearly stated; and when reasons for the requests are provided.

Relying on rewards as a source of power defines the leader-follower relationship in purely economic terms and may make subordinates feel manipulated. Regardless of the value placed on them by leaders, rewards may result in low subordinate compliance if they are not personally valued or deemed sufficient for the task. Likewise, depending on too much expert power may breed contempt for the leader or create a feeling of "nonworth" among subordinates. Subordinates may feel intimidated and refrain from expressing their views or ideas to one in authority. Leaders who depend on referent power to influence subordinates' behavior have the loyalty and trust of their subordinates, and they lead by example. Not all subordinates, however, will have equal trust in and loyalty to the leader, and some subordinates may find little or no personal affiliation or appeal in the leader's personal characteristics.

In the final analysis, any source of power used by assistant principals will meet with varying degrees of resistance by teachers. To maximize task commitment, the use of referent and expert power is preferred over legitimate power. To attain teacher compliance, legitimate and reward power are preferred. Use of coercive power ensures compliance, but results in many negative side effects. Therefore, to maintain informal power, a leader should apply legitimate power judiciously, pick fights carefully, act politically, pay off past obligations, and back down on issues that do not impact the leader or the organization negatively.

Practical Sources of Power for Assistant Principals

Assistant principals can and do use all five sources of power in several contexts. First, assistant principals schedule teaching and class assignments. Some teachers prefer to teach only one subject per semester or year. Others thrive on diversification. Some teachers prefer to teach slower learners whereas others prefer advanced placement or honors students. Assigning teachers to certain courses and ability levels may involve the use of reward and coercive power when rewards are given for performance and compliance and when the threat of not granting requested assignments is used as coercion.

Second, many assistant principals have budgeting power and can reward department heads and teachers with the acquisition of requested materials or with the permission and funds to attend professional conferences. Making certain teachers' requests a low priority can be viewed as exercising legitimate or coercive power, depending on the assistant principal's rationale.

Third, the process of evaluating classroom performance, perhaps the most important instructional task of the assistant principal, can be stressful for many teachers. Professionally and ethically, fair and objective assessments should be made. But the evaluation process is one in which reward, coercive, legitimate, and expert power can be used. Rewarding compliance in areas outside of teaching by providing positive evaluations should not be practiced. Likewise, using classroom evaluations as a means to exact conformity or gain favors is a form of coercive power that should be avoided. By using both legitimate and expert power in the teacher evaluation process, assistant principals can make objective, unbiased evaluations of teacher performance through the utilization of their superior knowledge and skills.

Fourth, assistant principals who have a major voice in hiring new personnel can use their expert power to evaluate and select the best candidates. When candidates are hired, the use of coercive power to maintain loyalty may be tempting, but the temptation should be resisted. In addition, assistant principals should not try to influence new teachers' behavior based on the role the assistant principal played in awarding the job.

Fifth, assistant principals can use referent power to attain goals or change teacher behaviors through their own personality traits and through their association with influential people. When there are openings in administrative positions, or other avenues for personal or professional advancement for teachers, assistant principals can exercise referent power by providing recommendations for advancement. Of course, the assistant principal has the option of applying coercive and legitimate power in the same situation.

Finally, assistant principals can exercise their expert power by recommending teachers for tenure or for annual employment contracts prior to tenure. In most cases, teachers' anxiety is high over the tenure issue because coercive power or legitimate power can be applied in these situations. The assistant principal's actual or perceived influence with the principal or central office administration can be viewed as referent power, but such an association also provides the opportunity to apply coercive power.

As can be seen from these examples, the assistant principal has many opportunities to abuse power. Assistant principals who want to use power for the good of both the organization and the people in it, will choose to enhance their leadership skills and knowledge through continued professional growth and a constant evaluation of their own motives. In this way, they will become true leaders who understand the long-term effects of their own actions.

Leadership Through Influence and Persuasion

The ability to lead through influence and persuasion is an effective leader behavior. Effective principals and their assistants rely more on influencing and persuading teachers to achieve their goals than they do on their positional authority. These leaders establish a leader-follower *covenant* rooted in mutual trust, respect, and loyalty, and nourished through shared beliefs, values, and goals. This "all for one and one for all" attitude is "custodial" in nature and is characterized by the mutual desire to safeguard one another's welfare and to promote one another's interests. Central to this relationship is the leader's ability to *personally know* followers' needs, goals, and aspirations, and then to carefully consider these personal variables when making decisions. It is this personal knowledge that allows leaders to influence or persuade their followers to do their bidding.

Influence

According to Yukl (1994), "Influence is the essence of leadership" (p. 223). There are many different forms of influence. Influence can come as a *simple request,* which is successful when the task is part of the follower's assigned duties and within the follower's capabilities. Another form of influence is the *legitimized request.* Here the request is based on precedent or policy; although the follower is influenced to follow through on the legitimized request, task commitment is low. An *inspirational appeal* results in high task commitment and arouses enthusiasm by linking the follower's needs, values, or aspirations to the request.

Consultation, another form of influence, includes the follower in the decision-making process. Yukl (1994) relates that "this process illustrates the apparent paradox that you can gain more influence by giving up some influence" (p. 226). Here task commitment is high. *Exchange* involves the explicit or implicit offer of a reward for completing a task. This form of influence is most beneficial when the follower is indifferent or reluctant about completing a task. Task commitment is moderate. *Personal appeal* is a form of influence whereby a leader resorts to friendship or loyalty in getting another to accomplish a task. The stronger the relationship, the greater the probability this form of influence will work. We call this *blue chipping,* that is, calling in past personal favors; a leader can ask for only so many blue chips before the other begins to sense manipulation. Here task commitment is moderate.

Ingratiation is a form of influence whereby the leader gains favor with the subordinate through deliberate efforts to do so. Yukl and Tracy (1992) warn that such tactics can be viewed as manipulation, but when the comments and actions are sincere and merited, ingratiation can be effective. Task commitment is moderate. *Pressure* includes warnings and close supervision of the subordinate's work. Pressure may be initially effective with those who are lazy or indifferent, but, in general, pressure should be used only as a last resort. Task commitment is low. In addition, pressure undermines working relationships and may lead to covert behavior. *Coalition* as a form of influence involves several people acting together to trigger the compliance of another. Task commitment is low.

Applying these different forms of influence allows leaders to "energize" others without using legitimate authority. Using influence is more likely to be successful when a follower believes that the request is *intrinsically* desirable, that it is the *correct* or *proper* thing to do, and that it coincides with the follower's *value system.*

Persuasion

Persuasion is defined as a leader's ability to change behavior, initiate action, and gain consensus through facts and logic, or through the discrediting of facts and logic. Successful persuasion depends on the degree of *trust* and *respect* the parties have for one another, and on the way in which the persuasive appeal is presented. Nonthreatening appeals promote interest and openness, and followers are more likely to be swayed by them (Weller, 1999).

When leaders apply *rational* persuasion, they use an effective and powerful skill to change another's behavior. Rational persuasion is most effective when the appeal is carefully made to another by using facts and logical reasoning to point out the *direct benefits* to the follower of the requested behavior. The degree of respect the follower has for the leader, the amount of credibility the leader has with the follower, and the degree to which emotional influences can be suppressed by the follower, is the degree to which rational persuasion is effective. Generally, rational persuasion is moderately successful in changing behavior, especially when compliance rather than commitment is sought. When rational persuasion is used in conjunction with some form of influence, it becomes a highly effective leadership skill (Yukl, 1994).

Roles and Responsibilities of
Assistant Principals: Survey Results

To find out what assistant principals do in their jobs and how they feel on a variety of topics, we surveyed 100 assistant principals from urban, suburban, and rural schools and found, in general agreement with the existing literature, that the primary responsibilities for assistant principals continue to be discipline and attendance counting. Approximately 77% of the respondents identified discipline and attendance as their major job assignments, whereas 13% indicated discipline or attendance were secondary to their primary responsibilities of improving instruction or overseeing the vocational education program. Schools with more than one assistant principal generally had one assistant principal primarily responsible for curriculum, instruction, or vocational education, and one assistant principal primarily responsible for student discipline and attendance.

What Assistant Principals Do in Their "Spare Time"

- Supervise students (98%)
- Complete routine reports, enforce policy, and write grant proposals (92%)
- Participate in the selection of teachers, department heads, and assistant principals (87%)
- Evaluate teacher and staff personnel performance and provide remedial assistance (78%)
- Coordinate and/or conduct staff development programs and mentoring or peer tutoring programs (62%)
- Develop the school's master schedule (57%)
- Coordinate and place student teachers and paraprofessionals (52%)
- Prepare the school's budget (7%)
- Act as the school's liaison to community and civic organizations (5%)

SOURCE: 2000 Survey of 100 Practicing Assistant Principals From Urban, Rural, and Suburban Schools

---

The assistant principals were asked to list other duties or responsibilities assigned by the principal or contained in their job descriptions. The 68% who responded to this question listed a variety of additional assignments, which ranged from supervising students (98%) to acting as the school's liaison to community and civic organizations (5%).

A few respondents, approximately 30%, commented on their additional duties. Typical of these comments is the following:

> While my title is Assistant Principal for Discipline, I'm expected to evaluate teachers, coordinate extracurricular programs, coordinate school-community relations, write grants, and represent the principal at meetings he does not want to attend. I'm spread too thin but I can't let discipline "go to pot."

A number of respondents indicated that many assigned responsibilities required new knowledge or skills. Twenty-five percent, for example, felt they lacked the necessary leadership skills essential for some of their assigned duties. One commented, "My basic course in educational leadership theory is most valuable, but I need more." Approximately 65% of the respondents indicated that in addition to other skills, they needed skills in working with teams, improving instruction, and developing curriculum. One comment perhaps best captures the frustration and demands associated with the position of assistant principal:

Comments by Assistant Principals on the Variety of Roles They Play

"An assistant principal is essentially a 'jack-of-all trades and master of none.'"

"I've thought about trying to write down every thing I do in a day's time as I do it, but I can't justify the time loss. Let's just say I stay *very* busy."

"I wish that I could spend more time with students other than those in trouble. That's why I went into the educational field to begin with, and I really miss that interaction."

"At the end of some days, I feel like I've been pecked to death by ducks. Somebody is always in my face wanting something."

"I see the variety of tasks I'm asked to perform as a way of getting to know the total school program. I want to be a principal and I want to be exposed to as much as I can in my role as an assistant."

"I like the job because I never know what will come up in a day's time. I never get bored."

SOURCE: 2000 Survey of 100 Practicing Assistant Principals From Rural, Suburban, and Urban Schools

---

My primary job is student discipline, but I'm asked to help teachers improve, place student teachers, develop the master schedule, strengthen the curriculum, attend meetings for the principal, work on the budget, evaluate personnel, and complete reports. Sometimes I'm flying by the seat of my pants and my day starts at 6:30 a.m. and ends at 7:00 p.m.

**Areas in Which Educational Leadership Courses
Did Not Adequately Prepare Assistant Principals**

- Motivating teachers
- Resolving conflict
- Developing curriculum for the "real world"
- Working effectively with teams
- Improving instruction
- Dealing with the "politics" of the job

SOURCE: 2000 Survey of 100 Practicing Assistant Principals From Rural, Suburban, and Urban Schools

Table 1.1 Job Description for Assistant Principal

Callaway City School System
Job Description
Assistant Principal

Qualifications:	• Master's Degree
	• Valid Leadership Certificate
	• Minimum of three years successful classroom teaching experience
	• Alternatives to the above qualifications deemed appropriate by the Board of Education
Primary Duties and Responsibilities:	• Assist in all matters assigned by the principal
	• Be responsible for student discipline and campus supervision
	• Supervise student and staff attendance
	• Supervise the In-School Suspension program and serve as hearing officer
Secondary Duties and Responsibilities:	• Assist with teacher observations and evaluations
	• Assist with school staff meetings
	• Coordinate public information for the school
	• Contribute to school improvement plans
	• Assist with planning staff development programs
	• Develop teacher and student handbook
	• Coordinate field trips
	• Evaluate department heads and clerical staff
	• Counsel with parents, students, and staff when necessary
	• Assist in developing the master schedule
	• Supervise extracurricular activities and athletic events
	• Assist in the selection of instructional materials
	• Assist in evaluating all school programs when necessary
	• Supervise lunchroom and transportation programs
	• Assist in supervising school physical facilities

Table 1.1　Continued

	• Assist in evaluating the instructional programs • Stay current on effective teaching practices and ways to improve student achievement • Assist in preparing the school budget • Serve as the one in charge during absence of the principal
Terms of Employment:	Ten-, eleven-, or twelve-month year depending on needs of principal. Salary set by the Board of Education.
Evaluation:	Evaluation conducted yearly by the principal and/or superintendent. Criteria for performance evaluation will be those on the job description and others assigned.

Table 1.1 presents a typical job description of a solitary assistant principal in a high school of approximately 600 students. As seen in the table, the *primary* responsibilities of this assistant principal are student discipline and attendance. The *secondary* responsibilities listed on the job description include many of the responsibilities associated with the leadership and managerial functions attributed to effective leaders. It is apparent that a cadre of knowledge and skills is essential to effectively perform the array of responsibilities associated with the assistant principalship, but the majority of assistant principals responding to the survey indicated they lacked the necessary training to perform many of these responsibilities.

The job description of an assistant principal who is primarily responsible for instruction and curriculum is presented in Table 1.2. This job description is for an assistant principal in a high school of approximately 2,000 students who serves with two other assistant principals, one being primarily responsible for student discipline and attendance. As seen in Table 1.2, the primary responsibilities fall within the expectations of leaders focusing on the improvement of instruction and curriculum. Many of the duties are identified as those associated with providing effective instructional leadership and also require tasks associated with effective managers.

Developing Leadership Competencies

How can one best develop leadership competencies? Certain aspects of leadership can be acquired by participating in training, observing role models, engaging in work experience, reading research and theory, and practicing self-leadership. Manz (1991) found that practicing self-leadership provides a testing ground for learning and developing leadership competencies. That is, one must first want to be a leader and then make a conscious effort to change one's current behavior patterns. Second, one must make a personal commitment to perform leadership tasks daily and with the knowledge that official rewards or incentives will not be forthcoming. Third, one must create "mental activities" for practicing leader behaviors by planning leadership activities in advance, rehearsing leadership activities through "mental imagery," building in "natural" rewards for success, and then practicing self-criticism and reflection on task completion.

Observing effective leaders is an excellent way to develop leadership competencies. Following or "shadowing" respected leaders over time allows one to witness firsthand how leaders apply their skills in various situations. Allowing time for after-the-fact reflection and discussion is important. Apprenticeship or administrative assistantship is still another way to develop leadership competencies. Here leaders identify and then place potential leaders in positions as apprentices or administrative assistants. Leaders guide and model while the apprentice actually performs leadership tasks and gains practical experience. In this role, leaders encourage, inspire, tutor, and mold their charges into future leaders.

Reading theory and research-oriented journals is a time-honored way to gain knowledge about leadership. Less appealing to most practitioner-oriented students of leadership, theories and research provide the essential foundation on which good practice is derived. Those ignorant of theory and research are akin to those who are ignorant of history: doomed to repeat the mistakes of their predecessors.

Leadership Theories: Building a Theoretical Base for Practical Applications

The leadership theories discussed here are not meant to be exhaustive, but do represent those that have had a major impact on the thinking and behavior of others. The selected theories presented below are grouped according to their associated characteristics and intended to serve as references for leadership preparation.

Behavioral Theories. Behavioral theories investigate what effective leaders *do* or how effective leaders *behave*. Behavioral theories seek to identify which behavior patterns make leaders more effective. Three common descriptions of leader behaviors are *autocratic, democratic,* and *laissez-faire.* The autocrat expects compliance

Table 1.2 Job Description for Assistant Principal of Instruction and Curriculum

Lamar County School System
Job Description
Assistant Principal of Instruction and Curriculum

Duties and Responsibilities

1. Develop the master schedule.

2. Evaluate teachers and department heads.

3. Coordinate staff development programs.

4. Coordinate peer coaching and mentoring programs.

5. Coordinate the placement of student teachers.

6. Evaluate student test scores and improve instruction and the curriculum as needed.

7. Assist the principal in conducting meetings of the School Governance Council.

8. Coordinate the Parent Teacher Association program.

9. Coordinate the business partnership programs.

10. Assist in maintaining a school culture emphasizing academics, student achievement, and teaching excellence.

11. Keep current on the recent research on improving instruction, student learning, and curriculum trends which promote student achievement.

12. Perform all other duties assigned by the principal.

Supervisor:	Principal of the school
Terms of Employment:	Eleven-month contract with salary based on highest degree and years of teaching experience
Evaluation:	The principal will evaluate job performance based on the job description and any other duties he/she assigns.

without questions and uses threats and punishments to achieve goals; decision making and power are centralized. Democratic leaders delegate authority and share power; teams are an integral part of the decision-making process and organizational goals and objectives are jointly developed. Laissez-faire leaders grant complete freedom of action to subordinates. They see their primary role as providing resources and moral support.

Another behavioral theory is the two-dimensional theory of *initiating structure* and *consideration for subordinates*. Researchers sought to identify leadership behavior "patterns" that yielded effective performance. Leaders who emphasized initiating structure focused on achieving performance goals, defining and organizing tasks, establishing communication channels, setting work deadlines, and pushing subordinates to work to capacity. Those leaders who emphasized consideration for subordinates exhibited trust, respect, warmth, and concern for subordinates' welfare. They were friendly and fair and listened to subordinates' ideas and concerns. The most effective leader is one who can provide a balance of these two aspects of leadership.

Trait Theories. Trait theory holds that leaders are different from other people, with research focusing on those personal characteristics and traits that promote leadership effectiveness. Trait research initially identified five general categories impacting effective leadership: (a) capacity (intelligences and verbal facility), (b) achievement (scholarship and knowledge), (c) responsibility (initiative, persistence, integrity, honesty, and self-confidence), (d) participation (sociability, flexibility, cooperation, and humor), and (e) status (socioeconomic position and popularity). Later trait research reconfirmed the presence of many of these traits, but findings concluded that the traits of *intelligences, dominance, self-confidence,* and *high energy levels* were most prevalent in effective leaders. Most recently, effective leadership traits have been classified into three groups—*personality, motivation,* and *skill.* Personality traits include self-confidence, stress tolerance, emotional maturity, empathy, and integrity. Motivation traits include being task oriented, and holding high values and expectations. Skill traits include technical administrative expertise, ability to conceptualize, and interpersonal relations. These traits do not necessarily guarantee successful leadership, but can best be viewed as competencies to be developed or acquired.

Contingency Theories. Efforts to determine the one best set of leader traits and the one best set of leader behaviors in *all* situations provided inconclusive results due to the complex nature of leadership. The theory that effective leadership is *contingent* on the situation(s) in which leadership occurs is more prevalent today. Contingency theories state that the most effective type of leadership depends on the leader's ability to analyze the nature of the situation and then apply the leadership style that would be most effective in that situation.

Fiedler's contingency theory (1967) holds that leader effectiveness results when leadership style is matched with the leader-follower situation *and* with the individual(s) involved. Two leadership styles promote effective results: (a) *task motivated,* which is effective when structure is needed and efficiency in performance is required, and (b) *relationship motivated,* which is effective when building a positive interpersonal relationship is required. Three factors determine leadership style: (a) the degree to which the leader is accepted by the follower (the degree of confidence, trust, and respect the follower has for the leader); (b) the degree to

---

Readings on Behavioral Theories of Leadership

- *A Theory of Leadership Effectiveness*, by F. E. Fiedler (1967). New York: McGraw-Hill.
- "Patterns of Aggressive Behavior in Experimentally Created Social Climates," by H. Lewin, R. Lippit, and R. K. White (1939), in *Journal of Social Psychology, 10*, 271-299.
- *The Management of Organizational Behavior* (5th edition), by P. Hersey and K. H. Blanchard (1988). Englewood Cliffs, NJ: Prentice Hall.
- *Leadership and Supervision in Industry,* by E. A. Fleishman, E. F. Harris, and R. D. Burtt (1955). Columbus, OH: State University Press.

---

which the task is understood by the follower; and (c) the extent to which the leader possesses the ability to influence the follower through legitimate, reward, and coercive powers. Effective leadership results when the "right mix" occurs among these multiple variables.

Hersey and Blanchard (1988) relate that effective leaders accurately assess the maturity level of their followers (their competence and motivation to perform) and then apply one of four leadership styles—telling, selling, participating, or delegating. The leader's style must vary with the situation and the follower's personal attributes to achieve the desired outcomes. There is no single "best" leadership style for all situations.

Transformational and Transactional Leadership Theories. Transformational theory maintains that leadership is a *process* by which leaders and followers raise each other to higher levels of morality and motivation. Leaders appeal to followers' higher ideals and moral values and stimulate higher-order needs in followers. Followers have trust, admiration, loyalty, and respect for the leader. Leaders transform and motivate followers by (a) making followers aware of the importance of their jobs and of the quality of their job performance; (b) motivating followers to place their self-interests behind those of the organization; (c) articulating a

---

Readings on Trait Theories of Leadership

- "Personal Factors Associated With Leadership: A Survey of the Literature," by R. M. Stogdill (1948), in *Journal of Psychology, 25*, 35-71.
- *Bass and Stogdill's Handbook of Leadership* (3rd edition), by B. M. Bass and R. M. Stogdill (1990). New York: Free Press.

vision, promoting it vigorously, and modeling expected behaviors; (d) individual-izing consideration of followers' needs and goals; and (e) stimulating followers' intellectual interests.

Transactional leadership involves the daily exchanges of incentives and re-wards for compliance. This is a quid pro quo type of leadership in which job secu-rity, tenure, good evaluations, and raises are provided for subordinates' support, cooperation, and compliance. Research findings on transformational and transactional leadership are mixed, but seem to indicate that effective leaders use a combination of transformational and transactional behaviors.

The Effective Schools Research and the Implications for Effective Leadership

One of the most intriguing aspects of the effective schools movement is the lack of a clear and universally accepted definition of school effectiveness. The lit-erature on school effectiveness generally agrees that effective schools are those that make a *difference* in student performance on standardized tests of achieve-ment. Edmonds (1982) provides a general definition that embraces the gestalt of the effective schools movement. He defines effective schools as those in which stu-dents from lower socioeconomic backgrounds perform as well on basic skills tests as do students from mid-level socioeconomic backgrounds. As the research on effective schools expanded, a wider array of assumptions about schools in general accumulated. These assumptions are (a) schools are responsible for the academic success or failure of their students; (b) students are capable of learning regardless of their ethnicity or home or cultural background; (c) students from low socio-economic status families do not need a different curriculum, and poverty does not excuse failure; and (d) differences between schools impact student achievement, and those differences can be controlled by the school.

These assumptions resulted from a new line of research that focused on pro-cesses of schooling, unlike previous research, which focused on the quantities of *resources available* to schools and individual *student characteristics*. Researchers believed that success on standardized tests was not restricted to basic skills mas-tery, and that test performance was not an accurate reflection of the overall mis-sion of education. Effective schools are now defined as those that can meet the social, emotional, physical, and academic needs of students. Interest in the social and emotional development of students began to take on greater importance as educators reexamined their value to the overall mission of education and the implications for their impacting student test performance. As a result, defining school effectiveness based on student performance on standardized tests alone began to be seen as inadequate. Effective schools are now defined as those having

---

Readings on Contingency Theories of Leadership

- *A Theory of Leadership Effectiveness,* by R. E. Fiedler (1967). New York: McGraw-Hill.
- *The Management of Organizational Behavior* (5th edition), by P. Hersey and K. H. Blanchard (1988). Englewood Cliffs, NJ: Prentice Hall.

---

programs that positively impact student attitudes, self-esteem, social responsibility, higher-order thinking skills, and test performance (Stedman, 1987). Effectiveness results from a combination of many policies, programs, behaviors, and attitudes within the school itself.

The Research on Effective Schools

Early research on inner-city high schools yielded the following effective school variables:

- Strong leadership by the principal, especially in instructional programs and activities
- High expectations by teachers for student success on achievement measures and in classroom performance
- Emphasis on developing basic skills and increasing the time spent on teaching and learning
- A safe and orderly environment in which to teach and learn
- Frequent and systematic evaluation of student learning (Stedman, 1987)

As effective schools research intensified, it expanded to middle and elementary schools. As a result, an expanded set of effective school variables emerged. Cuban (1990) notes that effective schools have the following characteristics:

Readings on Transformational and Transactional Leadership Theories

- *Leadership and Performance Beyond Expectations,* by B. M. Bass (1985). New York: Free Press.
- *Leadership,* by J. M. Burns (1978). New York: Harper & Row.

- Instructional leadership by a principal who understands and applies the theories and practices of effective instruction
- A climate in which all staff members hold high expectations for student success and mastery of the basic skills
- A clear school mission that encompasses school goals and assessment procedures and a commitment to student learning by all staff members
- A safe and orderly learning environment that allows students to learn and teachers to teach in an oppression-free atmosphere
- Classrooms where time on task is emphasized by spending the maximum amount of time on planned activities to master basic skills
- Frequent monitoring of student performance and use of evaluation results to improve teaching and learning
- Positive home-school relations that foster parents' support for the school's mission, involvement in school programs, and active participation in their children's learning

Research by Levine and Lezotte (1989) identified characteristics of effective schools that are tangential to the actual teaching and learning process:

- Schools with site-based management that practice teacher empowerment and allow teachers the latitude to solve site-based problems
- Central office support for making decisions and solving school problems that impact instruction
- Strong leadership at the school level
- A planned and well-coordinated curriculum that is scoped and sequenced and focused on the holistic needs of students
- Staff stability which provides a strong, cohesive work unit
- Comprehensive staff development programs that are teacher led and address the specific needs of teachers
- Parent programs designed to help parents help their children with homework, attendance, and discipline
- Schoolwide recognition of student academic success and teaching excellence
- Collaborative teacher planning to promote the sharing of knowledge and ideas and provide continuity in the curriculum and in student learning experiences
- Shared vision, mission, and goals to promote collegiality and to foster a sense of community

The effective schools movement has its critics. In an analysis of the research on effective schools, Grady, Wayson, and Zirkel (1989) found that the results were primarily based on studies conducted in urban elementary schools. The results, they reported, are unclear and some are spurious. In addition, they noted the use of weak research methods, the fact that subjects such as art and music received less attention than did academic subjects, and the fact that the information that the shared governance variable associated with effective schools has increased the conflict between teachers and administrators over how much control teachers should have in the area of instructional leadership.

Implications for Leadership

Research results on the principals of effective schools are also mixed. Bossert (1988) relates that four primary variables contribute to principal effectiveness: (a) setting instructional goals and requiring effective instructional practices, (b) exercising leadership to accomplish goals, (c) using effective management practices, and (d) exhibiting excellent human relations skills. Some research on effective school principals has tried to link principals' effectiveness to the bureaucratic model by stating that strong principals must be highly structured to implement effective school characteristics, but no conclusive findings exist as to what type of structure is needed or what processes must be structured. What has evolved from the research is the following: (a) Leadership is important for promoting effective schools, (b) no single leadership behavior or set of leadership behaviors has been identified as enhancing academic achievement for all schools, and (c) effectiveness seems to be linked to appropriately matching situational variables, such as the curricular and instructional programs, with the leadership style of the principal. That is, principals who are effective tend to delegate authority, jointly establish school goals, "guide" the instructional process, and allow teachers to make certain decisions about the teaching and learning process.

Current Research on Student Learning and the Implications for Effective Leadership

Researchers have long suspected that some instructional practices promote student learning more effectively than others. Wang, Haertel, and Walberg (1993) analyzed approximately 11,000 statistical studies and interviewed 61 educational researchers and arrived at a "reasonable consensus" on the most significant influences impacting student learning. They found that *direct* influences, the amount of time teachers spend on instruction and the quality of "social interaction" they have with their students, have greater impact on learning than *indirect* influences, such as school and state-level policies and organizational structures such as site-based management.

Variables having the most impact on student learning were psychological, instructional, and contextual. The current emphasis on improving curriculum, restructuring school governance, developing school culture, and reforming education is focused on variables that have less direct impact on student learning.

Moreover, the research shows no strong, direct link between student performance and a principal's leadership behaviors. At best, the principal's influence on student learning is indirect and situation specific. Principals' effectiveness or ineffectiveness may result from congruence or incongruence between leadership style and follower-situational factors, personality characteristics, student and community demographic factors, and turnover rate of teachers and teacher teams.

Leadership Effectiveness Indicators

Determining leader effectiveness is a multifaceted and complicated task. Leadership effectiveness indicators are many and varied throughout the literature. There seems, however, to be a general agreement that effectiveness is best determined by the *outcomes* resulting from certain leadership activities. These outcomes are as follows:

- *Personal perceptions and personal judgments of others.* Followers' perceptions of the leader—and whether or not those followers are able to be effective under that leader—form an indicator of leader effectiveness.

- *Subordinates' satisfaction.* The degree to which subordinates' needs and aspirations are met contributes greatly to their opinion of leader effectiveness.

- *Goal attainment.* The level to which organizational goals are achieved provides an objective criterion for assessing leader effectiveness.

- *Preparedness to address challenges or crises.* Does the leader successfully handle unexpected challengers or crises that, if handled differently, would leave a major negative impact on the organization or the followership?

- *Types of decisions.* Decisions made by leaders impact the loyalty and commitment of their followers and their work lives in general. Decisions have both direct and indirect effects. Direct effects have an immediate, personal impact on followers, whereas indirect effects take time to assess, are less personal in nature, and often cause a chain reaction. Whether a decision has direct or indirect effects on the followership, the leader's decisions allow subordinates to rise in glory or go down in flames.

- *Implementation of change.* Leaders who successfully implement change are able to motivate, build self-confidence, assist their followers in gaining new knowledge and skills, maintain harmony and cooperation, and use resources wisely and efficiently. When the desired result of change is realized and accomplished in a timely and "hassle-free" manner, leaders are judged to be effective.

Skills and Knowledge for Effective Assistant Principals: Survey Results

Approximately 70% of the 100 assistant principals surveyed indicated that "people skills," "good communication skills," "knowledge of leadership theory," "techniques for improving curriculum and instruction," and "working with teams" were the most essential skill and knowledge areas for effective assistant principals. Other skills, listed by less than 40% of the respondents, included the ability to work with "community, civic, and business leaders," "knowing the informal leaders and networks in the school," "curriculum development," and "conducting effective meetings and managing one's time." One respondent commented, "Many 'survival' skills are not taught in degree programs. Being diplomatic, dealing with different personalities, and being flexible and patient are essential to this job." Another respondent commented, "Your time is 'eaten alive' by the demands, conflict, and controversy caused by others. I have to be 'political' in dealing with teachers, parents, and my principal to be effective. I didn't get these skills in graduate school."

Let's Review

Leadership effectiveness can be viewed as competencies to be developed, and begins with practicing self-leadership, which includes nurturing the desire to improve, to change one's behavior, and to model the behaviors of recognized leaders. Leadership development is supplemented through apprenticeships and the study and understanding of leadership theory and research. Effective leadership indicators vary, but generally include the quality of work life leaders provide; the type of decisions they make and the goals they achieve; their ability to plan, organize, and coordinate; the degree of subordinates' satisfaction with the leader; and the leader's ability to motivate others and introduce change and innovation. A key leadership behavior is the ability to persuade and influence others to achieve the leader's goals without applying formal authority or resorting to manipulation or bartering.

Exercises

Exercise 1: Power Source Profiles

Reread the section on formal and informal power sources; then think about *superiors* with whom you have had recent experiences (depending on your current position, these superiors may be principals, assistant principals, or department heads). Select one you deem to be effective and another you deem to be ineffective. Answer the following questions in the context of situation, task, and personalities involved:

- Provide specific examples of the power sources most often used by the two superiors.

- Were these power sources effective? Why? Why not?

- What sources of power would *you* have used to be more effective? Why did you choose these power sources? Provide specific examples.

Exercise 2: Leadership Knowledge and Skills

Your superintendent has asked that a group of prospective teacher-leaders, of whom you are one, develop a list of knowledge areas and skills necessary to be an effective assistant principal. To acquire this information, you decide to *interview* certain leaders to gather data-based information. Interview your principal, assistant principal, and a department head to complete this task. Compare your results with those found in this chapter.

Exercise 3: Effective School Plan

Your superintendent has appointed you to a committee to develop a plan to make your school an "effective school" within 3 years. As chair of the committee, you decide to set priorities for meeting this objective for each of the 3 years. As you open the first meeting, you quote from the superintendent's letter:

The committee has the following goals:

1. Develop a program to train effective *leaders.* Most lack the essential skills. You fix it!

2. Develop a program to train *teachers* to be effective in the classroom. Many are not. You fix it!

**Skills and Knowledge Needed to Be Effective
As an Assistant Principal (in priority order)**

1. People skills
2. Good communication skills
3. Knowledge of leadership theory
4. Techniques for improving curriculum and instruction
5. Ability to work with teams
6. Ability to work with community, civic, and business leaders
7. Knowing the "politics" and networks within the schools
8. Ability to conduct effective meetings
9. Ability to manage one's time
10. Flexibility
11. Knowing how to be "diplomatic"
12. Patience and empathy
13. Common sense
14. Ability to maintain a good rapport and working relationship with colleagues

SOURCE: 2000 Survey of 100 Practicing Assistant Principals From Rural, Suburban, and Urban Schools

---

3. Develop a comprehensive plan to *evaluate* the effectiveness of your committee's improvement plan. Be thorough.

Explain the steps you would take with committee members to set priorities and develop an improvement plan.

Case Study: Improving Classroom Instruction

Sally Lonering was in her office, door closed, working on the school's budget. As principal, Sally was responsible for the total operation of the school. Money and attention to detail were the most important factors to the superintendent, bar none. Sally knew she should spend more time on improving instruction, but delegated this responsibility to Harry Tinker, her assistant principal. Harry was capable, she thought, even if he jumped from interest area to interest area. Besides, she had sent Harry to a recent daylong workshop on how to improve classroom instruction.

Harry was delighted when Sally proposed that he draft a 3-year plan to improve teacher classroom performance. This allowed him the opportunity to delegate more responsibility for student discipline to department heads. Harry didn't like dealing with discipline. Harry's award as Teacher of the Year when he was a classroom teacher gave him the confidence he needed to develop a comprehensive staff development program for making teachers more effective in their classrooms. Harry felt a bit uncomfortable when he tried to present the completed plan to Sally because every time he attempted to see her, she was busy with reports, talking to custodians and cafeteria personnel, improving office efficiency, or engaging in public relations activities. Her stock response was, "See me tomorrow, I'm keeping this school above water."

Harry never did get to discuss his plan with Sally, but his big day came when he presented it to faculty members at their first teacher workday. Sally was there to make room arrangements, attend to refreshments, and oversee all the AV equipment needed by Harry for his first presentation. Harry was proud of his work. He had colored graphs, sample training materials, and complete agendas for all the staff development sessions. "Yes," Harry thought, "this is going to be my ticket to a principalship."

After the meeting, Harry and Sally reflected on the outcomes. Both thought the presentation went very well. In fact, Sally commented on the quality of the graphs and the organization of the presentation. But both began to recall certain particulars about the presentation, and Sally asked Harry to make a list for further reflection. They noted that the teachers were less than enthusiastic about the prospects of self-improvement. No teacher volunteered to either chair or serve on the staff development programs evaluation committee, and both were surprised that not one teacher had asked either Harry or Sally any questions after the presentation concluded. Sally then said, "Note Ms. Thwartall's remark: 'The fluff was great.'"

If you were asked to provide advice to Sally and Harry about what they should be concerned about, what advice would you give? Be specific in your answers by providing information presented in this chapter.

2

Making the Transition
From Manager to Leader

In This Chapter

As a matter of practicality, assistant principals must come to grips with issues surrounding the manager-leader paradox. Because assistant principals are generally required to perform more management than leadership tasks, the move from manager to leader requires a personal commitment, the allocation of time, and the drafting of a "personal plan" to develop core, effective leadership competencies. Although leadership development opportunities may be rare for some assistant principals, there are opportunities that can be taken advantage of and even created. Most often these opportunities center on variables such as teachers' job satisfaction and morale and the development of teachers as leaders. Job satisfaction impacts performance and output and is related to tasks performed, work environment, and factors associated with human psychology.

The Manager-Versus-Leader Debate

Distinctions have been made between managers and leaders, but debate continues because of the overlap of certain behaviors and functions required of both leaders and managers. A person can be a manager without being a leader, or a leader without being a manager. No one has proposed that managing and leading are equivalent. Bennis and Nanus (1985) provide insight when they state, "Managers are people who do things right, and leaders are people who do the right thing " (p. 21). One can be both a manager and a leader, but this depends on the *person* in the position and the *responsibilities* required of the position. Therefore the

29

type of person holding the position and the job responsibilities required of the position may define the leader-manager debate in specific instances. The reality of the situation is that a leader must lead the organization *and* manage the organization as well.

Managers

Managers have been described as functionaries who focus on the microconcepts of an organization and concern themselves with enforcing policy and structuring the work environment for better productivity. They are concerned with the daily problems of subordinates and making sure rules and regulations are followed. Managers pay attention to detail; they are concerned about *how* things get done; they are organized; and they reward, praise, and marshal resources for others to do their work. Managers work closely with others, and their effectiveness largely depends on their specialized knowledge and their interpersonal skills.

Managers, according to Schermerhorn, Hunt, and Osborn (1998), use positional authority, fear, barter, manipulation, and the bureaucracy of the organization to get others to perform their assigned tasks. Managers receive their authority from the organization's line staff chart and resort to their legitimate authority to gain involuntary compliance through threats or punishments or by withholding or granting favors. Barter involves verbal contracts with subordinates for work in exchange for resources or favors. Managers use manipulation by creating "false hopes," making "artificial promises," or appealing to the good nature of subordinates. Fear is created when managers remind subordinates of performance evaluations or other issues relating to job security. Managers learn how to use the bureaucratic structure to their advantage. That is, they bend the rules for some and not for others while simultaneously reserving latitude for themselves. As discussed in Chapter 1, this, too, is the use of power or authority. Some managers make policy enforcement their reason for being and flaunt it through their scepter of authority, whereas others are loyal to rules and regulations and see this as organizational commitment, job security, and their route to advancement. Subordinates who are subjected to these behaviors will provide *compliance* (the required minimum) at best. At worst, they will display "spiteful obedience" (Bennis & Nanus, 1985).

Managers are *liaisons* who are responsible to their superiors and held accountable for "getting things done." Managers are responsible for the effective and efficient task accomplishment of others. They must possess the necessary expertise to assist others in performing their work *and* to maintain the credibility and respect of subordinates. Effective managerial performance therefore requires good human relations skills. Well-developed human relations skills keep managers from resorting to authoritarian behaviors that have a negative impact on morale, job satisfaction, and respect among subordinates. The manager who develops such skills is developing as a leader, and the organization generally recognizes such development through promotions to jobs requiring more leadership skills and fewer managerial ones. In the case of the assistant principal, the development of such skills may be the pathway to a principalship or a central office position.

Characteristics of Effective Managers. Research has found that those in management positions can be more effective in their tasks by practicing certain behaviors and deemphasizing others. Hammer and Champy (1993) note, for example, that in "progressive, quality-oriented" organizations, managers emphasize teamwork, encourage individual initiative, and practice joint decision making. Drucker (1995) relates that effective managers "help," "support," and "facilitate" others to excel while placing less emphasis on controlling and directing the work of others. Also noted in the research is that effective managers rely less on their authority and power to enforce rules and regulations, and more on providing satisfying experiences that motivate subordinates to perform at higher levels.

The manager's work is highly fragmented in nature. It involves a variety of tasks that consume an average of 10 minutes or less per task; there are constant interruptions during conversations, which are usually short, rapid, and disjointed; and most interactions stem from confusion, frustration, or conflict (Yukl, 1998). Assistant principals in charge of discipline and supervision of students need only think of the number of interruptions that occur while dealing with a routine discipline incident or while supervising students in the cafeteria during lunch to recognize themselves in these descriptions of a manager. Effectiveness in these situations requires conflict management skills, good listening and communication skills, and the ability to empathize and respect the opinions of others.

Managers are "here-and-now" oriented because they have to focus on daily work life and spend their time putting out "campfires" before they become "forest fires." They are troubleshooters whose time is not their own, and they must practice "management by walking around" to solve a myriad of problems that randomly occur. Assistant principals know that when they walk down a hall of the school, they will be approached by several students or teachers who need information or have a "problem." Time not spent on people problems is consumed by paperwork, telephone calls, and meetings. Bass (1990) notes that over 80% of managers' time is spent on specific issues and problems affecting their immediate sphere of influence (as opposed to leaders, who spend the majority of their time on general issues or problems affecting the future of the organization). For these reasons effective managers are highly organized and knowledgeable in time management techniques.

Time Management Techniques

- Use a calendar to coordinate meetings and appointments.
- Keep the calendar with you at all times.
- Plan your day before it begins, either on the afternoon before or the morning of the day.
- Prioritize your activities as you complete them.
- Designate a time of day for routine activities such as returning phone calls, planning your day, opening mail, and so on.
- Make a decision on each piece of paper as you receive it—handle each piece of paper only once, if possible.
- File paper in a well-organized filing system.
- Plan outgoing communication.
- Record incoming communication.

Decision Making and Planning. The decisions managers make are often made in an atmosphere of confusion, frustration, and high-pressure demands. Instead of having time to carefully analyze or reflect, they must frequently make decisions with incomplete information, stopgap measures designed to "stop the bleeding" until superiors can be consulted or a crisis averted. Decisions can be sustained, modified, or overturned by superiors. Decisions frequently made by managers are those authorizing minor deviations from rules or regulations and those focusing on operational problems in the manager's sphere of influence. As a result, planning is usually informal and short range in nature. Planning as a formal, long-range process with written goals, objectives, and implementation strategies falls outside the responsibilities of most frontline managers.

For assistant principals to make the transition from manager to leader, they must be willing and able to step outside their immediate frame of reference—the student sitting in front of them who has just been engaged in an altercation with another student, for example—and not only see the big picture but also develop and implement a plan to improve it.

In the case of discipline, for example, it is easy to get caught up in incident after incident and go home exhausted at the end of the day, only to show up at school the next morning to find the same type of discipline incidents waiting to be dealt with. The assistant principal who is destined to remain an assistant principal may be doing an excellent job of organizing his or her time so these incidents flow smoothly and no time is wasted. He or she may, in fact, be complimented on this orderly flow and on the way students and parents are handled. The assistant principals destined to move on to other leadership positions, on the other hand, will analyze the types of discipline incidents, the possible causes for the incidents, and

---

How to Keep Decisions From Being Overturned

- Review policy, rules, and regulations *before* a crisis occurs.
- Be proactive by solving small problems before they turn into big problems.
- Gather as much relevant information as possible before making a decision.
- Seek input from those who have different perspectives on the problem before making a decision.
- Apply policies, rules, and regulations fairly and equitably.
- Inform the principal of any decision that might be called into question and provide the reasoning that formed the basis for the decision.

---

such factors as the time of day the incidents occurred, searching for patterns that may reveal clues on how these incidents could be avoided in the future. This evolving leader, for example, may discover on looking at the discipline data that 15 incidents out of 45 in the space of 2 days occurred before school began in the morning. Further investigation reveals that some of the teachers assigned to early morning duty had not shown up at their duty stations. With this information the assistant principal has what is needed to resolve the issue that has contributed to 33% of the discipline problems occurring at the school over a period of 2 days.

The temptation in the managerial assignments of the assistant principal is to "relax" into those assignments with no questions asked. In fact, there is hardly time to think as one problem after another bombards the assistant principal. Anyone watching the assistant principal do the job will marvel at the frantic pace, the barrage of problems, and the ratio of those problems to the number of hours in a workday. Many of those observers will resolve never to become an assistant principal. Those destined to remain managers or assistant principals will revel in the feeling of being "needed." How could the school function without them? Leaders, on the other hand, will find the time to get to the root causes of the problems by analyzing the data for patterns. It is this ability to see "the big picture" that separates managers from leaders. These "big picture" leaders will plan, using a formal process with written goals, objectives, and implementation strategies.

Role Effectiveness. Manager effectiveness is often related to how well one meets the role expectations held by superiors *and* subordinates. Bass (1990) found that managers are often placed between conflicting demands and expectations of superiors and subordinates, and are then forced to choose between the separate role expectations held by these two groups. Manager effectiveness therefore largely depends on how conflicts or problems are resolved to each party's satisfaction, relative to the manager's behavior, within the role expectations held by these parties. Manager effectiveness is also related to task objectives. That is, certain tasks may require managers to behave inconsistently with role expectations held by superiors or subordinates; that is, managers are forced to choose between effective task completion and role expectations. Role choice often places managers in compromising situations because their effectiveness and job security largely depend on the satisfaction of superiors and subordinates.

Role effectiveness may be impacted by complacency. Complacency is being self-satisfied and unaware of existing problems or discontent in the workforce. Unchanged responsibilities, lack of personal challenges, and longevity in the position lead to a status quo disposition of complacency where change is viewed as threatening. Habits are formed and become deeply rooted, and new ideas or ways to improve are resisted. This resistance and stagnation often leads to discontent on the part of superiors, and manager replacement soon follows (Stewart, 1982).

Low turnover in the workforce may be an indicator of manager effectiveness. Superiors often view stability in the workforce as an indicator of job satisfaction and high morale (Stewart, 1982). On the other hand, there may be high levels of discontent, but job scarcity and other economic factors may mask employee dissatisfaction.

Leaders

Leadership and leaders are great topics of fascination that stir excitement and interest in people because of the mystical and enchanting aura that surrounds them. Examples of the leadership phenomenon are many and come from military, political, religious, and civic leaders who impacted their nations and the world both positively and negatively. As discussed in the preceding chapter, ideas about leadership focus on questions about leader characteristics and definitions of leaders. Leaders are usually defined according to the sum total of one's own experiences, and definitions vary from perspective to perspective. That is, definitions of what a leader is remain individual in nature and are expressed in terms of what "makes sense" to those experiencing this "enchanted mystery."

The generic aspect of leadership is that a leader-follower relationship must exist. Leaders do not lead in isolation. Some argue that leaders have certain traits, behaviors, interaction patterns, role relationships, and administrative positions and responsibilities. Others argue that leaders create an *influence process* to accomplish their goals by applying different *methods* of influence. These methods vary depending on the situation and personalities involved. Influences can be rooted in emotional appeals, social and psychological theory, professional and ethical standards, economics and politics, or reason and analytical thought.

Generally, however, leaders plan strategically, delegate authority, motivate others, coordinate programs and activities, and use influence and persuasion to achieve their ends. Leaders focus on developing human potential, forming bonds and relationships with subordinates, and gaining voluntary commitment among followers. Leaders are viewed as being fair, honest, and trustworthy, and they work in the best interests of their followers. Leaders also inspire, challenge, shape ideas, and originate. Leaders have been said to be "movers and shakers"; others define leaders as "guardians" or "caretakers" who are caring, empathetic, people oriented, and concerned with the economic and psychological well-being of their followers.

In essence, leaders perform functions that impact the organization on a "large scale" because they are concerned with and are responsible for the "global" issues and aspects of organizational life. Leaders are responsible for the overall effectiveness and efficiency of the organization and delegate authority to managers for the daily operations, problems, and crises confronting it.

Characteristics and Practices of Effective Leaders. Etzioni (1988) relates that effective leaders work on changing attitudes and behaviors, create high expectations for others, and provide an atmosphere where others can succeed and excel. Yukl (1998) notes that leader effectiveness is best determined by the consequences of a leader's decisions on followers, specifically, how decisions impact job satisfaction, morale, and the commitment to meet organizational goals. Other indicators of effectiveness include advancement to higher positions of authority, improvement of subordinates' work life, and recognition from external sources.

The following list of effective leader behaviors includes practices and behaviors deemed essential for those in leadership positions:

- *Delegating:* Empowering subordinates to make decisions, solve problems, and expand their sphere of influence by taking initiative, being creative, and assuming more responsibilities

- *Planning:* Creating vision, mission, and long-term goals for the organization and developing a strategic plan that incorporates resource allocations, priorities, and the means for evaluating goal attainment

- *Monitoring:* Evaluating personnel performance, the quality of outputs, progress toward meeting the goals of the organization, and trends and issues impacting the effectiveness and efficiency of the organization

- *Supporting and Mentoring:* Facilitating the work of others, providing moral and fiscal support, counseling and listening to complaints and problems, coaching and mentoring, and helping others advance and develop professionally

- *Consulting:* Seeking advice from others before implementing change, encouraging suggestions for improvement, practicing joint decision making, and using the ideas of others in planning and decision making

- *Motivating:* Creating enthusiasm for work, achieving the vision and goals of the organization, and inspiring others to maximize their human potential

- *Problem Solving:* Identifying root causes of problems, finding solutions based on facts and accurate information, and acting in a timely manner to resolve problems and crises

- *Informing:* Disseminating accurate and timely information about plans and decisions that affect people and their work and fulfilling requests for information about resources and assistance

- *Networking:* Developing social contacts, building an internal and external network to gather and disseminate information, and building relationships for support and assistance

- *Rewarding and Recognizing:* Providing monetary rewards or promotions for superior performance, achievement, competency, and innovations and providing praise and recognition for performance, loyalty, achievement, contributions, and effort (Adapted from Yukl, 1998)

Developing a Personal Approach to Leadership. Because there is no one leadership style or set of behaviors deemed universally effective, cookbook approaches to leadership are rarely effective. What is needed for effective leadership is the *individual* approach based on self-knowledge, an understanding of effective leadership knowledge and skills research, and experiences that allow for trial and error as one proceeds to polish and refine one's practice of leadership.

Leadership self-knowledge is knowing one's own strengths and weaknesses and one's tolerance for limitations in others, and having a well-defined philosophy of life and leadership. Knowledge and skills of effective leadership include the study of leader behavior patterns, role expectations, and traits. Skill areas include good human relations and communications skills. Experiences include practicing leader behaviors and actions, and observing recognized leaders as they practice their craft.

Highly effective leaders integrate the right mix of managerial and leadership behaviors as required by the situation and personalities involved. In addition, these leaders work hard to gain a *personal knowledge* of their subordinates that provides them with a clear understanding of what motivates each of their subordinates, what challenges they expect from their work, and their personal and professional goals. Practicing "management by walking around"—having lunch and coffee with subordinates, and engaging in chitchat during chance encounters—provides insight into what makes subordinates tick.

Other practices you can use to promote leadership effectiveness are as follows:

- Develop or assess your leadership philosophy and determine if your philosophy is appropriate for the subordinates for whom you are responsible and the tasks they perform. Effective leaders continuously reflect on how people respond to leader behaviors and then adjust their behaviors accordingly.

- Use the list of effective leader behaviors presented above to guide your interactions with subordinates in fulfilling your responsibilities.

- Use the vision and goals of your school or school system to guide your planning, goal-setting, and decision-making activities. Develop action plans for self- and school improvement in a variety of areas.

- Delegate authority; foster teamwork and collaboration; provide timely and accurate information; and reward, recognize, and praise superior performance and competency.

Moving From Manager to Leader

Desire, Commitment, and Initiative

Regardless of the principal's leadership style, the essential first step in becoming a leader is to make a conscious decision to assume leadership roles and practice leader behaviors. Desire, commitment, and initiative are the key motivational factors assistant principals need to make the transition from manager to leader.

Initiative is a key leadership quality that excites and stimulates others and is contagious and admirable among a followership (Burns, 1978). Taking the initiative, "seizing the moment," motivates and inspires others to follow and accomplish difficult tasks. The wry statement attributed to George Washington, "An army of asses led by a lion is vastly superior to an army of lions led by an ass," is worthy advice for assistant principals making the leadership transition. *Desire* and *commitment* are essential to stay the course and promote stability and admiration in the followership. Desire and commitment, according to Machiavelli, provide the leader with the necessary "armor" essential for successful statecraft, for "among other evils which being unarmed brings you, it causes you to be despised by your subjects" (p. 39).

Theory and Research

A firm understanding of the basic theories of leadership is essential for effective practice. As those who don't understand the past are doomed to repeat it, those without an understanding of leadership theory will repeat the mistakes of their predecessors. Leadership theory provides the all-important knowledge base leaders need to plan and execute the daily demands of leadership. Knowledge of theory allows leaders to choose the wisest course of action before they act and increases the probability of their success. Lunenburg and Ornstein (1996) note the value of leaders understanding and applying leadership theory, and argue its importance in another dimension as well—its use in *reflective thinking*. Theory, these authors maintain, provides leaders a base for judging the effectiveness of their own performance. That is, effective leaders reflect on their behaviors and use feedback from others to assess the impact and "meaning" of their behavior on others. Reflective thinking used in conjunction with theory allows leaders to understand their behaviors and then modify their conduct to enhance their effectiveness. Leaders are less likely to act arbitrarily when they reflect on their actions from a research-based perspective.

Being a constant consumer of research is equally essential for leadership success. Staying abreast of the most current findings in areas impacting leader behavior is essential if leaders are to practice their craft more effectively. Subscribing to research journals, being active in professional associations, and attending conferences and workshops are ways leaders can keep current and include research in their practice.

Building a Leadership Plan

Various criteria can be used to build a leadership plan, but we believe that the most expedient criterion is situation specific. That is, assistant principals should look to the evaluation criteria currently used in their own school to assess job effectiveness as a template for planning an individual leadership program. Evaluation criteria are statements delineating what is *valued* and *expected* at the local level. Meeting these criteria is essential for job security and promotion. Local criteria will not provide opportunities to apply all effective leadership behaviors, but they will allow assistant principals to gain leader experience in areas most valued at the local level. Taking the initiative and expanding those areas to incorporate additional leader behaviors provides the competitive edge for those on the fast track to the principalship. To do this, assistant principals should develop individual improvement or action plans.

Selecting additional leader behaviors will depend on existing opportunities; first and foremost, however, the availability of opportunities will depend on the predominant leadership style of the principal. The most commonly defined styles of leadership are authoritarian, laissez-faire, and democratic. *Authoritarian* leaders emphasize bureaucratic authority, rely on their positional power to motivate, believe in disciplined compliance to policy and an impersonal approach to leadership, and seek additional avenues to control and direct the behavior of others. Authoritarians believe in the sanctity of authority, view loyalty to the organization and themselves as the most essential quality of subordinates, and are managers more than leaders.

Laissez-faire leaders are few in number and primarily found in organizations employing highly motivated, goal-oriented, independent thinkers who need excessive freedom to be creative and pursue their own agendas. Universities and research centers are where laissez-faire leadership thrives, because this type of leader is mostly a facilitator who functions as a leader only when asked or compelled. Many argue that this leadership style is inappropriate for schools, which are public agencies governed by federal, state, and local policies.

The *democratic* style of leadership involves participative governance, teamwork, and teacher empowerment. Leaders practicing this leadership style are people oriented, use their influence and persuasion (as opposed to authority) to achieve their goals, delegate responsibility, and work to meet the needs of subordinates and organization alike.

Assistant principals will have more opportunities to expand their leadership roles under democratic leaders. These leaders are more willing to delegate authority and involve others in decision making and problem solving, as they are more flexible and open to new ideas. Those with authoritarian principals will find their best opportunities to develop additional leadership competencies during large-scale change initiatives or when working with small groups where leader behaviors that run contrary to the principal's are not easily detected. Under such authoritarian leadership, assistant principals often find the leadership variables of initiative, determination, and commitment sorely needed and severely tested.

Modeling and Reading Research

Leadership plans can be enhanced by incorporating and modeling behaviors of recognized leaders. Observing and then modeling these behaviors expands one's leadership experiences. Practicing reflective thinking based on the actions of role models provides valuable insight into leader behavior and allows one to establish a habit recognized as good practice. Models for leadership can be found in the school system, in the community, and at the state and national levels of government.

Reading research published in recognized professional journals on a regular basis allows assistant principals to keep current on the latest best practices in the field. As consumers of research, assistant principals can continuously update their leadership plans with new ways to expand their leadership experience by testing research findings in a field setting. By attending professional conferences and workshops and being active in professional organizations, assistant principals can establish professional networks *and* gain firsthand information about effective practices. Keeping current on the research is essential because practices considered leader competencies today may be deemed less effective tomorrow.

Conducting Action Research

Action research is a valuable tool for testing new hypotheses, programs, and practices at the school level. Action research methods are the same as experimental research methods but with one all-important difference—the lack of random sampling and hence an inability to generalize the experimental results to a wider population. When new research findings appear in the literature or at conferences, assistant principals who are keeping current can apply action research methods in their own schools to determine their effectiveness with their own teachers or students. Incorporating action research into a leadership plan expands the range of possible experiences and allows assistant principals to actually test the latest research "in their own backyards."

Action research allows assistant principals to replicate empirical studies and test the results in their own situations. Researchers have long valued the accumulation of findings over time as a way of proving or disproving theory. Replication is the practice of taking an existing study or piece of research and conducting the study as described in a journal or book with a like population. Assistant principals can, for example, replicate studies conducted on situational leadership or transformational leader theory (discussed in the preceding chapter). The findings of action research projects may or may not coincide with the findings of the literature. When findings run counter to the published research, it may be due to variables such as sampling techniques, inadequate time or resources to conduct a true replication of the study, or the fact that the investigated phenomenon really does not work with the experimental population. Regardless of the outcomes of the study, assistant principals conducting such research have gained important new knowledge about those who are *now leading* and they can modify their approaches to leadership accordingly.

Making Time for Leadership

Making time for leadership activities may be difficult at best for assistant principals whose primary responsibilities are discipline and attendance and whose other duties are mostly managerial in nature. Regardless of the job assignments, assistant principals must make time for acquiring leadership competencies as they fulfill their current job responsibilities, and there are many opportunities to do so. For example, assistant principals spend most of their time interacting with others in face-to-face meetings; resolving conflicts and crises; serving as counselors, mentors, and confidants; resolving problems; and making decisions that affect others. Despite the lack of a *formal* leadership role attached to the assistant principal, these activities require leadership behaviors and provide assistant principals the opportunity to take the initiative to develop additional leadership competencies.

See the appendix to this chapter for a sample of a personal improvement plan for assistant principals. The Comprehensive Leadership Plan allows assistant principals to develop leadership competencies in their own school or school system, at their own pace, and with their own job description or responsibilities as a point of departure. Moreover, the plan can serve as a guide for identifying opportunities to apply leader behaviors and then test and reflect on the outcomes. By using real-life situations as a proving ground, assistant principals can modify and refine leadership skills under actual working conditions.

Developing a Skills and Knowledge Base

There is no single set of instructional leadership practices deemed to be universally effective, but elsewhere we provide some starting points for school administrators who target instructional improvement as their major goal (Weller & Weller, 2000). These starting points have direct application for assistant principals who seek to gain experience and prepare for the principalship. Taking a leadership role in the instructional area is an essential first step for assistant principals who aspire to the role of principal.

First, assistant principals should ask to be given an active role in the evaluation of teachers. Evaluating teacher performance allows assistant principals to acquire leadership experience in coordinating, planning and goal setting, problem solving, interpersonal communications, mentoring, and rewarding and praising. For example, through the coordination of teacher observations and participation in preobservation conferences, assistant principals help teachers plan and prepare for classroom observations by reviewing their lesson plans and helping them overcome individual problems. Postobservation conferences allow assistant principals to practice their interpersonal skills as they praise teachers for exemplary performance or plan and problem-solve with teachers on ways to remediate weaknesses. Here assistant principals have the opportunity to serve as mentors, as coordinators for peer coaching or tutoring programs, or as developers of staff development activities.

Second, assistant principals should become troubleshooters proactive in seeking out potential problems and addressing them before they can negatively impact teaching and learning. Such problems can be detected through attending team or committee meetings, engaging in chitchat with teachers, talking with parents and students, and attending community functions.

Third, assistant principals must become experts at providing essential and timely classroom resources to teachers, including textbooks, supplemental materials, computer software, and copy machine privileges. Effective leaders circulate a "wish list" for teachers to specify their needs in priority order. When money becomes available—and instructional leaders become experts at finding "available" funding—assistant principals should purchase these items for teachers in the order they have specified.

Finally, instructional leadership is demonstrated by creating and maintaining a climate, or *ethos*, promoting instructional excellence. Assistants aspiring to leadership roles must make academics the major topic of discussion with an emphasis on achieving quality in teaching and learning. They should talk freely with teachers about academics, improvement of instruction, high expectations for student learning, and curriculum revitalization, and they should recognize and reward teacher and student achievements.

Promoting Job Satisfaction: Survey Results

We surveyed assistant principals and asked what practices they currently employ to promote teachers' job satisfaction or morale. Our survey results indicate comprehensive efforts in this direction. The majority of the respondents listed the more traditional intrinsic motivators of praise, recognition, and demonstration of concern and empathy. Interestingly, no respondent mentioned intrinsic motivators dealing with self-esteem or self-actualization. Also omitted from the responses were mentions of providing clear, accurate, and timely information; increasing responsibilities or promoting greater job autonomy; or redesigning work assignments or responsibilities.

Efforts to improve job satisfaction included banquets to recognize and reward teacher achievements, a teacher-of-the-month award, a bulletin board dedicated to teachers and their achievements, teacher representation on administrative team meetings, the introduction of shared governance, teacher-led focus groups, seminars for professional and personal improvement, money for teachers to attend conferences and workshops, more planning time, and securing parent and community volunteers to free teachers from lunchroom and bus duty. Despite the many things assistant principals are doing to improve teacher morale and job

---

What Do Assistant Principals Do to Promote Teacher Job Satisfaction and Morale?

- Praise
- Recognize
- Demonstrate personal regard
- Invite teacher participation in problem solving and decision making
- Provide a safe and pleasant working environment
- Promote good working relationships
- Help teachers develop professionally
- Work with teachers to deal with unfair treatment or policies
- Help teachers obtain promotions to department heads or instructional lead teachers

SOURCE: 2000 Survey of 100 Practicing Assistant Principals From Rural, Urban, and Suburban Schools

---

satisfaction, many of them made comments about the difficulty of finding the time to do so; finding the time is essential for a leader, however.

Job satisfaction, or morale, is essential to promoting effective instructional outcomes. Some, including ourselves (see Weller & Weller, 2000), maintain it is the *most* important factor in promoting quality outcomes from teachers and staff members alike. Job satisfaction depends on a mixture of psychological, task-related, and environmental variables. Lunenburg and Ornstein (1996) note that job satisfaction depends on the degree of importance administrators place on human resources. That is, the more administrators value their people, the higher the levels of morale and job satisfaction.

What are the most common job satisfiers? Newstrom and Davis (1997), in a summary of the research, report that pay, job autonomy, challenge, variety, and significance are the most important *task* job satisfiers. *Environmental* satisfiers include safety, professionalism, pleasant working conditions, fair and equitable treatment, and trust and respect. *Psychological* satisfiers include job security, friendships and good working relationships, rewards and recognition of achievements, responsibility, and personal development.

More recently, job satisfaction has been viewed as a function of attitude and perception. Newstrom and Davis describe attitudes as feelings or emotions toward people, offices, or "things," which contribute to the perceptions people hold about their work, their work life, their peers, and their supervisors. Perceptions are personal beliefs that trigger actions and reactions to problems, situations, and

---

What Assistant Principals Say About Their Efforts to Improve Teacher Morale

"I know all that stuff about Maslow and Herzberg, but I don't have time to apply it the way I want to. Besides, my principal is not the 'warm and fuzzy' type. She is a no-nonsense person who believes that teachers have jobs to do. If they don't do them, she'll see that they perform, or it's the road."

"Bottom line, teachers know the pay is low when they enter the profession. No one made them become teachers. All I hear is 'We need more money.' Making teachers happy is fine if you have the time, but I don't. Besides, who said that happy teachers are more effective?"

"When nine teachers met with the principal at once, he got the wake-up call loud and clear. Since then, he has been more attuned to teacher needs and has made me realize the importance of satisfied teachers."

"I truly know job satisfaction is important. Believe me, I was a teacher for seven years. But my degree program in leadership never taught me the practical application of theory on motivation—just theory."

"My principal is not really into job satisfaction theory. When I talk to him about some of my ideas, he either says, 'Let's talk later' or 'Let's wait until the teachers press for it.' I have my job to do and I do what I can in what little time I have to give the teachers 'uppers,' but I can't go against my principal. I need his recommendation for a school of my own and I need to keep this job."

SOURCE: 2000 Survey of 100 Practicing Assistant Principals From Urban, Rural, and Suburban Schools

---

the environment. When perceptions toward one or more work attribute are negative, the potential for conflict is high, morale is low, and poor performance generally results. Positive attitudes and perceptions promote productivity, morale, and job satisfaction. Effective leaders seek ways to provide positive "mental sets" for subordinates so they can view their jobs and workplace more positively. Positive mental sets require leaders to help subordinates see the positive side of their situations such as long-range or indirect benefits.

Bardwick (1991) investigated job satisfaction and attitude and found that subordinates hold one of three broad types of work attitudes:

1. *Earning:* Subordinates believe that rewards, praise, promotion, and recognition must be earned. Superiors have the right to judge work, but rewards must be fair and equitable and reflect work performance. Morale and job satisfaction levels are high.

2. *Fear:* Fear of job loss, demotion, and unfair treatment force subordinates to focus on self-preservation and take a cynical attitude toward their work and the future. Job satisfaction and morale are low.

3. *Entitlement:* Subordinates believe they are entitled to rewards, recognition, and promotion. When these entitlements are not forthcoming, apathy sets in, and low morale and job performance result.

Fear and *entitlement* attitudes can be mitigated when superiors and subordinates *jointly* develop an accountability system with fair and equitable standards of excellence and rewards. This joint collaboration helps lessen fears about job performance and increases the probability that rewards and recognitions will be fairly applied.

Hoy and Miskel (1996) note that job satisfaction is *cumulative* in nature because it takes several contributing variables over time to develop. Job satisfaction can dissipate more quickly than it can develop. Job dissatisfiers are individual in scope, with salary, working conditions, and relationships with peers and subordinates being the most common. For teachers, job dissatisfiers are poor interpersonal relations with peers, students, and administrators; lack of praise, recognition, and reward; lack of responsibility and autonomy; unfair policies and administrative practices; and unsafe working environments. Other factors that negatively impact teachers, report Lunenburg and Ornstein (1996), are lack of participation in decisions about curriculum, instruction, and school policy; lack of respect and not being viewed as competent; and being required to perform extracurricular duties without pay or other compensation.

Assistant principals are challenged to find ways to promote teachers' job satisfaction. Most teachers, however, have many things in common, and the following examples provide a starting point to increase teacher morale:

- Praise, recognize, and reward when warranted and with sincerity
- Involve teachers in solving problems and making decisions about the school policy and instructional program
- Provide ways in which teachers can use their talents and creativity to enhance the school's programs

- Develop learning programs such as seminars or focus groups where teachers can develop professionally and personally and where keeping current in their fields is both fun and stimulating

- Adopt the mind-set that teachers can be leaders, and help teachers acquire some of the essential leadership knowledge and skills for future administrative positions

Passing the Torch: Developing Teachers as Leaders

One of the most important responsibilities of leaders is the obligation to pass the torch of leadership to those coming after them. In education, teachers constitute the largest group of potential leaders and are an unlimited resource for promoting school effectiveness. In many schools, however, little is done to capitalize on or enhance teachers' leadership capabilities. Very few are offered or assigned competent leadership roles in the school. Assistant principals can take the initiative to promote the teacher-as-leader concept by identifying teacher leaders and then providing them with opportunities to lead others and gain leadership experience.

The idea of a "community of leaders" is the keystone of the teacher-as-leader concept. Many teachers enroll in leadership programs to attain leadership certification or have natural leadership ability, but choose to remain in the classrooms to which they are dedicated. These teachers' talents should be utilized to contribute to the overall improvement of school programs. Leadership opportunities and responsibilities abound, and only a limited imagination on the part of school administrators keeps teachers from realizing their leadership potential.

Teachers as Leaders Defined

Definitions of teachers as leaders are many and varied. Schlechty (1990) defines teachers as leaders when they strive to influence peers to become more effective in classrooms and when they themselves become active in school governance committees or chair committees that undertake educational reform. Wilson (1993) relates that teachers' leadership is evidenced in the future behavior and successes of their students and that successful teachers motivate, challenge, and encourage risk taking and creativity in their students. Here teachers are to students what principals are to teachers.

Teacher Leadership Roles: A New Perspective

Viewing teachers as leaders requires a paradigm shift in the concept of leadership. Assistant principals must first be willing to view teachers as leaders rather than as subordinates under contract with specific duties to perform. Next, assistant principals must advance the paradigm shift by recalling their years as teachers and the frustrations they experienced with their attempts to lead improvement initiatives in their own schools and classrooms. Most likely, whatever frustrations existed then still exist now for teachers. Finally, when assistant principals reflect on the leadership characteristics of their teachers and the opportunities that exist for teachers to lead, old stereotypes and assumptions can be replaced with new mental models of the teacher as leader. The actions that follow such a shift in perception often result in teachers who begin to see administrators differently as well. As the joke in the box on the following page indicates, it's definitely time for such a shift in our thinking.

Conventional Teacher Leadership Roles

Teacher leadership roles include department head; administrative assistant or intern; lead teacher; master teacher; and chairperson of committees, task forces, or teacher instructional teams. Ad hoc appointments to positions such as director of summer school or of an alternative school are some of the more recent leadership positions that are being delegated to teachers. Some of these positions carry positional authority, but others are functional positions that necessitate the use of a teacher's ability to influence others through personality, interpersonal skills, or special skills and knowledge.

Means for Developing Teachers as Leaders

Assistant principals can help teachers develop leadership experiences in their school by creating opportunities and taking initiative in the following ways:

- Encourage teachers to speak openly and honestly about issues they strongly believe in and to work with others to improve all aspects of schooling
- Delegate authority to teachers to solve problems and make decisions that impact the efficiency and effectiveness of their classrooms, grade levels, and departments
- Encourage teachers to conduct action research, to be creative and innovative, to take risks, and to plan and coordinate improvement programs with other teachers
- Reward, praise, and recognize teacher leadership efforts
- Encourage teachers to discuss leadership ideas and initiatives with peers and administrators

---

Perfect Analysis

A man in a hot air balloon realized he was lost. He reduced altitude and spotted a woman below. He descended a bit more and shouted, "Excuse me, can you help me? I promised a friend I would meet him an hour ago, but I don't know where I am."

The woman below replied, "You are in a hot air balloon hovering approximately 30 feet above the ground. You are between 40 and 41 degrees north latitude and between 59 and 60 degrees west longitude."

"You must be a teacher," said the man.

"I am," replied the woman. "How did you know?"

"Well," answered the man. "Everything you told me is technically correct, but I have no idea what to make of your information, and the fact is I am still lost. Frankly, you haven't been much help so far."

The woman responded, "You must be an administrator."

"I am," replied the man, "but how did you know?"

"Well," said the woman, "you don't know where you are or where you are going. You have risen to where you are due to a large quantity of hot air. You made a promise which you have no idea how to keep, and you expect me to solve your problem. The fact is you are in exactly the same position you were in before we met, but now, somehow, it's my fault."

(Author unknown)

- Encourage teachers to take leadership roles in the community and in professional, civic, and social organizations
- Conduct staff development programs for teachers on leadership theory and its application to school problems

A Teacher Leadership Development Model

Assistant principals can take the lead in developing and nurturing the teacher-as-leader concept by implementing a six-stage process:

1. Informally talk with teachers about their interest in leadership positions. Point out that many of their daily classroom activities with students are leadership behaviors, for example, planning lessons, organizing instructional materials, teaching through group work and individual tutoring, seeking student input on preferred learning activities, and evaluating both their performance and that of their students.

2. Gather information about teacher interest in leadership through conversations and questionnaires to assess teachers' current and future leadership aspirations. This information then becomes the basis for developing structured staff development programs that allow teachers to explore leadership opportunities and acquire skills and knowledge associated with leadership behavior.

3. Conduct seminars and interest groups that focus on paths to leadership positions and the knowledge and skills essential for these positions. Informal counseling sessions can help teachers identify leadership positions that are closely aligned with their current and future aspirations.

4. Create opportunities in the school for teachers to become leaders. Providing teachers with student teachers, establishing peer coaching networks, and placing teachers as chairs of committees and teams are all ways to introduce teachers to leadership responsibilities.

5. Assist teachers in finding leadership positions in other schools, in the school system's central office, and on committees in the community and school system.

6. Serve as a mentor to those seeking an assistant principalship. Provide release time for teachers to "shadow" assistant principals, and delegate administrative responsibilities to these teachers as they practice the craft of building-level leadership and prepare for an administrative position.

Helping Teachers Demonstrate Leadership Skills

Assistant principals can help teachers demonstrate the leadership trait of risk taking by giving permission and encouragement for new and innovative programs or teaching methods and encouraging teachers to show initiative and a desire for self-improvement by seeking national certification. As team leaders, teachers can develop leadership skills that apply to group leadership. These include building commitment and self-confidence, creating opportunities for others to excel or lead, resolving conflict, leading by example, and removing obstacles imposed by others so the group can achieve its goals (Buckner & McDowelle, 2000).

Teachers can also practice interpersonal skills essential for effective leadership. These include effective listening, writing, and oral communication skills and the ability to provide objective and prompt feedback to others. Being responsive and empathetic to the needs and concerns of students and peers is also an essential leadership trait. Assistant principals should encourage teachers to be data oriented in solving problems and resolving conflict. Effective leaders seek data to solve problems and gather a variety of information from a variety of sources prior to making decisions; teachers must, however, be provided with experiences to practice these skills, and assistant principals should provide such opportunities while they serve as mentors to these teachers.

Let's Review

Assistant principals are both managers and leaders. Managers are functionaries who pay attention to detail, enforce policy, structure the work environment, address daily problems, reward and praise, and marshal resources for others to do their work. To become leaders and move up in the administrative ranks, if that is their desire, assistant principals must plan and implement strategies to develop leadership skills and knowledge, and their position affords them plenty of opportunities to do so. Assistant principals must become proactive and spend time shaping ideas, changing attitudes, challenging others to do their best, creating high expectations, and maximizing the talents of others. Assistant principals must enhance the effectiveness of their schools by taking advantage of the leadership skills of department heads and lead teachers and the teacher-as-leader concept.

Exercises

Exercise 1: Manager or Leader?

Refer to the portions of this chapter on manager and leader behaviors and tasks. Observe your assistant principal and your principal for a total of 4 hours each (this may take a week or more) and note the behaviors and tasks associated with each position on separate sheets of paper. Then indicate how each person observed could be more effective in his or her behaviors and tasks. How could both parties become more effective leaders and spend less time as managers?

Exercise 2: Evaluating Yourself as a Leader

Again refer to the sections in this chapter that discuss manager and leader behaviors. Keep a daily log of your activities for 5 days or more. Omit no activity in your daily log. Examine which activities are associated with leadership and which with management. Draft a plan to incorporate more leadership behaviors in your daily routine over a 4-week time period. Draft another plan to refine or perfect your current leadership and managerial activities.

Exercise 3: Job Satisfiers and Dissatisfiers

Ask four of your peers to write down their current job satisfiers and dissatisfiers. Compare the lists and then ask each peer to develop a plan on how to increase job satisfaction and decrease job dissatisfaction. Again compare the plans. Are they similar? If so, discuss these results with an administrator of your choice and note the administrator's reaction. Some questions to ask your administrator include: (a) What can be done to improve job satisfaction? (b) Can my colleagues and I help? (c) Do you think you might be able to use these results?

Case Study: Why Do Good People Always Go?

Hayden Goodlead (Mr. G) is the director of the Regional Education Service Center and is a former school superintendent. Being of the old school, Mr. G believes that the organization is supreme—all must do all for the organization. Mr. G is good with figures. Some say he keeps the budget in his back pocket. Mr. G believes in a day's work for a day's pay and that rules exist for a purpose—a good purpose. Joe, a general consultant at the center, is Mr. G's "fair-haired boy." Joe idolizes Mr. G and uses him as a role model for leadership. Mr. G loves attention, and he quickly notices Joe's admiration. Mr. G makes Joe head of the Planning, Research, and Evaluation Department after Joe helps the area high school get a $10,000 grant for the Driver's Education Department.

When Mr. G makes Joe department head, he says to Joe, "The secret to success is to be loyal, mind your own business, and run a tight ship. You have six consultants over there in your department, and I know you will do a good job. Any problems, come see me." Joe, kind of timid at first, eventually says: "Mr. G, if it's all right with you, I'll take your lead in running things. That way, I can't go wrong." Mr. G smiles, nods approvingly, and says, "Get to work, Joe. Time is money and people need to work from 8 to 5 with no slacking off on company time. Hear me?"

Joe has an opening in his department and Elaine Eager has excellent credentials for it. She has a PhD in research methods, has worked for a big-name testing corporation for 5 years, and has written a best-selling book on research and evaluation methods. She is so good that Joe and the other members in the department can't believe she wants to work at the service center. Joe tells Stan to be on his best behavior when he interviews Elaine. Stan is the one Joe trusts the most in the department. Stan idolizes Joe much as Joe idolizes Mr. G and talks to him frequently about how to advance in the organization. Joe delights in helping Stan with grant-writing questions and responding to his inquiries on how to be an effective leader.

Stan does as he is told. He "sells" Elaine on the job, and Joe offers Elaine a contract. Elaine, always eager to settle things, signs the contract and says she can start tomorrow. As Elaine is about to leave Joe's office, Joe says: "We start at 8 a.m. sharp and quit at 5 p.m., theoretically. Mr. G likes to see people here at 7:45 a.m. and work until you get a job done—like 5:30 p.m. or so. The employees' handbook is with my secretary. Read it. It's Mr. G's good book, and it's one we all follow, to the letter. See you at your desk at 7:45 a.m."

Next day, Elaine introduces herself to the other department members and then gets busy with her first assignment. At lunch, she learns that Bill and Sue are planning on leaving in 3 weeks when their contracts expire. Carol is also looking for a job but has 6 months until her contract expires. Stan, she learns, is very happy with his job and plans to retire at the service center. No one, however, will give precise reasons on why they are dissatisfied. Bill, the most informative, just says: "Wait and see. The honeymoon won't last long."

During the second week of the third month of Elaine's employment, Joe calls her into his office at 8:03 a.m. Joe is sitting at his desk, and before Elaine can speak Joe says: "We have to reach an understanding. Wait until I finish before you say anything, OK? Now, on three occasions you entered your office at 8:05, 8:07, and 8:10 in the morning. Then you got coffee, talked to the secretaries and the rest of the staff, and your productivity began at 8:30 on each of those days. Lunch is from 12 to 1 p.m. On two occasions, you were more than 10 minutes late. Your expenses exceed the maximum allowed for mileage and meals by $5 over the past 2 months. Mr. G does not like that; therefore I do not like that. This is an efficient operation. Now you may speak."

Elaine is dumbfounded. Finally, she says: "Joe, I guess you are right. But as you know, I take work home, I have established good working relations, and you said last week that my work is 'excellent.' I'm at a loss for words."

Joe then says, "Stan helps me keep track of things. He stands on the front loading dock and sees who comes in on time. Good man, that Stan. Anyway, if you want a salary raise this year, you need to reread Mr. G's good book. Now I have work to do and so do you. Good day."

Elaine goes to her office, makes a telephone call, and at the end of the day meets Joe for an appointment she scheduled through Joe's secretary. Elaine tells Joe that she has a job offer she cannot refuse with the federal government in Washington. Because she knows he will hold her to her contract, she offers to pay the service center her monthly salary until a replacement can be found. Joe, knowing that some grant monies come from the federal agency Elaine will be working for, says it is not necessary for her to pay the service center.

The next morning, Joe meets with Mr. G and repeats his conversation with Elaine. Mr. G shakes his head and then says: "Joe, why do we lose good people? I know! They use this excellent training ground as a way to gain valuable experience to enhance their own résumés. They know of our outstanding reputation and use us to feather their own nests. Well, Joe, that's OK. Our reputation just spreads and spreads. Now get out there and find some more excellent people. You do a great job, Joe. I'm proud of you."

1. If you were to asked to give advice to Mr. G. about how to run the service, what specifically would you tell him?

2. If you were asked to give advice to Joe about leadership, what specifically would you tell him?

3. If you were asked to give advice to Elaine about what questions to ask on a job interview, what specifically would you tell her?

4. After you provided advice to both Mr. G and Joe, do you think there would be behavior changes in either one? Why? Why not?

(This case study is a true experience, with some minor modifications, that one of us personally lived through.)

Appendix

Comprehensive Leadership Plan

Part I: Leadership Categories and Behaviors

Directions: Part I lists 10 leadership categories associated with effective leaders. In the space under Behaviors, list the specific behaviors you choose to develop over a specific time period. As you develop these behaviors, continue to expand the list.

Categories	*Behaviors*

1. Delegating:

2. Planning:

3. Monitoring:

4. Supporting and Mentoring:

5. Consulting:

6. Motivating:

7. Problem Solving:

8. Informing:

9. Networking:

10. Rewarding and Recognizing:

Part II: Self-Knowledge

Directions: Part II contains four fundamental areas of knowledge essential to effective leadership. Provide information relevant to these four areas. Work to strengthen identified deficiencies by developing your own self-improvement plan.

1. Philosophy of Leadership (in 50 words or less)

2. Knowledge of Leadership Theory

3. Knowledge of One's Strengths and Weaknesses

4. Research Journals and Professional Organizations

Part III: Job Evaluation Criteria

Directions: Part III presents four questions essential to expanding your development of leadership competencies. Using your job description, list your primary job responsibilities and then answer the following questions. Use the answers to these questions to plan ways to increase your leader competencies.

1. List your job responsibilities in rank order of what is important to you as an administrator.

2. List your job responsibilities in rank order of what is important to your principal.

3. List your job responsibilities in rank order of what is important to teachers.

4. Are there differences in areas of importance on your list? If so, develop a self-improvement plan for including as many leader competencies as you can while meeting the expectations of yourself, your principal, and teachers. Refer to Parts I and II as starting points for your plan.

Part IV: Modeling Leader Behavior

Directions: Part IV contains four activities designed to enhance your leadership competencies. Give careful thought to each question and develop a specific plan for each activity.

1. Identify two recognized leaders in your school system or community and state why you consider them exemplary leaders.

2. List the specific behaviors you will model from the two leaders of your choice.

3. Specifically state how you will model these behaviors, under what conditions, and so on.

4. Specifically state how you will evaluate the effectiveness of the modeling activity and how you will use the evaluation results in fulfilling your responsibilities.

Part V: Action Research

Directions: Part V is designed to assist you in applying action research to fine-tune your leadership abilities. Answer the following questions.

1. Identify a leadership style that is closely aligned to your leadership philosophy and then locate an empirical study on that leadership style. Replicate the study in your school. Are your results similar to those reported in the study? Why? Why not?

2. Do you believe that a person can change his or her leadership style? Why? Why not?

3

Informal Leaders and
Groups in the Schools:
Developing a Power Base

In This Chapter

This chapter examines the nature of informal groups as sources of influence that compete with an organization's formal leadership for control, resources, and power. Informal groups have their own leaders, values, beliefs, codes of conduct, and membership roles and responsibilities. Informal group leaders coexist with formal leaders and use overt and covert tactics to achieve their goals and support their members in times of conflict. Informal groups have their own communication networks and use these networks to both assist and resist formal leadership. The grapevine and rumor are two of the most common forms of communication among the membership of informal groups.

It is essential for assistant principals to know how to identify and work with the school's informal leaders and groups, to be knowledgeable of the power games and tactics used by these groups, and to identify informal group networks and use their communication systems to be more effective school leaders.

Informal Groups and Leaders and
Communication Networks: Survey Results

To determine the extent of knowledge about informal power structures in schools, we asked assistant principals the following questions:

- Do informal groups or cliques exist in your school?
- What is the difference between the ways you use power and authority in dealing with informal groups and individuals?
- What knowledge or skills do assistant principals need when working with informal groups or teams of teachers?
- Do coalitions exist in your school?
- What roles do grapevines and rumor play in communication in your school?

Overall responses to the questions were low (48%). Over 35% of the respondents indicated that informal groups, or "cliques," existed in their schools and that these groups did impact their group members' behavior. One comment, representative of many others, noted "unfamiliarity" with informal groups and their leaders, but added, "This is something assistant principals should know about."

The second question asked if the respondents could differentiate between the use of "power" and "authority" to accomplish their tasks. Less than 20% of the respondents had a clear understanding of the difference between these two concepts. One respondent indicated, "While I'm not sure of the difference, I probably should know this." Another comment best captures the conventional interpretation of power:

> Power allows one to control another's fate and to coerce those to do what they are unwilling to do via threat of punishment. I may not have the "authority" to do something, but my position gives me the "power" to do many things.

In response to the question of what knowledge or skills are essential when working with groups or teams of teachers, over 55% of the respondents replied that a knowledge of conflict management and goal-setting skills were necessary for effective team performance.

The assistant principals were then asked about their knowledge of "coalitions" and "political games and tactics." Although less than 45% reported knowledge of coalitions and political games, over 70% indicated that this would be "important to know." Several respondents noted the playing of power games by certain faculty members in their school.

A final question focused on the presence of grapevines and rumors in the school. Over 90% of the respondents acknowledged their presence, but few indicated how to effectively combat rumors. Rumors were a concern to most respondents because of the negativity associated with them.

Assistant Principals on Informal Power Structures

On the existence of informal groups, or "cliques," and their leaders:

"I'm not sure I would have known that these informal groups and leaders existed if my principal had not clued me in. I thought they were just social cliques."

On the differences between power and authority:

"I have the authority to make certain requests or demands on teachers based on the responsibilities I must fulfill as an assistant principal, and I have the power to make teachers do things they may not want to do, such as teach a certain grade or subject."

On the knowledge or skills needed to work with informal groups:

"You need to understand how you can help a group of teachers evolve into a productive, work-oriented group."

"I still don't understand why some groups succeed and are productive while others seem to make little, if any, progress."

On coalitions and political games:

"In my school, anything that has *change* associated with it gets 'flagged' by the heads of the English and social studies departments. These departments get all excited, hold meetings, and are the most negative in faculty meetings."

"We have a few teachers who go out of their way to do favors for the administration. Some call it 'brownnosing,' but they want favors in return."

"One of our teachers is related to a board member and lets us know it all the time. She expects special treatment and she gets it."

On grapevines and rumor:

"Rumors around here focus on character assassination, to one degree or another. I wish I knew how to prevent them."

SOURCE: 2000 Survey of 100 Practicing Assistant Principals From Rural, Urban, and Suburban Schools

The Nature of Informal Groups

Informal groups are a fact of work life, and they develop spontaneously to meet the unfulfilled needs of the membership. Informal groups do not appear on any line staff organizational chart, but each group has its own leader; its own power structure and rewards system; and its own values, norms, and codes of conduct. In essence, the informal group is a bandit within the formal organization because it is unofficial in nature.

Informal groups are primarily social in nature, but they engage in political activities when their group autonomy is threatened or when one of their members is targeted unfairly. Informal groups also engage in political games and tactics to achieve their goals or to foster change in the formal organization. Informal groups can positively or negatively affect work effectiveness, efficiency, job satisfaction, and morale (Hoy & Miskel, 1996). On the other hand, formal organizational groups have official legal status; their operations are controlled by formal, sanctioned authority; they focus on the "good" of the overall organization; and they achieve their goals through official policies, rewards, and punishments.

The *dynamics* (from the Greek word meaning "force") of an informal group depend on the situation or issue at hand *and* on the degree of importance it has to the group's leader or membership. Informal groups have power, and group action occurs when the group's existence is threatened; when its values, norms, or beliefs are challenged; or when a member is unfairly treated or put "at risk" by formal authority. Action can be overt or covert in nature and may or may not lead to the replacement of the organization's formal leadership.

Members of informal groups have similar tasks, needs, aspirations, and values. These similarities promote a bond of friendship that provides the "glue" that holds the group together. Members who continuously seek special favors or who strive to promote self-interests soon fall out of favor with the group's membership because these members place themselves and their interests *above* the common good of the group.

Informal Group Member Roles, Status, and Leaders

Roles of Members. How and why informal groups emerge significantly impacts the roles group members play, the status individual group members hold, and the leadership of the group. The roles group members play vary between groups, with roles usually emerging over time to fill each group's specific needs. Roles therefore belong more to the group than to the individual. Fisher (1980) states,

Role networks exist where members are "social chameleons" who have an assigned "duty" and know when to be "on stage." Role behavior is sanctioned and limited by norms and values, and all players know their appropriate regions of role performance. (p. 176)

Some of the more common roles group members play are "joker" (harmonizes, relieves tension, and motivates), "information giver" (provides facts, hearsay, and rumors), "special interest pleader" (champions causes and issues, and seeks to promote group action), "spy" (provides reliable information from formal organizational sources and other informal groups), "gossip" (transmits the day-to-day activities of the formal organization and embellishes on their accomplishments and importance), and "silent member" (follower, supporter, sympathizer, and compromiser).

Member Status. Status in informal groups is not always easily distinguishable, but hierarchies do exist. The characteristics that give rise to status generally vary from group to group, but status within groups always focuses on one salient, universal characteristic: *the particular value the member has to the group.* Other factors impacting group member status are (a) the relationship a member has with the group's leader as compared to other group members; (b) the degree to which the group depends on or views a member as being helpful; (c) the technical expertise, knowledge, or skills of a group member; and (d) the personal characteristics of a group member. "This hierarchy of status levels, then, is a rank ordering of members' roles relative to one another, but the roles are not judged according to some absolute standard or scale ranging from good to bad" (Fisher, 1980, p. 192).

Leaders of Groups. Leaders are at the top of the status hierarchy and are at the center of all group interaction. Leaders usually emerge through group consensus and generally meet one or more of the following criteria: (a) charismatic personality or excellent interpersonal skills, (b) special knowledge or skills, (c) multiple information sources, (d) strong relationships with other influential people, (e) natural leadership ability and an ability to provide rewards or favors, and (f) standing or status outside the workplace.

Leader "switch" in a group may occur on a temporary basis depending on the issue or problem needing resolution, but consent must be given by group members for such a switch, and there is a tacit understanding that "temporary" leadership will be freely surrendered when the issue is resolved. Blau and Scott (1962) relate that group norms and values are rigidly honored, that any attempt by a group's members to violate the accepted codes of conduct will be disciplined, and that permanent leadership is attained through the consent of the governed. Informal leaders can be valuable assets to an organization's formal leadership, or they can use their influence to work against the goals of the organization. Group leaders can, for example, help promote job satisfaction and motivate group members to achieve the goals of the organization, instill respect for authority, and encourage their membership to work within the policies of the organization. Leaders can also serve as information conduits that allow formal leadership to provide timely and accurate information in times of uncertainty or when information is too "sensitive" for formal communication channels.

Informal Communication Networks

Informal networks exist in all types of organizations and have similar patterns of information flow. Information networks exist among both individuals and groups, and their value depends on the accuracy, speed, and credibility of the source(s) of their information. These informal networks allow small groups of people to maintain contact and exchange information about mutual interests. Networks exchange information downward, upward, and horizontally, and they keep members informed about organizational life. Networks gain access to information through members' contacts with influential people, members' community ties, and members' friendships with a wide variety of people.

Downward information flows from group leaders who provide timely and accurate information about issues, problems, policies, or changes affecting their membership. Early sharing of information promotes high morale and trust in subordinates, as well as loyalty between leader and followers. Yukl (1994) notes that downward information flow from group leaders helps prevent unnecessary stress and thwarts the spread of rumors by providing facts from credible sources. Group members greatly depend on their leaders to provide information when formal leadership withholds information or when poor communication channels exist between legitimate authority and the workforce.

Upward information flow is essential to organizational effectiveness and efficiency. Those in authority need information that is timely and accurate. Yukl (1994) relates that upward information may be used as "impression management" by subordinates seeking advancement, special favors, or increased stature. Some midlevel administrators are hesitant to communicate problems or failures to their superiors due to the possible negative connotations that may be attached to their leadership abilities. On the other hand, problems may require special knowledge or a higher level of authority to resolve the problem. Lack of personal information flow may compound problems, jeopardize careers, and promote poor quality work. The balance between too much and too little upward information requires judgment that is best attained when a working relationship is built on mutual trust and respect.

Horizontal information flow is accomplished through "boundary spanners," members of two or more groups who provide information between and among groups. Boundary spanners have prestige and influence because of their information and connections with several sources within the organization. Boundary spanners can provide information to other peers or superordinates, and they build valuable relationships and reciprocal networks based on their ability to provide accurate and timely information (Yukl, 1994).

Monitoring information flow is a way formal leaders can identify informal groups and their leaders. Determining informal group membership can be accomplished by observing the interactions of those in the workplace and by asking individuals to name their "most trusted" coworkers. Network charts can often be drawn from compiling this information. These network charts provide knowledge of both individual group membership and of those group members who interact with members of other groups (crossovers or boundary spanners). Figure 3.1 provides an example of a network chart.

As seen in Figure 3.1, Bill and Sue, who are members of Group I and Group II, respectively, are also "crossovers." Crossovers provide a communication channel between the two groups. In Group I, Bill also has the most interaction among members of his group and is a strong candidate for group leader. Sally is an "isolate," one who is least informed and rarely consulted for input. In Group II, Sue has the most interaction among group members and Pam is the isolate for this group. Because of the frequent interaction between Bill and Sue, and because of their crossover interaction, Bill and Sue are most likely the leaders of their respective groups.

Building Community Networks

To promote leadership effectiveness, it is essential that assistant principals identify informal groups and their leaders and build a series of reliable networks in both the school and the community. Luthans and Lockwood (1985) found that networking is directly related to a leader's advancement in an organization and that networking behaviors can be grouped as either *social* or *instrumental* behaviors. Practicing both social and instrumental behavior is essential for successful leadership. Social behaviors include the following:

- Participation in informal discussions (at social events, encounters in the workplace, and before and after meetings), about family, friends, associates, and mutual interests with peers and superiors

- Participation in lifelong sports, friendships with community members, and civic organizations

Figure 3.1 Network Chart of Group Member Interaction With "Crossover" Member Interaction

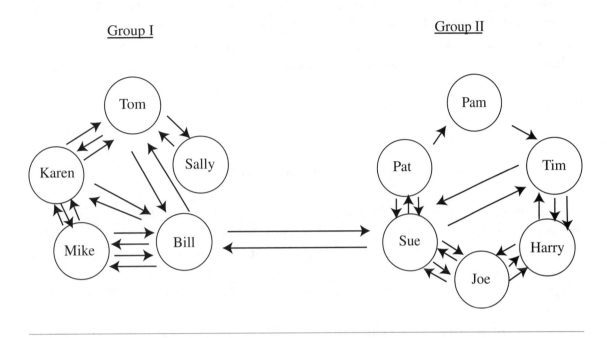

- Attendance at professional association meetings, engagement in chitchat with peers, and membership in the association's committees or task forces

Instrumental behaviors are those that promote self-interest and gain favorable recognition from superiors. Instrumental behaviors are as follows:

- Providing valuable information or doing favors for others without requesting something in return
- Providing assistance to others by sharing or taking responsibility for inaccurate information, failed projects, or incomplete work
- Providing resources not readily available or in demand, being flexible with your time to accommodate others, and helping others with difficult assignments or tasks
- Showing sincere appreciation for favors granted, providing political and social support for others, being recognized as a "team player," and recognizing the special accomplishments of others
- Avoiding negative comments about others, avoiding association with rumors, and behaving in ethical and professional ways

The members who are most valuable in networks have something special to "trade." Kaplan (1984) states that networks continually trade valuable assets among their membership, and the more assets a member has, the more valuable the member becomes. Important information and access to needed resources are the most highly valued trading variables in networks. Members also acquire value when they gain "mutual dependency" through initiating joint projects, volunteering for special assignments, or providing special or scarce resources that benefit the network.

The Grapevine and Rumors

Grapevines are part of the informal organizational structure that fill a gap created by insufficient communication. The term *grapevine* originated during the Civil War in connection with the stringing of telegraph lines from tree to tree covered in wild grapes. Many of the messages passed along were incorrect and triggered rumors, which, it was said, came from the "grapevine" (Newstrom & Davis, 1997).

Grapevines are a result of the natural need to communicate and be informed. Newstrom and Davis (1997) present several factors that *encourage* grapevine activity:

- Excitement or insecurity
- Lack of top-down communication
- Involvement of friends or associates
- Impending change or policy decisions
- Personality or position of a person

Grapevine information is approximately 75% accurate and spreads rapidly. Three factors are essential for trustworthy grapevine information. First, the original source of information must be credible. Secretaries or those closest to the origin of the information are deemed most reliable. Second, as information spreads, facts are embellished and the credibility of the source of the information becomes the test of its accuracy. Third, information must coincide with past patterns of behavior or with "expected" forms of behavior (Weller & Weller, 2000).

Positive aspects of grapevine information include updating subordinates on organizational developments that impact daily work life, providing subordinates a safety valve to release emotional tension, and building subordinates' morale by providing timely and accurate information (Weller & Weller, 2000). Additional benefits for school administrators include the following:

- Providing feedback from teachers about the morale and attitudes of others
- Allowing for the assessment of teachers' attitudes toward a proposed new policy or major change without making formal inquiries
- Allowing information to be carried when the formal communication system has purposely omitted that information from dissemination, for example, the possibility of school system consolidation or the downsizing of personnel

The negative aspects of grapevine communication are rumor and speculation. Rumor and speculation spread quickly because facts cannot be verified, information becomes distorted, and different parts of a rumor or speculation are emphasized by different people. Regardless of the negative effects of grapevines, effective school administrators know grapevines exist and use them to their advantage. The most effective way administrators can use grapevines is by knowing the leaders of informal groups in the school or identifying their information sources. "Leaking" information to these sources will ensure wide and rapid spread of information on the grapevine.

Rumor is a message devoid of fact or evidence and is the untrue or unverified part of grapevine information (Weller & Weller, 2000). Rumor is perhaps the most rapid form of communication and is instigated by wishful thinking, inaccurate information, and selective listening. The term *speculation* usually does not convey the negative aspects associated with *rumor*. Speculation is more often associated with informed projections that require some knowledge or facts. Speculation may be wishful thinking and have only hope as its source, however.

Rumors are rife, notes Bass (1965), when (a) people feel threatened or insecure; and (b) there are inadequate facts, inaccurate information, or clandestine activity. Bass also notes that when formal communications are infrequent, provide incomplete information, and are slow to be transmitted, rumors are transmitted instead.

Three characteristics of rumors make them an appealing as well as rapid form of communication:

- As rumors spread, details are omitted to make them easier to repeat.
- Rumor focuses on specific detail, and people emphasize or embellish different aspects of a rumor.
- Different people tend to listen for different things in a rumor. This is a function of their own bias, and they repeat the rumor in the context of that personal bias or interest.

Rumors can destroy reputations, trigger conflict between individuals or groups, and cause hostility and covert activity. Newstrom and Davis (1997) report that rumor can initiate excitement about impending change or the positive aspects of new programs or policy. And rumors can have a positive effect on morale.

Assistant principals must learn how to combat damaging rumors with facts. Administrators are cautioned about initiating untrue rumors, because credibility and trust are essential leadership qualities. Culbertson, Jacobson, and Reller (1960) make the following recommendations to school administrators on how to confront rumors:

- When rumors arise, provide facts immediately to demonstrate the inaccuracy of the rumor.

- Develop skills in assessing rumors. Often rumors are symptoms of group fear, tension, hostility, anxiety, or aspirations. Touching base with informal group leaders can often provide administrators with reliable information regarding the source and cause of rumors.

- Develop a formal and comprehensive communications system that allows teachers, parents, students, and community members to have continuous, accurate information about school programs and activities. Information that is accurate, factual, and timely decreases the probability of rumors.

Power and Authority in Informal Groups

Power is the "force" or "control" over the behavior of others that makes them comply with the will of those in power. Often coercive in nature, power is usually used when voluntary compliance is not given or when overt resistance is evident or foreseen. *Authority* derives from legitimate control over others through an officially sanctioned position in the organization. Brewer, Ainsworth, and Wynne (1984) note that every organization has a two-tier structure—one formal and one informal. Formal structures are controlled by legitimate authority: power sources that are vested in the leader's position and that come from the organization's line staff chart. Formal authority is used to control and regulate behavior and to achieve organizational goals. As just discussed, informal structures are groups with collective values, expectations, and norms of behavior. Informal structures have leaders who emerge with power and authority derived from member consent. In both formal and informal structures, someone sets the rules, defines the limits, and rewards and punishes.

Authority, according to Hoy and Miskel (1996), implies a certain degree of voluntary compliance to legitimate commands. Authority is more a function of influencing and persuading others to voluntarily comply with the leader's expectations. Blau and Scott (1962) note that authority stems from the values held by group members, and that these values legitimize the power relationship within the group. This legitimacy encourages subordinates to comply or to voluntarily suspend resistance to the leader's commands.

Those with formal authority have a legally sanctioned position in an organization and are required—and have legal protection—to perform certain duties (Daft, 1991). Kotter (1985) notes that formal authority promotes compliance, but does not foster initiative, creativity, or risk taking among subordinates. Assistant principals have formal authority to enforce school system policy and school regulations and to require teachers and students to obey legitimate requests or directives. As members of the organization, teachers and students have the obligation and duty to obey because they have voluntarily "joined" the school in exchange for the desired benefits that are provided by the school. Subordinates *obey* superiors, according to Schermerhorn, Hunt, and Osborn (1998), because they are quite willing to *obey* authority. Their obedience, however, is conditional. The conditions of obedience are these:

- The directive is clearly stated and understood by the subordinate.
- The subordinate is capable of performing the task with existing mental and physical abilities.
- The directive coincides with the goals of the organization.
- The directive is consistent with the subordinate's personal interests, values, and beliefs.

In most instances, subordinates voluntarily obey directives from those in formal leadership positions. This voluntary compliance is known as the *zone of indifference*—a zone in which each person makes a conscious decision to comply with a directive that the person deems "legitimate" or "bona fide." Zones of indifference are not constant, but are situation specific. When requests for compliance fall outside the zone, an individual may or may not choose to obey the directive. Usually, noncompliance is rooted in a person's value system when the request is considered to be unlawful, unethical, or unprofessional. Rewards or incentives, more so than legitimate or coercive power, expand the zone of indifference (Schermerhorn et al., 1998).

Informal authority, according to Daft (1991), is primarily rooted in the personal characteristics of the leader. That is, the leader's personality, special knowledge and skills, or ability to influence and persuade. Other characteristics that enhance an informal leader's authority are (a) the ability to provide desired rewards or resources; (b) the ability to provide personal favors or advance one's career or status; and (c) the ability to fulfill highly personal needs such as friendship, love, and respect. Members give authority to the leader because of these personal attributes and, within limits, obey the leader's requests and follow the leader's inclinations. Zones of indifference also exist in informal group members, and they may or may not be as rigid or well defined as they are in formal groups. In an informal group, peer pressure or the personal fulfillment a member receives from the leader or group often provides more flexibility to the zone of indifference. It is important to note that when informal authority coexists with formal authority, the leader's ability to enhance performance levels of subordinates greatly increases.

Levels of Authority

In each organization, different levels of authority exist, and each level impacts the organization differently. Mintzberg (1989b) found that those in top management positions, such as school superintendents, are responsible for strategic planning, the formulation of policy, and the attainment and allocation of fiscal and material resources. Middle-level managers, such as principals and assistant principals, are responsible for interpreting and executing policy, delegating responsibility, meeting organizational goals, allocating resources, and enforcing rules and regulations. Lower-level managers, such as department heads, are expected to focus on technical matters, "keep the lid on things," and schedule and attend to the daily routines of organizational life.

The lower the level of authority, the more specific the tasks become and the more the people holding those positions are bound by policy, rules, and regulations. Assistant principals, as middle-level managers, spend a major portion of their day interacting with teachers on a wide variety of topics, continually solving problems, interpreting policy set by superiors, enforcing rules and regulations, delegating authority, and directing and coordinating the work of others. Acting in a position of formal authority, assistant principals are constantly confronted by the zone of indifference of individual teachers when they assert their legitimate authority. Care should be taken to ensure that assistant principals do not place teachers or others in situations that may compromise their values, their ethics, or their professionalism. To do so may weaken trust, loyalty, and respect, all of which are essential for effective leadership.

Trust and Loyalty: Essentials of Leadership

"Trust is the lubrication that makes it possible for organizations to work. An organization without trust is more than an anomaly, it's a misnomer, a dim creature of Kafka's imagination" (Bennis & Nanus, 1985, p. 43). Trust, like leadership, is difficult to define; but, as with leadership, we know it by its presence or absence.

Trust is generally acquired through consistent, predictable behavior under similar conditions over time. Trust results when one can predict the behavior of another.

"Trust is the emotional glue that binds followers and leaders together" (Bennis & Nanus, 1985, p. 153). Trust cannot be mandated, but must be earned. Followers trust leaders whose acts are predictable, whose values and beliefs are the norm of the organization's, and whose positions on organizational policy are made clear. Trust in administrators encourages teachers to take risks, be creative, and take initiative (Weller & Weller, 2000). Fisher (1980) adds that trust also requires the perception that the trusted one is capable of achieving the desired outcome.

Risk taking is an essential part of trust. Having trust in another involves the risk of failure, humiliation, disappointment, and ridicule. Consequently, regardless of the consistent, predictable past behavior of another, the possibility of inconsistent behavior always exists.

Loyalty, like trust, is difficult to define but recognizable when it is present. Loyalty is earned and implies allegiance and faithfulness. Loyalty expands the authority of formal and informal leaders and, according to Napoleon Bonaparte, is the most salient factor leaders need to ensure their success. Keegan (1987) notes that Napoleon had his subordinates' loyalty because he led by example, was always at the front of his army, put his troops' interests before all else, and asked no more of them than he himself could do. Pride, arrogance, and poor judgment breed contempt in subordinates and lead to the ultimate defeat of a leader and an army.

Loyalty implies commitment to an organization or individual. The greater the commitment to the vision and goals of the organization or to the values and beliefs of an individual, the greater the loyalty. In this context, loyalty to an organization is demonstrated by good attendance records, willingness to support organizational policy, and longevity in the workforce. Loyalty to superiors is demonstrated by job satisfaction, high morale, and high performance (Solomon, 1992).

Hoffman, Sabo, Bliss, and Hoy (1994) note that authoritarian principals are less likely to receive loyalty and support from teachers than nonauthoritarian principals. Controlling teachers through sanctions or threats of sanctions undermines authority and reduces the degree of loyalty and trust teachers have for principals. Conversely, when formal authority is used only to enhance teachers' job performance, loyalty, trust, and support for the principal increase. Loyalty increases for assistant principals, according to Henderson and Hoy (1983), when they demonstrate professional competence and autonomy from their superiors and accept responsibility for their own actions. Assistant principals can also increase teachers' loyalty and trust by acting ethically and professionally, providing the needed moral and fiscal support for teachers attempting the new and different, and helping teachers become more efficient in performing their instructional responsibilities.

Informal Power Coalitions

Although "politics makes strange bedfellows," power and politics, when mixed together, result in power coalitions. Indeed, states Mintzberg (1989b), power and politics are inseparable in contemporary organizational life because employees have three potential sources of power—resources, technical skill, and knowledge. When all three power sources combine in sufficient degree, the individual, regardless of position, has significant power and influence to become an "attractive asset" for informal group membership or for building power coalitions.

Those who build power coalitions are often already leaders of informal groups, or they are individual group members who are seeking positions of informal leadership, championing a special cause, or promoting self-interest. Those seeking membership in coalitions are generally dissatisfied with job-related issues or have unfulfilled personal needs that have not been addressed by the formal leadership. Coalitions, with their pooled resources, technical skills, and knowledge, often outweigh an administrator's position of authority. Coalitions are more likely to exist in schools with high bureaucratic structure, strict policy enforcement, and authoritarian leadership. Coalitions in these schools provide their members "psychological relief" from frustration and dissatisfaction, and offer them the potential to "right perceived wrongs" or improve working conditions. When those in formal authority fail to recognize coalitions and remain indifferent to their concerns or dissatisfactions, the ground becomes fertile for the sowing of intrigue and political games (Weller & Weller, 2000). As "spheres of power," coalitions choose when and where to exert their influence, and their actions may be overt, covert, or both.

Political Games and Tactics

Political games are power struggles, and they are played in all types of organizations. Political games are played between coalitions, interest groups, individuals, and administrators. Political games are divisive because they are intended to align individuals or groups against legitimate authority (Mintzberg, 1989a). When people become dissatisfied with their relationship with the organization, they have three choices: (a) remain and be loyal; (b) remain and voice their opinions, try to change existing conditions, or work to modify intolerable conditions; or (c) exit the organization (Hirschman, 1970). Those who choose to remain and voice their opinions or try to change existing conditions engage in political games. Political games are intricate, often subtle, and guided by rules that define the games being played. Each game has its main players, each player has specific reasons for playing the game, and participation in the game is almost always voluntary. Survival and success depend on the player's skill in planning and executing game strategy. Political games are often clandestine in nature; they target the leadership of the organization; and they seek outcomes that further self-interest. Political games may have positive effects. For example, they allow for the airing of grievances, and they may result in a voice in making policy, which forces leaders to confront salient issues affecting those engaging in the political games.

Power games are played for high stakes. Those who engage in political games and fail either self-select out of the organization, are pressured to exit the organization, or are severely punished. Failed attempts at reform usually result in more stringent policy and more stringent enforcement of policy.

Games Played by Individuals

Some political games are more informal than others and are played by individuals as opposed to groups. Informal games, defined as *tactics* by Vecchio (1988), are designed to achieve personal goals. Vecchio describes four tactics:

1. *Networking:* Forming relationships with those who have power or connections. Engaging in social chitchat and being "sociable" are the common forms of building a network to advance one's personal interests.

2. *Ingratiation:* Doing favors for others, especially those in authority. Over time, obligations accrue and a "norm of reciprocity" occurs. This behavior is viewed by authority as devotion to the job, loyalty, initiative, or other desirable traits.

3. *Information Management:* Acquiring information and then releasing or withholding information at critical times. Knowledge is power, and providing information establishes one as being "in the know."

4. *Impression Management:* Creating a positive visible appearance to form a favorable image. Dressing for success, making one's accomplishments known, and being known as knowledgeable, reliable, and resourceful are behaviors of impression management.

Games Played by Groups

Many political games are played by groups or leaders of groups, and have complex rules and specific strategic procedures necessary to "win" the game. Rules define how the game is played, what behaviors are expected, and what outcomes are expected. Mintzberg (1989a) describes the following political games most frequently played in organizations.

1. *Young Turks Game:* A game played for the highest stakes and designed to question or replace legitimate authority or restructure the organization. A major shift in the organization is the outcome desired by the small group of "young

Turks" who are close to the center of power. Organizational redesign or the replacement of leadership with their own ideology is their goal. The game is successful when leaders are weak or refuse to adjust to needed reform.

2. *Whistle-Blowing Game:* A brief and highly effective game played by one seeking change in the organization or leadership replacement. "Blowing the whistle" is disclosing information on another who, as a leader, committed illegal acts or displayed inappropriate behavior. The informant seeks promotion, prestige among peers, or greater group status.

3. *Expertise Game:* A game played by those having highly valued knowledge or skills. These players continuously let others know their value to the organization and claim uniqueness through their expertise. Mostly found in professional organizations, "experts" use their skills to attract a following, achieve their own ends, and create an image of being indispensable.

4. *Alliance-Building Game:* A game played among peers with one peer seeking the alliance of others to form a group or power block to address mutual interests. Groups may also ban together to form power coalitions to resist formal authority that may or may not remain in existence to foster future self-interests.

5. *Power-Building Game:* A game in which players ban together to amass information or resources for those in authority. Credible information or needed resources are brought to those in authority, which causes those in the positions of authority to trust those bringing the information or resources. Authority figures are then manipulated to "sponsor" group members for promotions. Those who are promoted then advance others to authority positions and, in turn, are given respect and loyalty for favors granted.

6. *Insurgency Game:* A game designed to resist formal authority or effect change through sabotage or the circumvention of the intent of policy. Confronting this type of behavior with authority or punishment causes subordinates to feel "wronged" and often triggers more overt or covert acts designed to weaken or dislodge formal authority. Using coercive or legitimate power to punish these types of insurgents often addresses the symptoms of discontent but does not address the root causes. Discontent often resurfaces and may lead to the overthrow of legitimate authority.

Political Traditions and Forms in Organizations

Two types of political traditions exist in organizations according to Schermerhorn et al. (1998). One tradition is rooted in Machiavelli's *The Prince*, which often advocates the use of illicit behavior, dishonest practices, and shrewd dealings to receive special favors or achieve personal goals. Politics, here, is played for self-interest; nonsanctioned or covert means are used to obtain sanctioned ends; and managers are labeled "political when they seek their own goals, use means not currently authorized by the organization, or use means that push legal limits" (Schermerhorn et al., 1998, p. 202).

The second tradition views politics as a necessary function, the "act of compromise," among competing self-interests in an organization. Compromise allows leaders to use their legitimate authority to achieve "socially acceptable" ends that promote both individual and organizational interests. Compromise is also turned to when the use of dictatorial authority has weakened a leader's standing with others; when policies or procedures are circumvented so as to reduce the potential of conflict that may be harmful to the leader's authority or to the collective interests of others; or when compromise can provide protection. Self-protection activities include stalling for time or delaying action to allow other forces to impact the situation; redirecting responsibility and diverting blame so as to avoid negative consequences for the actions of others; and using scapegoats such as lack of time or resources, weak peers, or incompetent subordinates.

Political Forms Model

Four political forms dominate and characterize the type of political activities found in all organizations. Political forms, of one type or another, are "nested" in an organization's formal structure and measured by the frequency and degree to which political games are played (Mintzberg, 1989a). The four political forms are the following:

1. *Complete Political Form:* Political games and intense power struggles are ongoing and pervasive. Authority, goals, and policy depend on informal power groups that can win individual issues as they arise. Authority is unstable, at best, and subordinate to political power. Conflict consumes the time and energy of the workforce.

2. *Shaky Alliance Form:* Political games are moderate and enduring, but confined. Educational organizations are primarily shaky alliances because authority exists for technocratic control and experts exist to provide products and services. This coexistence of power or influence triggers political activity as authority seeks to control and direct and experts strive for professional autonomy. When authoritarian leadership is present, conflict escalates, political games are played more often, and the balance of power is shaky at best.

3. *Confrontational Form:* Political games are intense, confined, and brief; political games are played by two rival groups or individuals who seek to dominate or win issues. Games are intense and high-stakes, with the victor clearly emerging in a short time period. Often confrontation is over control of resources, self-interest, gaining high status in a group, or job promotion.

4. *Political Organization Form:* Political games are moderate to intense and are pervasive and enduring. Large corporations are best characterized by this political form because political games and power struggles constantly permeate the entire organization.

Playing political games is dysfunctional behavior that may prove harmful to individuals, groups, and organizational effectiveness, but such games are part of life. Kellerman (1999) relates that the dysfunctional aspects of games include wasted time and energy; low morale; a hostile work environment; poor products and service; and a lack of trust, loyalty, and commitment to formal authority or to the organization.

On the other hand, political games can serve some positive purposes:

- Serve as a check on the misuse of legitimate authority through whistle-blowing or young Turks games

- Provide a forum for debate on salient issues that are important to subordinates but ignored by those in authority

- Serve as an information mechanism that signals to top administrators that those in middle management may be acting in their own self-interests or playing the expert game by keeping from superiors information that could be detrimental to their own self-interests

- Provide informal leaders an opportunity to test their leadership skills, demonstrate their leadership capabilities, challenge weak authority, or trigger needed change through alliance-building games

- Provide a mechanism to develop a power base for changes in policy that may meet strong opposition from superiors or subordinates; for example, when the expert game allows individuals and authority figures to gain broad acceptance of their ideas or arguments before promoting change or making unfavorable decisions

Political games can be kept to a minimum when those in formal leadership positions, including the assistant principal, practice the following:

- Build trust and loyalty among subordinates

- Be open to new ideas, and work to elevate the concerns of others

- Practice good communication skills; communicate essential information that is accurate and timely

- Practice a nonauthoritarian leadership style

- On an individual basis, assist others in meeting their personal and professional needs and aspirations in the workplace
- Practice joint decision making and teamwork

Let's Review

Formal organizations are officially sanctioned entities with formal authority, goals, rules and regulations, and a rigid system of control. Informal organizations are unofficial groups or social structures existing in the formal organization with their own norms, values, leaders, power relationships, and communication networks. Groups develop spontaneously, have status among their membership, and provide the personal or professional fulfillment lacking in the formal organization. Informal groups can positively and negatively impact the goals of the formal organization and the effectiveness and efficiency of work itself.

Leaders of informal groups emerge through group consensus; leadership may be based on personality, knowledge and skills, leadership ability, or available resources. These leaders can promote morale and job satisfaction and decrease resistance to change. Informal and formal leaders must cultivate and maintain followers' trust and loyalty to be effective.

Power and politics in organizations are inseparable and result in informal power coalitions. Coalitions may or may not play power games both among themselves and with those in formal authority. Power games are divisive; they are struggles to promote self-interest; and they are usually played for high stakes.

Informal networks exist between individuals and groups and are the source of grapevines, rumor, and speculation. Informal networks allow information to be spread rapidly and with varying degrees of accuracy. They fill a communications void created by an organization's formal leadership. Positive aspects of grapevines promote morale, job satisfaction, and acceptance of change. Negative aspects of grapevines include rumor and speculation, both of which can prove detrimental to organizational effectiveness.

Exercises

Exercise 1: Political Games and Power

Reflect on your past experiences attempting to meet personal or professional needs with those in authority. Answer the following questions: (a) What political game(s) did you play? Did you require the aid of others? Who? How? Were you successful? Why? Why not? (b) Describe a political game that you played or one in which you participated that was *unsuccessful*.

Exercise 2: Political Forms

Four political forms presented in the chapter are generic to all organizations. Using your current school (or another if you prefer), (a) identify the political form that best represents the school, and (b) provide at least two examples that substantiate your choice of forms.

Exercise 3: Roles in Informal Groups

Think of your current relationship with your peers and examine this relationship in terms of being a member of an "informal group." Answer the following questions: (a) What are the major common characteristics of the group members? (b) Who is the group leader and why is this person the leader? (c) What "roles" are played by members of your group? By you? (d) Has there been a leader "switch" in your group? What were the reasons for this switch?

Exercise 4: Power in Informal Groups

Informal groups have their own bases of power, and they can be assets or detriments to the achievement of formal authority's goals and objectives. Describe a situation in which an informal group (or two or more informal groups together) worked to either assist or work against the goals of formal leadership. Be specific in your answer. That is, frame your answer around the following questions: What was the goal of formal leadership? Who initiated the action for or against the goal? How did the group react to the proposed action? What were the specific steps taken by the group to achieve their ends? Was the group successful? Why or why not? What role did you play in this event?

Exercise 5: Communication Networks

Using the procedures discussed in this chapter, develop a network chart of informal groups in your school. Identify leaders and "crossovers," and ask one or two members from each group to verify the accuracy of your results.

Exercise 6: Grapevines and Rumor

Every school has several "grapevines." Think of a recent or current rumor or bit of information you have heard and then trace its source. Were you surprised at the original source of the rumor or information? Who was involved (what was the chain of information flow) in the grapevine? Where were you located in the information flow of the grapevine? How accurate was the information when you heard it? What bias was injected in the information between the time the original message was sent and the time you received the message?

Case Study: Interdepartmental Politics

Two weeks before school opened, Larry was hired by mutual consent of the principal, Mr. Quick, and the department head, Mr. Boring, to replace a recently and unexpectedly resigned member of the history department. Both interviewers were impressed with Larry's academic credentials, eagerness, and creative ideas about teaching. Vacancies were usually filled through a process of interviews by the principal and some department members, but a "warm body" was needed to fill the vacancy, and those usually assigned the task of interviewing were unavailable. Larry signed the contract as the 13th member of the department and promised to put "new life" into the curriculum.

At the first faculty meeting, Larry was warmly welcomed by Mr. Quick and Mr. Boring who both touted the department's good fortune in finding Larry at the "last minute." Mr. Boring pointed out Larry's creative mind and eager spirit. Mr. Quick noted the marked decline in social studies scores on the graduation test over the past 5 years, and reiterated the message that had been stressed in the interview that the department had to improve, and had to do so quickly.

Larry took Mr. Quick at his word and talked with Mr. Boring about introducing a new way to teach history—a topical or thematic approach. Mr. Boring, a devout lecturer known as "the simulator" to students, reluctantly approved Larry's request. As Larry was leaving, Mr. Boring said, "This is a good department. Mr. Quick is gunning for a superintendency and we do very well teaching history chronologically. It's the best way! Ask my students. All the kids love me! And don't forget to run this idea of yours by Mr. Stabber. He likes to be in on all department decisions and he fills in for me when I have to be absent. Good luck!"

Larry's meeting with Mr. Stabber went well, or so Larry thought. Mr. Stabber informed Larry that he also works part-time as an adjunct professor, that he would receive his PhD the following June, and that students must know American history chronologically if they are to do well in college. Mr. Stabber did say, "Try the topical approach if you must. I'll be interested in the results."

During the first year, Larry was busy and part of several cliques. He was invited to parties by Bill and Mary, was privy to the latest gossip by Ken, and heard the "straight scoop" and jokes from Pam and Harry. Larry felt as if he lived in front of the copy machine and he felt he was only one step ahead of his students while preparing for each unit. In June, Mr. Quick called to congratulate Larry on raising the average score of his students on the graduation exam by 10%. He told Larry he was going to "talk" with the other department members and get them "to do whatever it is that you are doing."

The first faculty meeting of the following year was "odd," thought Larry. People were pleasant, but no jokes or gossip were shared with him, and he knew he was not invited to the last big summer party. Mr. Quick noted Larry's achievement and then stated the following: (a) Copying and paper use will be on a priority basis and "all requests must be approved by me." (b) All new teachers will be evaluated five times a year, unannounced. "Department policy allows us to exceed the three observations required by the board," said Mr. Quick. Mr. Boring said, "In the social studies department, Mr. Stabber and Ms. Dullard, both teachers of the year some 9 and 10 years ago, will assist me in evaluating new staff. Our evaluation team expects to see lesson plans and good, time-honored teaching practices. Mr. Quick may ask me to coach those who need help or provide demonstration on excellent classroom teaching methods."

Larry was unconcerned. He was good, he had Mr. Quick in his corner, and Mary Dullard was his friend. Mr. Stabber attended all social functions and as long as you "stroked his ego," you were OK. Mr. Boring attended the socials as well and played poker too. As long as you talked military history, you were on the top of his list.

After the first month of school, Larry began to miss the Friday night poker parties at Ken's and the social gatherings put together by Mary. In fact, Pam and Harry were not sharing any jokes and he heard no gossip or "straight scoops" from anyone. He felt as if he was "taboo."

The sixth week of school was eventful. Mary Dullard entered Larry's first period class one minute before it started and said, "I'm here to observe. Could I have a copy of your lesson plan?" Larry complied, taught his class, and waited to see Mary after class for feedback. Instead of talking to Larry, she just winked and said, "I have class, and I can't talk right now." During the next 2 days, Mr. Stabber observed Larry. He, too, exited before Larry could speak with him, but he smiled and seemed to visually indicate "all was well." Consumed by his work, Larry forgot about the observations until the ninth week of school when Mr. Stabber entered Larry's first period class to observe once more. Larry's class went exceedingly well. He received a round of applause from the students; Mr. Stabber hastily exited the class during the applause, however.

The next day, Mr. Stabber and Mr. Boring visited Larry's classroom at the end of the day. Mr. Boring stated: "Larry, we have some major concerns about your teaching and your ability to 'fit in' as a team player in this department. As you know, state law does not require a reason for nonrenewal of contract. It is the consensus of this department, and Mr. Stabber fully concurs, that you should look elsewhere for next year's employment. Copies of our evaluation findings are with Mr. Quick. You should see him for any questions. We fully expect you to give your all for the remainder of this year. After all, you are a professional and you are under a binding contract. Good luck and good day."

Answer the following questions:

1. Was there an informal group with an informal power structure in the department? Who was in the group? Who was the leader of the group? What roles did the group members play?

2. If you were Larry and if you had knowledge of how informal groups operate, what, if anything, would you have done differently? Be specific in your answer.

3. What were some of the "early warning signs" Larry should have picked up on? Should Larry have been more concerned about being the new kid on the block?

4

Public Relations and Community Power Agents

In This Chapter

This chapter focuses on the importance of school administrators acting as public relations specialists to interact with powerful people in the community to make or influence school policy and practice. The nature, sources, uses, and types of community power structures are explored. Examples are provided to illustrate how community power agents, special interest groups, and social, economic, and political issues impact the decisions of school board members.

Because each community, regardless of its size, has a group of power agents or "influentials," attention is given to how those who have power or influence come into power positions. Three research methods are presented for identifying local community power agents, and suggestions are provided for building community support for the schools through these power agents. Techniques are provided for handling criticism from interest groups and power agents, and examples are given of how to construct surveys to measure public opinion about the schools.

The Nature of Power

"All life is a game of power" (Korda, 1975, p. 3). The word *power* comes from the Latin word *posse,* meaning "to be able." The most natural use of power is the application of one's mental talents or physical characteristics, which include special knowledge and skills, personality, and physical strength. Speech and writing are power variables associated with influencing and persuading others to achieve desired ends. Power, in and of itself, is *amoral.* It is neither good nor bad; it just is. It is the application of power that makes it good or malevolent to the perception of others.

Power is most commonly perceived as control or manipulation through authority. As Brewer, Ainsworth, and Wynne (1984) point out, authority and control hold organizations together and are essential to maintaining social order. Nothing, they maintain, gets accomplished without some form or some degree of power being exercised. No one is completely powerless, because we all have influence over others and use our talents or related attributes to persuade or motivate. Power is part of who we are and how we act.

All organizations, formal and informal, have defined power structures with formal and informal power agents. People in organizations compete for the attention and favor of the leader(s) and play political games to achieve their goals or to "survive." Leavitt (1978) relates that power is addictive. That is, one never gets quite enough power and there is a constant struggle for more power, despite the conflict that results from expanding one's power base.

> Power is often thought of pejoratively. We talk about power plays, power actors, and power politics. All three have implications of inequity and gamesmanship. And yet it is obvious to the executive that if we weren't pretty sophisticated about power and its uses, we would be dead in the water. (p. 136)

Burns (1978) relates that effective use of power is essential for effective leadership and that power should not be feared, but rather studied and then applied for maximum benefits. Central to the effective use of power are good communication skills and the knowledge of the limitations of one's talents. Brewer et al. (1984) note that the positive management of power exists when leaders recognize the existence of various power forms, work to apply power in positive ways, and use power and power agents to help themselves and others.

It is natural for humans to seek opportunities to amass more power, be it positional, monetary, or influential. Here the dominance-submission games are played and may involve immature, vile, and aggressive behavior. Those who are not reasonably skillful in playing in the power arena do not long survive as power players or influentials. To sustain or enlarge one's power base, one must be politically skillful and realize the subjective nature of power. That is, the use of power to achieve a goal or end may be viewed by some as good and by others as bad. Those on the side receiving rewards or advantages from power application view its use as good, whereas those lacking benefits or receiving punishment decry its use. Machiavelli advised leaders to be politically skillful in their use of power to survive. Machiavelli advised leaders that to succeed and survive, they must act sometimes like the fox, sometimes like the lion, and sometimes like the lamb. No single disposition suits all purposes, and the skillful leader applies the required behavior at the required time (Mansfield, 1985).

Leaders and Power

School leaders, relates Carlson (1996), often find themselves in precarious situations because they do not understand power forms and power bases. Administrators are outmaneuvered by teachers, parents, or community members who are admired in the school and community. They frequently fail to realize that power is an integral part of school-community relations and interstaff relations as well. Boulding (1989) found that those leaders who analyzed and understood power were more successful in achieving their goals and the goals of their subordinates. Kotter (1985) frames power in a political context: Successful leaders don the role of "benevolent politicians" and establish building-level networks and coalitions as supportive linkages between the school and community. Carlson (1996) places school leaders in the center of power relationships and political games played by teachers, parents, and community members. Administrators primarily have one power source, their position. But often positional power is not enough to counterbalance the different types of power held by others. Carlson relates that card players know a strong hand has aces, face cards, and high trump cards, and although you are not assured of winning, you are playing from a position of strength. But the rules of the card game change, and so do the power cards, since all sources of power are not equal. This is true in the school and community as well. Depending on the issue, different power agents exist and they activate their networks or coalitions to seek advantage, maintain their power, or expand their power base. Because power struggles are inherent in organizations, school administrators (at all levels) must recognize that part of their effectiveness as leaders rests on their ability to recognize, manage, and interact effectively with school and community power agents. Although positional power goes with all administrative positions, those who judiciously apply power understand that power is also held by others who have their own agenda and power base.

The Public Nature of Schooling

Schools are owned and governed by the local community, but are managed by representatives of a profession. This places schools squarely in the middle of a political arena rife with conflict and power players. Norton, Webb, Dlugash, and Sybouts (1996) note the "shared ownership" concept of public education that exists between stockholders (community members) and educators (the managers of this public organization). The public nature of schools calls for the community's elected representatives, the board of education, to enact policies and establish programs that coincide with the "popular will." Such activities serve to perpetuate the values, norms, and mores of the community's culture. Educators, specifically school administrators, are charged with implementing and managing school board policy. As the executive branch of school system governance, educators are duty bound to see that the wishes of the "public will" are fulfilled. Educators are also professionals who have a specific body of knowledge, distinct academic disciplines, codes of ethics, and research findings that guide their practice. With experience, these criteria satisfy the qualifications for those in any profession to have judgments about best practices and expert opinions. In education, the two major causes of conflict are (a) the community's legal right to control the educational system and satisfy its diverse needs and expectations; and (b) the obligation of educators to provide students with the best professional services and care possible in the context of their training, special skills and knowledge, and experience. The goal of shared ownership is lofty, and it rarely exists in practice. Because the power of statute clearly resides with the community and its elected representatives, the best that educators can do is exercise their power of "influence and persuasion" to fulfill their professional responsibilities and obligations. This places schools squarely in the political arena.

The Public Sector and Power

Democratic control, with its distinctive ways to allocate authority and enact laws and regulations, is unique to American public organizations. Elected bodies are political "winners" and make policies that "losers," those who were defeated, must accept. School boards use public authority to implement "their" policies, which may not represent the general "public will." As long as they stay in power, their will becomes that of the public. But the election process ensures that one "will" never dominates for long. Chubb and Moe (1990) call this *coercive action*, which means that public authority does not belong to one group or individual, but is "up for grabs," and belongs to the elected. Anyone who plays by the rules or gains enough support can be elected and exercise public authority, regardless of whether or not he or she represents the public will.

Central to power in the public sector is the presence of special interest groups and community power agents or influentials (those who have a power base and influence others independent of official office) who highly value public authority, try to capture it, and, after capturing it, set an agenda to promote their own goals and programs. In public organizations like school systems, the struggle for power (public authority) by interest groups is unending. Chubb and Moe (1990) state,

The result is a perpetual struggle for the control of public authority. During elections, the various interest groups (or power agents) struggle to place their partisans in public offices. Between elections, they struggle to influence how officials actually exercise their authority. Through it all, public authority remains a blank check on which everyone wants to write. (p. 29)

When power agents or representatives of interest groups are elected, their goals supersede those of the public.

Consequently, schools are controlled by those who set policy and formulate regulations. This reality, according to Norton et al. (1996), runs counter to the popular myth that local citizens "run" the schools through their elected school board members. Local schools are in actuality run by elected officials who, for the most part, have their own agenda or follow the agenda of those who are responsible for their election. In many instances, their source of power resides in one or more local community power agents whose influence extends over a wide array of community members.

The education profession provides services through personal relationships, and their members rely on their knowledge, skills, and experience to perform their responsibilities. Under the control of the school board, educators must adhere to board policy and, at the same time, perform their services as experts and professionals. Unfortunately, educators lack one criterion required of a true profession—having the autonomy to exercise discretion in applying their knowledge and skills, as required to best serve their clients (Knezevich, 1975). This discretion is in the hands of the local school board, the policies of which may thwart the application of "best practice."

Parental pressure and student opinion also restrict the exercise of educators' autonomy in providing best practice when service is perceived as less than satisfactory or runs contradictory to their judgment (Kawalski, 1996). When parents ban together to voice concerns through their parent-teacher organization (PTO), they become an effective interest group using the membership as power leverage. Administrators who work against parents or other concerned citizen groups because they have their own agenda or they view discontent as a challenge to their authority, only increase interest groups' dissatisfaction and determination. In these situations, teachers become frustrated; they feel pressured to engage in political trade-offs and unable to exercise their own professional judgment. This often causes low morale or job dissatisfaction and can force some to seek employment in schools with less political overtones (English, 1995). Nonetheless, the agenda for public school educators is largely set by politicians, local power agents, and interest groups who hold the keys of local political power and use this power to foster their own ends. Their major concern and primary area of involvement focuses on making decisions on issues regarding what schools *ought to do*, *who should do what*, and *how* (Kawalski, 1996). For educators, the question is not whether these power brokers will use their power, but how and when they will use their power to influence educational policy and practice.

Community Power Sources and
Special Interest Groups: Survey Results

The assistant principals responding to our survey were asked to do the following: (a) List any assigned duties or responsibilities regarding school-community relations. (b) List the knowledge and skills essential to effectively working with community leaders (power agents). (c) List the knowledge and skills essential to effectively working with special interest groups.

Over 60% of the survey respondents indicated that they were assigned one or more responsibilities associated with school-community relations. Almost one third of the respondents, 30%, either represented the principal at community, civic, or service organizations, or coordinated school programs in which community members and business and civic leaders served as advisors to the school's leadership team. The remaining 10% of the respondents indicated that their duties included preparing annual events calendars, news releases, and parent newsletters, and coordinating school activities with community organizations. These assistant principals served as the "bridge" between the school and the community, and fostered meaningful two-way communication between community leaders and the school.

It is important to ascertain what knowledge and skills are essential to working effectively with community leaders. Over 40% of the respondents indicated that knowing who the "real" community leaders were was essential for gaining community support for their school. Many respondents noted that certain people in the community have "lots of power" and that "some board members seem to listen to some people more than others." Approximately 20% of the respondents had taken a graduate-level course in school-community relations and noted that their community "has a power structure." Being able to identify those who are "power agents" is essential to gaining widespread community support for the schools. One respondent commented, "My course in school-community relations taught me to identify the local power agents. This helped me to convince my principal to select one [of them] as the chair of our Key Communicator Program." Another respondent stated, "Knowing who actually 'runs this town' allows me and my principals to make sure they are invited to school events and are asked to serve on committees." One respondent related, "As a result of the president of the local bank being on the principal's advisory committee, and his contacts with others, our school's effort to raise contributions for new computer software was very successful." A final comment perhaps best captures the responses of those answering this question:

Letting the general public know what you are doing [in education] and having representative involvement [in the schools] from business, government, and other community leaders is important to our school. But what is *really essential* is to know that each community has its own power structure, its own small group of power agents, and school leaders must know how to identify them and then get them on their side.

The respondents were then asked what knowledge and skills were deemed essential for working with special interest group members. Approximately 25% of the assistant principals surveyed responded to this question; one comment perhaps provides the best insight for the low response rate: "My principal meets with leaders of groups who have concerns with our school's programs or traditions. She says she is the one responsible for the school, its programs, and its activities. We don't get involved." Of those who did respond to the question, several comments were insightful. One respondent said,

Recently, we had a group who wanted a certain book removed from the library. They used confrontational tactics up front, got the clergy involved, and confronted the principal and then the superintendent. The board [of education] eventually resolved the matter, but my principals taught me how to 'defuse' the immediate crisis situation. Believe me, these skills are crucial when trouble knocks at the door.

Another respondent noted,

A leader of [a group of] disgruntled parents and community members confronted me when my principal was out and demanded an explanation for not having enough bilingual programs and a Latino counselor. I became defensive and tried to explain why we could only provide certain services. This "fueled the fire" and the property tax rate became an issue. It got out of hand and all I could do was refer him to the superintendent. Bad mistake for me since I discussed finances. Things would have been a lot better if I knew how to confront hostile leaders [of special interest groups].

The School's Political Landscape

The political landscapes in which schools operate are in constant change. Rapid shifts in population; the infusion of new businesses and industry; economic booms and recessions; and shifts in values, needs, expectations, and trends make local schools volatile institutions. In each community there are haves and have-nots, people seeking extreme or moderate change and people content with existing practices, and people of diverse cultural and ethnic backgrounds. As Norton et al. (1996) observed, these groups cause instability and discontent in communities, and educational leaders must be familiar with this aspect of the political landscape. Educational leaders must develop a working knowledge of the community and a sound relationship with community influentials and interest group leaders if they are to successfully navigate a terrain that is undergoing continuous reconstruction and the foundation of which is politics.

Wirt and Kirst (1992) note the importance of understanding the values and beliefs of subcultures that exist within the greater "community culture." They argue that values and beliefs are a subsystem of the overall political system through which accepted behaviors of the social order are legitimized. It is in the political system that values and beliefs are assigned priority and then converted to policy. During this conversion process, political activity becomes intense, with high stakes being anted up among the political players in the game. Policy, Wirt and Kirst maintain, represents the fulfillment of material values (such as money, land, or contracts) or intangible values (such as recognition, titles, or prestige), with both winners and losers waiting to compete in the next round of policymaking. The losers will seek to have their values replace those of the winners, and the winners will seek to maintain their powerhold and perpetuate their values, beliefs, norms, and mores.

The power used to influence policymaking that results in material and/or intangible gains for the power players is found within the existing power structure of the community. As Wirt and Kirst (1992) relate, power structures in communities exist in many forms, both formal and informal, and each has a sphere of power and a network to foster its influence over other power bases. Formal power structures are easy to recognize; informal power structures existing within the formal structure are more difficult to define, and informal power agents are more difficult to identify. What is certain is that, in any community, a power structure exists, and power agents and interest groups impact policymaking.

Community Power Structures

Understanding power structures and their characteristics, how these structures operate, and the personalities involved, is essential to being an effective school leader. The results of power structures' actions—through formal or informal means—directly effects school policy and programs and serves to limit or enhance the capabilities administrators have to promote quality education in their schools.

The study of community power structures comes from the discipline of sociology, but sociologists disagree as to the best method for investigating power structures, how best to identify power agents or influentials, and how power structures should be classified or typed. A power structure is usually defined as "an interrelationship among individuals with vested interests who have the ability or authority to control other people, to obtain their conformity, or to command their services" (Gallagher, Bagin, & Kindred, 1997, p. 22). McCarty and Ramsey (1971) identified four broad community power structures: *dominated, pluralistic, factional,* and *inert.* Each structure has some type of identifiable power ladder that functions as the basis for policymaking. Variations of these structures exist from community to community, but what is essential to administrators is that within each structure there exist common characteristics that can be identified, and the methods of power activity are generally consistent. The four community power structures are listed below:

1. *Dominated Structure:* Dominated communities have a dominant individual, group, or family, with governing boards being directed or controlled by the individual or group.

2. *Pluralistic Structure:* Pluralistic communities have power sources that arise from different bases or centers of power, with no single group or family dominating the policymaking process. Representatives from various groups or political parties, of different backgrounds and ethnicities, head various community boards and promote discussion and consensus. Basically, "What you see is what you get," and the minority agrees to yield to the majority opinion. The heads of community boards are respected; their opinions are sought; and they are looked to for information and direction.

3. *Factional Structure:* Factional communities have numerous interest groups (factions), the leaders of which struggle for control and dominance. There is much political group in-fighting for election to and control of community boards. In these communities, issues often trigger heated elections and debates, and cause split votes as a result of power shifts on the boards. Elections at times focus more on ousting incumbents than on the issues themselves.

4. *Inert Structure:* Inert communities are those where little, if any, political struggle takes place and where few agendas exist. The community lacks initiative and direction. Boards are content with the status quo and focus on maintaining existing conditions. The head of the community governing board is viewed as a catalyst and a person whose opinions and inclinations are sought and followed.

In each of these communities, governing boards are influenced by the community power structure, and the head of the community's governing board (mayor) is either influenced or controlled by the power structure. McCarty and Ramsey (1971) found that in dominated communities, superintendents are expected to fulfill the wishes of the controlling group. In pluralistic communities, superintendents are expected to follow the direction of the school board, while board members are influenced and informed by various community power agents, depending on the issue topics involved. In factional communities, superintendents have to use political expertise to avoid becoming linked with any one faction, so they provide information to all groups and speak to all sides of all issues. Inert community boards look for guidance from those in positional authority. Superintendents, as the chief administrators of the schools, supply direction and leadership for the school board. As McCarty and Ramsey warn, most communities are not clearly defined by these structure characteristics, but such charactaristics provide a framework for understanding the political mechanisms by which decisions are made and policy is formulated. Dolan (1996) found that in contemporary times, most communities are in flux, with various groups or individuals seeking control. Knowing who these power structure actors are is the first step to providing effective school leadership. Dolan adds that it is naïve for educators to think that school board members do not have individual or political concerns that greatly influence how they vote on making educational policy.

Another sociological view of community power structures is presented by Gallager et al. (1997), who identify three different types of community structures: *elite, pluralistic* or *diffused,* and *amorphous.* The elite structure is pyramidal, with the base representing the lowest form of power and the apex representing the highest form of power, which is in the hands of a small group of community influentials. Although each community is different, these power agents represent the professions; they are financial, industrial, and business leaders; and they are members of old families, leaders of religious denominations, and heads of powerful interest groups. Sometimes power is derived from political parties, ethnic groups, or other sources that have influence in the community. These community power agents exercise control over matters of basic public policy that impact their well-being or interests. Prior to any major community project, such as a vote on a school bond issue, seeking their support and counsel is vital to success.

Dolan (1996) notes that in some elite power structured communities, a two-group power structure exists, which resembles the *orthodox pluralism model* in that the elected representatives of the community are the true power agents and the formal government structure is the center of community power. Here the mayor and the community council are the most powerful actors in making policy and influencing other community members' behaviors and attitudes. This does not mean these official leaders are uninfluenced by other economic, political, and bureaucratic notables. What it means is that these notables lack sufficient power or influence as groups or as individuals to override the orthodox pluralism structure which actually "runs the town."

Pluralistic or *diffused* communities are those with several power groups. Each group has a leader and exercises control and influence over its primary area of interest or concern. In this power model, is it not one or two groups that form the center of power, but several groups that exercise control over issues pertaining to their sphere of power. For example, the group concerned with expanding the arts and cultural activities in a community is not the same as the group concerned with economic and financial development. The heads of these groups usually do not cross interest lines unless they have mutual concerns. Likewise, a member of one group is usually not a member of another. Education may be the notable exception, because its mission involves a broad range of interest areas.

A variation of pluralism is the sociological theory of *institutional politics.* Dolan (1996) notes that the power structure is already in place: The center of power for schools is the school board, the center of power for local government is the mayor and city council, and so on. Institutional politics holds that power resides in institutions that have the public trust to execute their missions through their established hierarchy of leadership. Dolan adds that this power structure, like other structures described by sociologists, have two "faces" of behavior. The "formal face" behaves and conducts business as expected, and the "informal face," which is social in nature, conducts business in social settings such as country clubs or other private organizations.

In the *amorphous* structure, power is basically dormant. Unless a major challenge to their power exists, power agents are satisfied with the status quo. In these communities, there is little external or internal pressure for change, and those with formal authority are almost identical to those with informal power and influence.

These three power structures are prototypes, and most community structures vary in discernible ways. Power structures vary from time to time within communities; structure variation is most likely in bedroom communities (suburban communities) where frequent shifts in population occur. For example, in new and growing communities where families reside for 10 to 12 years due to job assignments, there is usually a "rudimentary" pluralistic power structure. This structure then gradually emerges as a more traditional pluralistic structure, complete with specialized power groups. Leaders of these groups are often family members who remain in the community and have gravitated to an interest area. Over time, the community may evolve into an elite power structure with one or two centers of power, with power agents being longtime community members or coming from established families, and professions such as business and finance.

For educators the implications seem clear. To successfully gain support and acquire the necessary resources to promote quality education programs in schools, administrators must identify community power agents and influentials, and then develop structures by which their influence and participation can be used to promote school goals. This is especially true in a contemporary society in which "factionalization" is most common. Our social order, states Kawalski (1996), has become a highly mobile and factional one in which the general population has a wide range of diverse needs and interests. These needs and interests often become focal points for powerful special interest groups who seek to promote their own ends. When interest groups get their representatives elected to community boards, such as the board of education, board meetings often become a forum for winning support for specific issues and passing school policies based on partisan decision making.

Special Interest Groups

Special interest groups are a product of our democratic way of life, and the actions of these groups are an accepted form of political behavior. Those seeking to dominate the decision-making process strive to unseat the incumbent through the ballot box. A former majority quickly becomes the minority and must adhere to the new policies of those now in power. Special interest groups, according to Dilenschneider (1994), are always in the minority, and seek to make their concerns known and achieve their ends through both overt and covert means. Special interest groups constantly struggle to gain recognition and exercise authority; they come in all shapes and sizes; they advocate an array of social, political, and economic interests; and they all have a singular goal—to win.

Special interest groups use debate, open confrontation, the election process, and political games to advance their agendas. Some interest groups are cooperative in nature and seek to influence or achieve their ends through overt means such as debate, compromise, or other cooperating practices within the system. Other interest groups resort to covert methods to gain control or intimidate. Dolan (1996) relates that, regardless of the methods used, interest groups seek to impose their values and ideologies by either influencing decision makers or controlling the decision-making process itself. Each community has a cadre of interest groups, and effective school administrators learn how to recognize and work with the different types of groups with an intent to impact educational policies or programs of the school.

Kotter (1985) advises those who are targets of special interest groups to prepare for extreme measures, because most interest groups are willing to play political games or use covert means to further their cause. In education, many interest groups want to dominate educational thought and advocate radical change through extreme measures to get their way (Dolan, 1996). Educators have a professional and moral obligation to resist what goes against best practice and is not in the best interest of students. History has taught us that dominance-seeking interest groups provide little, if any, common ground, and conflict is inevitable. Confrontations with such groups yield winners and losers, and desires for revenge. Educators are not always the winners.

Consequently, it is important for educational administrators to prepare for conflict with special interest groups. Dolan (1996) found that educators can prepare best by taking each interest group seriously and giving group leaders individual attention. Some interest group leaders simply want a forum to express their concerns, and principals who hear them out often defuse a potential conflict situation. An interest group may be a one-time phenomenon that surfaces and exerts its influence or makes its concerns known and then disbands after receiving satisfaction. Some groups are trend oriented and others are permanent fixtures in the community that continually seek to perpetuate their own interests. Some interest groups serve as "watchdogs," focusing attention on the appropriateness of books in libraries or materials in classrooms. Some groups target curricular programs such as sex education while others target the teaching of religion or values. Emotionally charged, these groups attract the media and seek their support. They accomplish their goals through a change in policy or programs. When special interest groups become involved in school affairs, lawsuits may result, jobs may be lost, and there will be great expenditures of personnel time and fiscal resources. These all impact the school negatively in terms of public relations; emotional trauma and frustration result from win-lose conflict strategy.

Some special interest groups can have a positive effect on schools. These groups include the PTO, church-affiliated groups, band and athletic booster clubs, Kiwanis, and other civic or service-oriented organizations. Educators have special interest groups as well, including the National Education Association, the National Association of Secondary School Principals, and the American Association of School Administrators. Each of these groups provides fiscal advantages, professional direction, and other areas of assistance. One thing about interest groups is certain. They are composed of people who feel strongly about their cause and are united in their effort to see their goals materialize. Unfortunately, most interest groups cannot achieve their goals without controversy (Gallagher et al. 1997).

Ways to Deal With Special Interest Groups

Today controversy is grist for the mill of the media, and interest groups do generate controversy. Controversy is also associated with poor public relations, dysfunctional organizations, and inadequate leadership. Controversy also indicates dissatisfaction with the status quo, and educators, like others, feel comfortable with "business as usual" and thrive on routine. Sometimes change is required in education, and controversy can promote needed change. Educators, also a special interest group, are defensive when confronted with change and can react negatively to interest groups seeking change—when external pressure is applied, regardless of the validity or nonvalidity of the change, educators view themselves as under attack and react much the same as any interest group assuming a defensive posture. How one group reacts to the changes of another group sets the tone and defines the limits of overt and covert action.

How to Effectively Confront Special Interest Groups

Although no single formula exists for working with all types of special interest groups, there are some general guidelines to follow to diffuse potentially high-conflict or inflammatory situations. Gallagher et al. (1997) and Dolan (1996) provide the following general guidelines:

- Value controversy and respect divergent opinions. Look at your own biases and admit that they exist. Personal biases close minds to some well-meaning advice and points of view. Bias makes one view others as complainers or "boat rockers" and tends to make one dig in the heels more deeply. Kudlacek (1989) reports that, for every irate person willing to express his or her views, many more exist with similar views who lack the skill or courage to express them.

- Define your school's vision, mission, and goals. School administrators must know the purpose, goals, and values of their educational programs. Weller, Hartley, and Brown (1994) state that when vision, mission, and goals are not established through a community-wide process, educators trying to defend their role and programs find themselves on shaky ground. When the community is not involved in developing vision, mission, and goals for the school, ownership and the necessary universal buy-in are lacking. This puts school administrators at a distinct disadvantage in times of conflict with special interest groups because they lack their first line of defense—"We as educators are promoting the purpose and values of the community."

- Know the goals and the key players of special interest groups in your community. Most interest groups have a political agenda. Some are hidden, but others are announced. Some have greater impact potential on school governance than others. To work effectively with interest groups, administrators must know their agenda, their leadership, and how they operate. Gathering this information requires networks and linkages that provide direct, reliable information about interest groups goals. Members of the school's internal special interest groups, such as active parents of the PTO and booster club members, often belong to external interest groups or know community members who belong to such groups. Information networking is one of the most reliable ways administrators can gain accurate, current information about these groups and their areas of dissatisfaction. Effective school administrators are media oriented and read the local newspaper with an eye on community issues and names and organizations associated with issues generating dissatisfaction and support for schools (Weller, 1999). These proactive administrators are members of civic organizations, attend organization meetings regularly, and develop their own information network and community linkages.

• Know how to respond to special interest group demands. Several approaches are recommended for effectively dealing with interest groups. Stevenson (1995) maintains that, in using the following approaches, two considerations are essential. First, ask yourself how important it is to maintain good working relations with the interest group. Second, ask yourself how strongly you believe in the position you will take on the issue under consideration. The following five suggestions for dealing with interest groups' demands can be used singularly or in combination:

1. *Evasion:* Most frequently used, evasion is least effective in working with interest groups. Ignoring an issue or group leaders only serves to delay the inevitable, and can increase group hostility. Some argue that issue evasion is a primary cause of interest group development. Evasion is mostly used when the group is perceived as lacking power or influence, but sometimes members of one interest group are members of another group and evasion triggers support for an issue from other more powerful and influential interest groups. Evasion may be considered when the issue of the group has no effect on the school and when maintaining a good working relationship is not important.

2. *Conciliation:* Letting a group have its way can be dangerous or beneficial. When groups have agendas that coincide with the mission and purpose of the school, giving in may maintain or foster a positive working relationship and prove beneficial to all involved. But when schools lack clear vision, mission, and goals, giving in is dangerous, especially when conciliation results in exceptions to existing policy. An exception for one group usually leads other groups to seek exceptions for their causes. Unless school administrators know and are guided by established goals and values, making exceptions is dangerous, because controversy will result and charges of favoritism will be made. Conciliation should only be used when maintaining good working relations with the group is an all-important consideration.

3. *Bargaining:* The give-and-take approach to dealing with interest groups is the most common approach used by educators. This approach is flawed because no one comes away feeling good about the outcome, and the message is sent that the administration will give in on key issues. In bargaining, the problem is not resolved, but is temporarily shelved and will likely appear later. This approach, often used to quiet controversy and media attention, is used when both parties feel that neither party will have a total win. Bargaining is useful, however, when the issue is important to the school, and when maintaining a good working relationship is of equal importance.

4. *Opposition:* Programs or policies sought by special interest groups that are directly in opposition to the school's mission and values should be firmly opposed. Opposition is called for when the school does not need to maintain good future

working relationships with the group. Opposition results in a win-lose situation and educators must be prepared to lose and confront the effects of that loss. Should the interest group lose, it is likely the issue will resurface or be repackaged. Stevenson (1995) notes that sometimes interest groups that fail to achieve their cause are perceived as weak and attacked by other interest groups. When this happens, they usually become ineffective and disband.

5. *Consensus:* Given the public character of schools, there are few situations where school administrators can afford to offend community-based groups. Consequently, administrators must try to reach a win-win outcome, especially if the goals of the group do not run counter to those of the school's mission. Consensus building is the best way to achieve a good working relationship with any group. By working together, both parties strive to resolve conflict and mutually agree on solutions. Consensus building is a difficult and time-consuming process, and both parties must be willing to explore options and select the one that best satisfies the needs of both parties. When seeking a win-win outcome, it is best to enter the process with a realistic mind-set (Weller, 1999). That is, the best one can hope for is a win-win situation. One party will always gain more, if not much more, than the other party. A 50-50 split is not a realistic outcome. The key to managing the "big win" versus the "little win" is that both parties recognize the outcome up front and agree to any perceived inequity once a solution is reached. However desirable, consensus cannot always be reached and should not always be tried for. Some groups will remain firm in their convictions, and others represent causes that are dramatically opposed to the mission of the public school. In these cases, consensus is not an option.

Although the five above-mentioned approaches to responding to interest group demands are effective, other variables can assist school administrators in resolving conflict with community interest groups. These are as follows:

1. Practice good listening skills. Good listening first requires an open mind and the acknowledgment of one's bias or prejudice. Next, good listening requires concentrating on the message and intent of what is communicated and not on facts or details. Concentration means being highly interested in the speaker's message; paying attention (no daydreaming or forming conclusions in advance); refraining from emotional involvement (let reason, not emotion, work); empathizing with the speaker's point of view; and observing body language, facial expressions, and tone of voice.

2. Establish a key communicator program. Developing your own community grapevine is essential to keeping informed and being proactive on issues impacting education. Supplement your community contacts with names of community influentials supplied by teachers and friends. Ask each person to supply a

list of five to seven people who others go to for information and advice about education-related matters. Members of the PTO and booster clubs are essential for a comprehensive source list. Teachers' and staff members' names will often appear on the list. Use these people as regular information providers and make sure they are well informed about school programs and receive updated information. Their interactions with other community members serve as one of the best public relations sources you have.

3. Involve leaders of key special interest groups in planning for change. People want to be involved in planning for the new and different, and they generally support that in which they have a vested interest. Involving interest group leaders in the school allows them to be part of the solution instead of the problem. Leaders and members of interest groups should be appointed to school committees and advisory groups. This gives them a platform to discuss their concerns, receive recognition for their interest group, and learn firsthand what is happening in the school. Sometimes it is beneficial to place on committees antagonists or members of groups who oppose a specific change. Although caution is urged, extreme views are sometimes made moderate by those with a more balanced position (Kudlacek, 1989).

A concluding remark about confronting special interest groups and strategies used to defuse conflict situations is related to one of the quality management tools of Deming (1986). Benchmarking other communities and schools is a sound and reliable way to gain information on how others address the demands of interest groups. With few exceptions, interest groups do not vary their behavior patterns or their tactics. Visiting other schools and learning first-hand their experiences with special interest groups provides school administrators with viable ways to confront interest group demands on a variety of issues. Stevenson (1995) found that proactive administrators develop contingency plans and scenarios on how to handle group confrontations on "hot topics" that generate controversy and conflict. These scenarios are often case studies reported by others (through the newspaper or journals, and at professional associations) with their demographic characteristics and other variables rearranged to accommodate those of the local situation. Role-playing scenarios then provide excellent practice for real-life confrontations.

Community Power Agents

How can configurations of power, influence, and authority be determined? How does one find out "who governs?" There are a number of research methods derived from sociology that help identify community power agents and the seat of community power. Power agents or community influentials, broadly defined, are those who have power or influence over others in the community, mostly independent of those with positional power associated with elected or appointed office (Gallagher et al., 1997). Frequently, power agents are those who exert considerable influence or control over decisions regarding social, economic, and political matters. They obtain their power from a variety of sources, including family background, financial status, property or business ownership, and political leadership; they might be media executives, clergy, bank presidents, or members of one of the professions. These community influentials have "connections" as members of informal and formal groups, and their power is sustained through mutual interests. Power agents usually conduct their affairs quietly and behind the scenes, and use a secondary group of influentials to negotiate matters and relay information. Their inclinations and counsel is best sought if major community change is in the offing.

Because schools are public organizations financed through public monies, education is a primary concern of community power agents. Gallagher et al. (1997) point out that politically smart school superintendents know who the community power agents are; seek their advice; and heed their warnings when seeking to implement major educational change, pass school bond referendums, or increase local property taxes. Power agent support is essential to a successful, low-conflict undertaking of these emotionally charged issues. Power agents operate under the political practice of reward and punish. Rewards are given for going along with their wishes; punishments include withholding needed support to accomplish a specific task such as passing a school bond issue. With power agents, "back-scratching" is common practice, and as Gallagher et al. (1997) state, "Instances are legion where sound social proposals have been defeated because they run contrary to the interests of the power structure, whereas socially undesirable proposals were adopted because they represented the wishes of the power group" (p. 24).

Identifying Community Power Agents

Three methods are commonly used to identify community power agents. Because each method has its strengths and weaknesses, the selection of a method primarily rests on which key underlying assumptions the researcher chooses as being most viable for uncovering power agents. These power agent identification methods are *positional, decision-making,* and *reputational.*

The Positional Approach

The key assumption with the positional model is that those who occupy key leadership roles in major social, economic, and political areas of the community are, in fact, the power agents of the community. There are difficulties with this model because some leaders do not utilize their power potential in issues that go beyond their elected or appointed responsibilities. Some positional leaders choose not to involve themselves with issues that are tangential to their primary duties, but the theory holds that someone has to be responsible or have "influence" over key decisions in "low-interest" issues, and that person is most likely the positional leader. Moreover, positional leaders who do not have influence over a broad range of issues tend to seek advice from others when making decisions. Major issues have subissues, and before a sound decision can be made, all factors need to be considered. The criteria used to identify community leaders by position differ from community to community. Most researchers rely on the title of the position to identify the leader, with few other supporting criteria. The positional approach lacks a method of identifying and consistently applying supplementary criteria, which makes this approach suspect and the least preferred of the three methods (Kaiser, 1993).

In an unpublished study, one of us has used the positional approach to identify influentials in a community of 20,000 people. Experience suggests that the use of this model alone does not allow one to identify the majority of the "real" community power agents. Experience verifies the weaknesses of the model and emphasizes the fact that each community is different in its power structure type. The positional model is more appropriate for small, primarily rural communities, where leaders in government, economic, and social areas are the key decision makers. As communities become larger—say, 25,000 or more people—the model is less reliable. In the study mentioned above, the mayor of the community was initially thought to be the leader of the governing body. After applying the decision-making and reputational research methods (discussed below), it was determined that, in areas regarding public policy and civil codes and regulations, the mayor was the "leader" of the community council. His advice was sought and heeded by the elected council members. But, in issues concerning economics and social problems, the mayor consulted the president of the local bank, two members of the clergy, the owners of the two largest industries, the chair of the chamber of commerce, a member of the oldest family in the community, and two of the most prosperous farmers. In this community, these were the power agents.

The Decision-Making Approach

The decision-making approach is based on the "pluralist" position rather than the "elitist," or positional, model of determining community power agents. The decision-making approach focuses on people involved in making key decisions about important issues in the community. Participation in decision making is the criterion for determining community leadership. The underlying assumption is that those who actively participate in decision making are the real leaders. Leadership is power (Kaiser, 1993).

Identifying power agents with this approach primarily involves applying documented research methods, that is, identifying major issues in the community over time and then tracing the decision-making process to the source to determine who was involved and what they accomplished. In this way, the researcher can identify the processes and actual participants rather than relying on the assumption that people with positional power make the decisions. Researchers carefully investigate past editions of newspapers and other public documents that identify key community issues and the people most often associated with these issues. Private club records and membership lists in civic and other types of organizations provide information about community members' interactions. Researchers also attend various community functions and observe "who associates with who" at meetings or social events focusing on specific issues. Observing interactions at open forums or panel discussions and examining minutes of committee meetings or government council meetings are valuable research practices for identifying who is involved in making decisions and how these decisions are made.

Some researchers argue that the decision-making model is more appropriate for determining the secondary level of power agents, those who are active in the public forum only as representatives of the "real" power agents, who prefer to remain hidden from public view. Some also argue that the decision-making model is more appropriate for identifying community networks and interlocking interest areas as opposed to identifying the real community leaders. One of us conducted a study of power in a suburban community of approximately 40,000 people. The decision-making model was applied and the results were inconclusive. The researcher identified the interest areas (government, economic, and social), networks, and high-profile people involved in discussions and debates, but found that most of these "actors" were not the real community influentials but only their representatives, who advised and befriended the key influentials. Only when the reputational method was applied was the researcher able to identify the actual power structure of the community.

In this study, nine community members composed the power elite. Much of the "business" of the community was discussed during weekend golf at the one local country club, and over early morning breakfast at one of the oldest local restaurants, where all nine power agents gathered once a month. Of the nine, one was a prominent businessman, one was a physician, one was a lawyer, one was the mayor, one owned much of the undeveloped land surrounding the community and several apartment complexes, one owned the largest construction firm in the community, one was a state senator, one was a local bank president, and one came from one of the founding families of the community and had inherited wealth through various means. Each had two or three close friends whom they turned to for advice and who usually represented them at community or civic functions by expressing "their" views or opinions. Members of this network relayed back to their respective power agent the impressions or feeling they received from others regarding their opinions or views.

In this community, the mayor relied heavily on the opinion of the other influentials regarding government issues. When issues developed regarding economics, the mayor listened carefully to those in state government, business, and real estate. For issues involving the social domain, such as building a new civic center, the mayor consulted the lawyer, the physician, and the founding family member. When it came to "running" local government, the mayor clearly dominated the city council.

The Reputational Approach

The reputational approach to identifying power agents is based on the assumption that those who have a "reputation" for power are, in fact, those who have the power. Power agents are identified by local "knowledgeables" in positions to know who has control and influence in the community. There are variations on the research methods used to identify power agents with the reputational model, but a two-step procedure is the most common and reliable despite the effort and time needed. The reputational method is generally held to be the most effective in identifying power agents in the community, especially when it is combined with the decision-making method. The two-step reputational research model is presented below.

Step 1: A list of "informants" is developed, and these informants are then asked to provide a list of community leaders. Informants are identified by a variety of sources, but the local chamber of commerce is the ideal starting place. From lists compiled by the chamber of commerce and other people recommended by chamber representatives, the researcher contacts these informants and begins the power agent identification process. Questions asked depend on the nature of the research topic. Educators would want to focus on those power agents influencing decisions on educational issues. The question might be asked, "Who are the people in the community whose opinions are most sought after and respected when it comes to matters impacting education?" A follow-up question could be, "If there were a major project—say, a school bond issue—that required a decision by a group of leaders who were widely respected, who would make up this group?"

The list is then presented to a panel of judges representing the major community areas of civic affairs, government, business, and social status. These names surface from talking with informants. The judges may be power agents themselves, but at this stage of the research that is of little concern and consequence.

The judges are high-profile people asked to pick 10 or more names from the list of people identified by the informants. Once the list is obtained from the judges, some criteria must be used to narrow the list to a manageable number. No single method exists to set criteria for deleting names of potential power agents, and this lack of criteria is a major weakness in the reputational model. Usually the lists of names will have duplications, and these potential leaders are immediately included in the pool. Names appearing on only one or two lists are deleted. If the list of names provided by the judges is not too large—say, 30 or fewer people—all names should be included in the pool of prospective leaders. If a cutoff point is necessary, the decision is arbitrary and based on intuition at best (another weakness).

Step 2: After the pool of potential leaders has been identified, researchers then interview each of these reputational leaders, or a sample of them if the list is too large. Questions asked these leaders center on their background, their community interest areas, their knowledge of and association with other community leaders, and their own evaluations of who makes major community decisions or greatly influences public opinion. Some argue that asking these leaders the question, "Are *you* a community power agent?" is vital to accurately identifying reputational leaders. Most interviewees will honestly answer this question by including themselves or providing a list of power agents.

One of us has conducted several reputational studies and found that the reputational method, when coupled with the decision-making method, provides highly reliable results. On several occasions, and at the conclusion of the study, community power agents contacted the author to discuss at length the research methods used to identify what they thought was a "well-disguised" group of citizens with a major interest in ensuring community growth, prosperity, and the perpetuation of its values and lifestyle. Inquiries such as these reinforce the validity of the reputational method.

An unpublished study by one of us can serve as an instructive example. After the reputational leader interview list was limited to about 20 potential power agents, and each candidate was interviewed once, a list of duplicated and triplicated names emerged. A second round of interviews took place with those whose names were mentioned two or more times. This second interview provided the researcher with a list of 8 potential reputational leaders. In the third round of interviews, one potential leader still denied he had any influence in the community, despite his name being mentioned most frequently by others, and despite his participation on committees and panels as reported in the newspaper and committee meeting minutes. The researcher asked one last question as the interviewee's patience was wearing thin: "Why were you so active in Rotary Club meetings and so positive and vocal about the effects of the proposed industrial park?" After a long silence, he complimented the researcher on doing his homework and said,

"Yes, I am what you call a 'power agent.'" Asking the researcher for the list of other influentials, he checked off each of the eight names, his included, and then circled five names. He said, "These are the names you are really after." As the researcher exited his office, the influential's parting words were: "Remember, you never *heard* those names from my lips."

Building Community Confidence Factors

Much of the conflict between school administrators and interest groups or power agents originates in the confidence community members have lost in education. Kawalski (1996) reports that the following factors lead to community dissatisfaction and promote conflict between educators and interest groups:

- Low-achieving or academically poorly performing schools
- High vandalism, discipline, and drug incidents
- Curriculum that runs counter to traditional community values and beliefs
- Poor attitudes among administrators and teachers
- Suspect decision-making process
- Lack of widespread participation in school governance

The image of today's public school has greatly diminished over the past decades. Kaiser (1993) relates that, since the 1960s, public displeasure has increased steadily with increased tax dollars yielding substandard student academic performance. Many community members view schools as unproductive and fiscally excessive; they want schools to be held more accountable for their practices and outputs. Some believe they know best how to make schools excellent. Each group has an agenda, and each agenda causes tension and conflict between school and community. Seitel (1992) discusses the need for school administrators to "lubricate" and "harmonize" interactions with community members. *Lubricating* is information sharing: keeping the public informed and up to date about school programs and outcomes. An informed public is a trusting and supporting public. Lubrication decreases the possibility of excessive tension or friction between educators and the community.

Harmonizing is being open, honest, and fair in all relationships, be they with students, parents, or community members. Honesty and openness breed credibility and decrease suspicion and discontent. Actively seeking community members' support and involving representatives from different organizations and ethnic backgrounds increases the credibility of a school's programs and practices, and decreases the potential for school-community conflict. When school decisions are made with broad community representation, the likelihood of community support for the school against interest group demands increases significantly.

Techniques for Handling Criticism

Criticism of school programs and practices can come from persons outside of interest groups as well as from power agents. Administrators hear complaints daily from parents, senior citizens, and others, and they should first seek to understand the motivation behind the criticism. Next, they need to be open and honest and take a positive approach when handling criticism. Kaiser (1993) provides additional salient tips to handle criticism successfully. These include: be a good listener, don't become emotional and remain objective, provide facts in responding to critics, be polite and professional, avoid discussing side issues, answer the questions posed, and follow through on the complaint. If the criticism is valid, ask the critic how the issue could best be resolved. Sometimes the suggested solutions prove the best, and such inquiries achieve on-the-spot involvement and allow the critic to leave the conversation with a positive attitude toward the school and the administrator.

Measuring Public Opinion

School administrators frequently find themselves attacked by interest groups or the media about the need for programs or for newly implemented practices deemed innovative but educationally sound. Pressure from interest groups and criticism from the media can be ameliorated through the use of survey results that provide an index of public opinion. Survey research assesses attitudes, preferences, and opinions, and informs school administrators and others how people think and feel about their school and specific issues. Survey research provides administrators with a dependable barometer that assesses public attitudes on proposed changes in school practices, providing data for sound decision making. Results from public opinion surveys, according to Gallagher et al. (1997), are one of the best ways to silence critics or interest groups, because such surveys indicate the opinion of the majority. Confronting critics with facts is the best way to defuse potential conflict situations. This is especially true for school administrators who must take the public will into account when making program or policy decisions.

Different types of survey research methods exist, but the mailed questionnaire is one of the best ways to determine community perceptions about schools.

When interviews are used to supplement questionnaire results, surveys are more reliable as sources of planning and decision making.

Borg and Gall (1983) note that educators can use scientific or unscientific survey methods to make programs and policy decisions. The primary difference is that "scientific" surveys use random sampling techniques, and their results can be generalized to the large population being sampled. Hence random sampling and generalizability separate scientific from unscientific survey methods. For the opinions of a group of 300 people or less, the entire population would likely be surveyed. But if opinions were sought from a population of 1,000 people, random sampling would likely be used to reduce the number of people needed for the survey and still represent the opinions of the total population. Formulas exist to tell the researchers the sample size needed, and sampling reduces the cost of the survey and the amount of personnel time needed to conduct the survey.

Rate of questionnaire return is a concern of researchers. Borg and Gall (1983) maintain that at least a 70% return rate is needed for confidence to be placed in the survey results. When a return rate is lower—say, 50%—it is necessary to conduct interviews with at least 10% of the nonrespondents, to check for agreement with respondent results on completed questionnaires.

Survey respondent bias is a major concern of researchers. Bias is a contributing factor to making research methods unscientific. For example, surveys in populations like a school's PTO are open to biased answers on opinion surveys. Parents who attend PTO meetings are generally supportive and positive about the school, and criticism would be unlikely from this "biased" population. Likewise, surveys from those attending conferences, group meetings, or forums, and surveys conducted by the radio and newspaper, are biased in that those who attend meetings or read newspapers either have a vested interest in the issue or feel strongly enough to respond. Results may not represent opinions held by nonattendees, nonlisteners, or nonreaders. Responses provide an indicator of how certain people perceive an issue, but results cannot be generalized to the larger population.

Other concerns researchers have about opinion surveys include the wording of questions. Educational jargon should be eliminated unless the terms are clearly defined. Attention should be given to how questions are framed, and leading questions should not be used, because such questions provide clues on how the question "should" be answered. Surveys going to ethnic populations should be printed in their predominant language, and demographic questions such as age, educational background, and employment should be asked only if this information serves an important purpose (Weller, 1999).

Mailed surveys have the advantage of reaching more people than telephone interviews, because those with private numbers and those without telephones are eliminated from the survey. Mailed surveys allow for candor, and open-ended questions provide an avenue for in-depth responses. Coding surveys is a consideration, especially when different strata exist in the sampled population and achieving an acceptable return rate is necessary. Coding practices vary. Some researchers use different-colored paper for different strata groups, some use letters, and some use numerals. Usually a certain percentage of the population will not return the first mailed survey, making a second or third mailing necessary. Coding can identify nonrespondents, so duplicate surveys are not mailed. All questionnaires should include a cover letter explaining the specific purpose of the survey and how the survey information will be used. A self-addressed stamped envelope should be included to assist a maximum return rate.

Constructing the Public Opinion Questionnaire

Constructing opinion instruments is a relatively simple task. Borg and Gall (1983) provide the following considerations for developing survey instruments:

1. Certain demographic information may be essential depending on the purpose of the survey and how the results will be used. Demographics most often assessed are race, sex, age, employment, years of education, and number of children in school by grade level.

2. The wording of survey questions is vital to the validity of the responses and to the return and completion rate.

- Questions should be concise, with no two questions on a single stem item. For example, do not ask questions such as, "Do you believe the school's lunches are nutritious and flavorful?" The stem item is designed to assess information about the school lunch, but asks about nutritional value and taste appeal at the same time. Respondents may answer "yes" with nutrition in mind, but "no" for taste. Regardless of the response, one doesn't know which food quality the respondent considered. The question is useless.

- Use clear and understandable language. Sometimes questionnaires are printed in a population's predominant language to facilitate response rates.

- Use terms people understand or define terms if they are essential to the survey. For example, if you are inquiring about people's attitude toward year-round schools, define year-round school and provide examples of how your proposed year-round school would operate.

- Avoid leading questions or questions that may cause the respondent to provide you with the answers you desire. For example, "If your taxes would be reduced, would you favor year-round schools?" Suggesting that taxes would be reduced usually causes a "yes" response to any question.

- Keep the number of open-ended questions to a minimum. Answers to open-ended questions take time to compile, and readers must have experience in coding key word responses. Training is needed to make sure readers are consistent in interpreting and coding respondent results.

- Pretest your survey with a sample of the population to which your survey is being mailed. The results will help you to clean up any confusing language, catch two-concept stem items, and make sure the survey is readable and understandable. Include these individuals in your mailings.

Applying the Results of a Survey

Most surveys seek information that impacts students and school operations, and because schools are owned by the public, the public has a right to know the results. Consequently, findings should be published in local newspapers and distributed to school committees and organizations.

Regardless of the results of the survey, school administrators should report the results in an honest, straightforward manner. If respondents feel that the school is delinquent in areas of proficiency or that problems exist, this information needs as much reporting space as do any accolades bestowed upon the school. Remember the reason for the survey instrument: to solicit honest feedback on the issues under investigation. Moreover, special interest groups probably know the school's shortcomings already. By providing open and honest communication to the community, the school increases community trust. Survey results also prepare administrators for dealing with areas inviting criticism. Administrators can use these results to plan for new programs or formulate strategy to defuse potential conflict situations.

Other Methods of Community Feedback

School administrators have additional means for receiving information from the community. *Open forums* and *conferences* are ways school administrators can promote frank discussion and receive valuable information about an educational topic of interest or concern to the community. School administrators can select topics for the forums or have community members designate topics. Often speakers or discussants are asked to present their views, and then people have the opportunity to respond. This interaction allows school administrators an opportunity to get a rough estimate of public opinion and a feel for areas of satisfaction and dissatisfaction. Forums and conferences also allow interested participants the opportunity to release tension and express themselves openly (Gallagher et al., 1997).

Advisory committees are groups of people representing a cross section of the community who can express the needs and opinions of those they represent. Different committees have different purposes, but generally they are asked to suggest ways to solve school-related problems and provide information about the concerns of those they represent. Their input helps administrators better understand the broad array of perceptions and needs among community members as they plan programs or make policy decisions (Kawalski, 1996).

The key communicator system is another effective way to take the pulse of public opinion. Kudlacek (1989) notes, "The best time-proven technique for staying ahead of issues is to tune into your informal community grapevine through the key communicator system" (p. 30). *Key communicators* are people who have standing or status in the community and may be power agents themselves. These individuals are in positions where they hear the opinions of others and can pass along vital information to school administrators. As members of an advisory or school committee, key communicators have the opportunity to keep administrators current regarding public opinion and rumors circulating throughout the community. As community influentials, they are in a position to provide trusted, timely, and accurate information and thereby shape public opinion.

Let's Review

Schools are controlled by those who set policy and those who have power and influence in the community. Each community has a cadre of special interest groups and a small group of community power agents or influentials who significantly impact the rules and regulations set by school board members. For school leaders to be effective in attaining their goals, acquiring adequate resources, and accomplishing the mission of their schools, they need to know the type of community they live in, understand the power structure in that community, and identify the community power agents so they can develop the rapport necessary to have them on their side. School leaders with the support and confidence of their community power agents have the community's confidence and the overall support of the board of education.

Interest groups apply various types of pressure to school leaders and to the board of education to enact their own agendas. When those agendas do not coincide with the mission of the school, effective leaders successfully confront these groups through proven conflict strategies that either turn these groups into supporters of their educational programs or redirect their discontent so that the school is no longer a primary target.

Effective leaders continually measure public opinion and use a variety of means to determine the areas of content and discontent among various segments of the public. Surveys, interviews, advisory committees, and key communicator programs are just a few ways school leaders keep informed about community issues impacting the schools.

Exercises

Exercise 1: Community Opinion

As assistant principal for instruction and curriculum, you have the complete trust of Mr. Miles, the principal. You have discussed research with him often, and he is much impressed with your research skills and knowledge. Today, however, his calm demeanor has turned into anger and frustration and he opens the conversation on a serious note.

Last evening, at the school board meeting, the superintendent was verbally attacked by three of the seven board members as being "unresponsive" to community demands for more extracurricular activities in the high school. This led to accusations that he was not demonstrating the "leadership" needed to make the high school a state-acknowledged School of Excellence. Three other board members strongly defended the superintendent's performance. The board chair, Ms. Katz, asked Mr. Miles to "find some data, some way, to get to the bottom of this mess." Ms. Katz could see that this conflict could lead to the superintendent's loss of a renewal contract. She wants factual data by next month's board meeting. Mr. Miles turns to you and says: "Drop everything and get me the data by next month before my job is in question."

As the researcher, you need accurate information in a short time period. You have no official advisory committee or key communicator program in place. How are you going to collect the necessary information for Mr. Miles? Be specific in your answer. If you devise an opinion survey, provide an example of how the survey would look, including all types of questions asked, and a description of who you would sample and why. Your high school is the only 9-12 school in a community of 15,000 people.

Exercise 2: Community Network

As the newly appointed assistant principal for instruction and curriculum, you need to understand the concerns of the different "populations" in your school's attendance zones. You decide that the best way to prepare against special interest group conflict and to continually meet the demands and needs of your community members is to develop a "communication network." Your principal has approved this undertaking, but has clearly stated that "the end product must be thorough in all respects." Develop a comprehensive "community network" program complete with committee names, people involved in the network, process of committee member selection, and members' roles and responsibilities.

Exercise 3: Community Power Agents

Yesterday, the superintendent asked you to conduct a community power survey. He was at a conference and heard other superintendents mention its importance. He knew you conducted a survey in another school system and has given you this 6-month assignment with an office in the central school office. The superintendent's last words to you were, "By next week, I want a detailed plan of *exactly* how you are going to conduct a power agent survey for this town of 35,000 people. I want this plan so well defined that even I would feel comfortable in implementing it." You responded that the plan would be on his desk next Friday.

Exercise 4: Special Interest Groups

As assistant principal for instruction and curriculum, you are working with a committee of parents and community members on developing a values clarification curriculum in Grades 9 to 12. You are using sources that the research labels "citizenship education" as the foundation for building the curriculum, which must be approved first by the teachers and then by the school board. The committee has approved its work and you are making a final review of the curriculum plan before it is presented to the faculty.

Suddenly, two women walk into your office and simultaneously shout, "Religion has no place in schools." One then adds, "If you don't throw this illegal nonsense out right now, we'll picket the school and hire a lawyer. Throw the plan out." What do you do now? What are the steps that you would take to try to defuse this already hostile situation? Remember that they are community members, you are a professional, and their feelings run deep.

5

Effective Communication and Listening Skills

In This Chapter

Effective assistant principals must communicate well to maximize their potential as leaders and managers. Their position as liaison between teachers and principal requires expert communication and listening skills. Moreover, they are required to communicate with a wide variety of publics to gain understanding and support. Effective communication skills help sustain the school's culture, build positive working relationships, and reduce the potential for problem or conflict situations. Effective assistant principals lead through influence and persuasion and must be able to accurately and concisely state what they need and motivate others to cooperate and be committed.

Why Assistant Principals Need Good Communication Skills

Effective assistant principals need good communication skills to achieve their goals, bring people together, minimize conflict, facilitate problem solving, and foster morale and commitment. Communication, both verbal and nonverbal, can attract or repel, and makes a difference between successful and unsuccessful school programs.

Good communication skills foster productive interactions among teachers, students, parents, and community members. Open and honest communication promotes credibility, reduces conflict and alienation, and builds confidence in leadership. Kindred, Bagin, and Gallagher (1990) relate that the word *communica-*

tion comes from the Latin *communicate,* which means "to share" or "to make common." Assistant principals depend on oral and written communication to bring about understanding and support for their ideas and programs. As a co-operative process, communication is the substance that determines the quality of interpersonal relationships and provides the foundation for successful school outcomes. Good communication skills are essential for change initiatives (Weller, 1999).

Communication as a Process

Communication is composed of verbal and behavioral symbols that convey meaning and describe ideas and feelings. These symbols shape perceptions, create concepts and images, and influence and persuade others. They are also used to hide and deceive, and to promote creative action, initiate change, and solve problems. Good communication skills, however good they are, will never compensate for inadequate leadership, poor judgment, or ineptness.

Effective assistant principals use communication skills to lead others through influence, persuasion, and consensus, rather than through positional authority or policy. When communication is not clear, reliable, and continuous, sociopolitical tension increases, and teacher frustration and dissatisfaction result. Morrison (1994) relates that continually sharing reliable information, seeking feedback, listening, and resolving conflict are essential communication skills for leaders.

Effective communication requires planning, and the communication method must be carefully selected to reach the target audience. The idea behind communication is to bring about a change in behavior through mutual understanding, acceptance, and support. Communication theory provides a six-step process for sending and receiving information:

1. *Source:* Message or ideas originate that the source wishes to communicate to another.
2. *Encoder:* The source formulates or encodes the message in symbolic form.
3. *Channel:* The channel is the device that carries the message—oral, written, or nonverbal.
4. *Decoder:* The message is received and interpreted by the receiver or decoder. Unfamiliar terms or symbols may cause misunderstanding on the part of the decoder.
5. *Receiver:* The receiver receives the message and may choose to formulate some type of feedback to the message.
6. *Action:* The receiver responds to the message.

Figure 5.1 A Generic Communication Model for Sending and Receiving Information

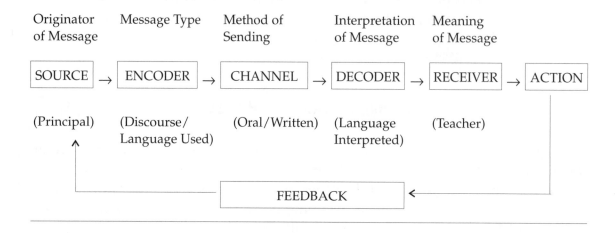

Figure 5.1 presents a model of the two-way communication process for sending and receiving information. The model is generic, and it applies to communication processes involving individuals and groups using verbal or behavioral symbols.

One-Way Communication

One-way communication refers to communication such as lecturing or speaking with no expectation of feedback from the receiver. This form of communication saves time, but its success depends on the sender's ability to use language that is clear, specific, and understandable. From a leadership perspective, one-way communication is perceived as being regulatory in nature, and it can result in selective compliance and fragmented implementation of policy on the part of subordinates (Clampitt, 1991). Assistant principals should rely on such practices as management-by-walking-around rather than on a tirade of lectures or a constant flow of memos that are thrown away by subordinates unread. Management-by-walking-around, a two-way communication opportunity, provides means to solve problems; answer questions in a personal way; offer immediate feedback to questions, concerns, or comments; and test for understanding. One-way communication, with its downward flow of information, regardless of the correct use of words, symbols, or cues, does not guarantee effective communication because it does not allow for dialogue or feedback, which are essential in the communication process.

Two-Way Communication

Two-way communication is a cooperative, reciprocal process wherein ideas and messages are shared through exchanges between sender and receiver. Burbules (1993) relates that dialogue, the mutual sharing of information, is central to informed decision making, encourages greater understanding of problems, and is essential in the implementation of shared governance and teacher empowerment.

Two-way communication facilitates commitment from both sender and receiver. Commitment develops when communication is mutually beneficial. Tolerance of and respect for the expression of opinion is essential in situations involving controversial topics, ideological differences, or personality conflicts. Committed communication allows leaders to receive constructive criticism that is essential for successful change, high teacher morale, motivated action, and the flow of creative ideas.

In the absence of open and honest communication, "filtering" takes place. Filtering, or selective listening, is the elimination of important information on the part of the receiver. For example, filtering may take place when receivers are not receptive to constructive criticism, when the message is threatening, or when a listener uses such filtering to protect or advance his or her position. Filtering contributes to the start of rumors and speculation (Burbules, 1993).

Rumor and Speculation

A *rumor,* according to Allport and Postman (1954), is a message devoid of fact and transmitted with great speed. Rumor is perhaps the most rapid form of communication and it depends largely on wishful thinking and inaccurate listening. *Speculation* is wild guessing or advance information built on little or no fact. Speculation does not usually convey the negative aspects associated with rumor. Rumors become rife when (a) people feel threatened or insecure and (b) there are inadequate facts, inaccurate information, or clandestine activity. Moreover, "when formal communications in an organization are infrequent, slow to be transmitted, or given less than complete credibility, rumors are transmitted instead" (Bass, 1965, p. 311).

According to Allport and Postman (1954), there are three characteristics of rumors:

1. As a rumor spreads, fewer details are provided, which makes it easier to repeat.

2. A rumor tends to focus on a specific detail. People will emphasize or embellish different aspects of the rumor.

3. Different people choose to listen to different things in a rumor, and this choice is largely a function of interest or bias. The rumor will then be repeated in the context of this personal bias or interest.

When a rumor arises, *facts* must be immediately used to refute or discredit the rumor. Ignoring a rumor tends to add credence to the story. Culbertson, Jacobson, and Reller (1960) make the following recommendations to school administrators on how to confront rumors:

1. Immediately provide accurate facts to demonstrate the inaccuracy of the rumor.
2. Develop skills in assessing rumors. Often rumors are symptoms of group tension, fear, hostility, and anxiety. Determine the needs that caused the rumor and address them.
3. Develop a comprehensive communication system that continually informs teachers, parents, students, and community members of the school's projects, programs, and activities. Change of any kind is fertile ground for rumor. By involving those affected by the change process, rumors and speculation can be eliminated.

Listening Skills

Studies on school administrators "have consistently shown that about seventy-five percent of the contacts an administrator has in a school day are one-on-one meetings" (Dolan, 1996, p. 113). For assistant principals, skill in listening is essential to effective leadership, with daily demands coming from teachers, students, parents, and community members. Hughes and Hooper (2000) point out that listening involves all parties in the communication process, but the receiver of the message must show signs of listening and understanding. These signs include eye contact, facial expressions, body language, and tone of voice.

Barriers to effective listening are many, but the greatest barrier is ourselves. Most people prefer to talk rather than listen because talking is more self-centered. The following barriers that can be learned and avoided are reported by Golen (1990):

- Listening for facts or details and not content
- Being distracted by noises during the conversation
- Daydreaming

- Being occupied with another topic or remembering an important task that must be completed
- Having little or no interest in the topic
- Focusing on the sender's physical appearance or mannerisms
- Thinking about the length of time the sender takes to communicate the message
- Concluding what the sender says before the message is concluded
- Getting emotional about the message
- Pretending to be interested in the message
- Being bored with the complexity or difficulty of the message
- Allowing personal bias or prejudice to interfere with the sender's message
- Avoiding eye contact and refusing to provide feedback
- Neglecting to clarify or seek clarification of the message

Poor listening costs an organization time, effort, and resources. Poor listeners often have to rework, spend time seeking clarification or redirection, and waste resources in doing so. They are often the object of jokes and can be omitted from important assignments that could enhance their careers. They are often characterized as being forgetful or inefficient.

Listening skills can be improved, but this takes time and effort. Many people can improve their listening skills by making a personal commitment to becoming better listeners. O'Hair and Friedrich (1992) suggest ways to improve listening skills:

- Develop a positive attitude toward the sender and the sender's message.
- Screen out noise—environmental and personal distractions that interfere with concentration on the message's content.
- Maintain eye contact and be alert for facial expressions and other nonverbal cues.
- Remind yourself that the message is important, and that you must hear it regardless of the topic or your bias toward the sender.
- Do not draw conclusions while the sender is speaking.
- Concentrate on what is said and how it is said. Difficult messages are sometimes conveyed in *paralanguage*, discussed later in this chapter.
- Provide periodic verbal and nonverbal feedback to the sender.

- Paraphrase the content of the message with your own interpretations and seek feedback from the sender.

- Relate new information to old information.

Communication Knowledge and Skills: Survey Results

In our survey of assistant principals, we asked what "formal" training, if any, they had in communication or listening skills. Of the 95% who responded to the question, over 65% listed "textbook" knowledge of communication skills, and less than 10% listed formal training in listening skills.

Other questions asked if the assistant principals had training in dealing with rumors, nonverbal communication techniques, or critics of school policies or practices. The responses indicated a lack of training in dealing with these issues on a practical basis. Several assistant principals lamented their lack of training in the area of dealing with rumors and noted the harm rumors cause. A majority of the respondents indicated that either their principal or members of their central office staff were designated as being responsible for addressing group or individual criticism. Several respondents noted the importance of having training in this area but also commented that they did not need an additional responsibility.

Another question asked if respondents had a crisis management plan in their school. Most respondents, over 65%, indicated that no such plan existed, but indicated that one was needed. Those respondents who indicated a school crisis management plan existed either had one that was developed by the central office or had developed a plan in conjunction with guidelines originating from the central office.

Communication for Persuasion and Influence

Much has been said about effective leaders leading through influence and persuasion. These leaders realize that language is power and that communication is neither neutral nor apolitical. Language is used to sway opinion and achieve goals. Language reflects the culture in which communication takes place, and this culture allows for the practice of *exclusion*. That is, people use language that is appropriate and acceptable, and endorsed and supported. Those who do not know the "language" are excluded. Even those who know the language are bound by this culture. Foucault (1972) states ". . . we are not free to say just anything, . . . we cannot speak of anything, when we like or where we like; not just anyone,

---

Assistant Principals on the Importance of Good Communication Skills

"Graduate work tells us the importance of communication [in leadership], but it's the same old textbook coverage. There is no practical application such as *how* to be a good listener or speaker."

"My formal training was on-the-job. I learned through making lots of mistakes. I had to learn that people don't always listen and that they hear what they want to."

"The biggest mistakes I've ever made have been errors of judgment related to communication. I've learned to be very circumspect in what I say and how I say it. If something *can* be misunderstood, someone is going to misunderstand it."

SOURCE: Survey of 100 Practicing Assistant Principals From Urban, Rural, and Suburban Schools

---

finally, may speak of just anything" (p. 16). In other words, our language is sifted through the culture in which we live and is used to ensure adherence to cultural norms.

Commenting on the power of language, English (1994) discusses the "law of situation," which dictates that authority is not determined by administrative hierarchy alone, but also by the situation and the person with potential to exercise competence and leadership in the situation. In this context, effective leaders are competent in language and therefore rely more on communication to influence and persuade others than on their authority to accomplish objectives. Authority intimidates, threatens, and makes subordinates feel inferior. The use of this type of power arouses negative feelings toward superiors regardless of how appropriate the use of authority may be. To be effective, assistant principals must learn to call on their own authority last.

Central to the art of persuading and influencing others are the attributes of *trust* and *credibility*. Trust is earned through consistent behavior over time, and credibility is achieved through competence and expertise. When subordinates deem leaders trustworthy and credible, influence and persuasion are highly effective leadership skills. In other words, it becomes unnecessary to use authority. Being a leader and learning the skills of a leader are hard work.

Persuasion and influence should be conducted in nonthreatening surroundings during face-to-face meetings, and should not be rushed. Loinberger (1960) presents a five-stage model for shaping attitudes and behaviors that is applicable for assistant principals as well as others initiating change:

1. *Awareness:* A person introduces a new idea or behavior with benefits clearly stated to the target audience.

2. *Interest:* The person provides information that entices the listener to examine the merits of the idea.

3. *Evaluation:* After careful examination of the merits of the idea, the listener evaluates the personal benefits of the idea.

4. *Trial:* The idea is tried for a brief period of time during which the person who originated the idea ensures that feedback and support are provided.

5. *Adoption*: The idea or behavior is adopted because the change is deemed good or personally beneficial.

Cognitive Styles of Communication

Carl Jung's work on cognitive style has direct implications for assistant principals trying to increase the effectiveness of their communication. The Myers-Briggs Type Indicator, a psychological type test, is based on Jung's theory of psychological type (Myers & McCaulley, 1985). The instrument is rooted in empirical research and used in a wide variety of fields, including leadership and management development. The Myers-Briggs Type Indicator and psychological type theory provide a method for understanding differences between individuals. This method has practical applications for assistant principals trying to understand how individual differences between people affect their preferences for receiving and sending information. Neither the theory nor the instrument can be mastered in a short period of time, but practical applications to promote leadership effectiveness for assistant principals will be immediately evident.

Nasca (1994) relates that, according to Jung's theory, there are two dimensions and four cognitive styles that can be used to promote effective communication. The two dimensions are (a) perception, or the way one views the world, and (b) decision making, or the way one processes information through *thinking* and *feeling*.

Four cognitive styles exist in each person, and each person has a preference for using one of the two cognitive styles categorized under each of the two dimensions. The four cognitive styles are *sensor, intuitor, thinker,* and *feeler.* These preferences interact to form four different combinations or cognitive styles.

1. The *Sensor-Thinker* prefers detail, fact, and sequential order in giving and receiving information. As a sender, the Sensor-Thinker delivers messages mainly using facts, practical examples, and concrete terms.

2. The *Sensor-Feeler* prefers communication that displays feelings of warmth and empathy. Communication with others has the personal touch and includes specific, humanistic examples.

3. The *Intuitor-Thinker* prefers theoretical, logical, and rational information, but not information that is highly detail oriented. Rational and general examples are provided in their communication with others.

4. The *Intuitor-Feeler* prefers warmth and empathy in communication, and emphasizes and is attuned to the personal touch in the message. Intuitor-Feelers can detect subtle words or symbols in communication, and they prefer communication of creative expression, personal experience, and personal challenge.

Assistant principals who use this knowledge of the different preferences people have based on individual psychological types can tailor information and messages to fit the needs and preferences of teachers, parents, students, and others. It is not necessary to administer the Myers-Briggs Type Indicator to each faculty member. Although this option may be desirable, it is not necessary if the assistant principal becomes knowledgeable in psychological type theory. Having a general understanding of this theory allows one to identify the psychological type of individuals based on clues and cues coming from them during the communication process. The study of psychological type can also broaden assistant principals' understanding of human differences and of *themselves*. It is invaluable for the insight it provides into human behavior.

Nonverbal Communication

Nonverbal communication is as important as verbal communication. A basic tenet of psychotherapy is that if you want to understand what a person is trying to communicate to you, then you should examine how that person's behavior makes you feel. Nonverbal behavior is generally defined as interaction with others that does not include words or symbolic messages. Harris (1993) provides examples of nonverbal *kinesis* communication such as raised eyebrows, firm handshakes, silence, and the shifting of posture. Behaviors communicating warmth and interest include smiling, touching, leaning forward, and eye contact. Positive movements strengthen rapport between people and foster open and honest communication. Eye-to-eye contact is direct and powerful. Prolonged eye contact indicates honesty, credibility, and sincerity; conveys attention to the message; and helps ensure understanding of content. But overly prolonged eye contact can be threatening and indicate that a more detailed response is needed.

<hr />

Readings on Psychological Type Theory

- *Manual: A Guide to the Development and Use of the Myers-Briggs Type Indicator,* by I. B. Myers and M. H. McCaulley (1985). Palo Alto, CA: Consulting Psychologists Press.
- *People Types and Tiger Stripes,* by G. Lawrence (1993). Gainesville, FL: Center for Applications of Psychological Type.
- *Developing Leaders,* by C. Fitzgerald and L. K. Kirby (1997). Palo Alto, CA: Davies-Black Publishing.

<hr />

Paralanguage, according to Luthans (1989), is an important form of communication that includes voice utterances that are not strictly verbal but add emphasis to a nonverbal message. These include grunts, sighs, laughter, yawning, and non-influences such as "ah" and "um."

Proxemics is also a form of nonverbal communication. Hall (1980) researched the importance of space in communicating messages and found that there are four personal "space zones" people use to communicate certain messages:

1. *Intimate Zone:* Two feet or closer implies an intimate relationship or that one is socially domineering.

2. *Personal Zone:* Two to four feet indicates that close association or a friendship bond exists, or that one is well acquainted with another.

3. *Social Zone:* Four to twelve feet indicates minimal acquaintance and that a definite reason exists for communication. Most business behavior is conducted in this zone.

4. *Public Zone:* Twelve or more feet represents detached interests, with little business being conducted.

The management of time can also be a nonverbal communicator. Vecchio (1991) notes the use of *chronemics* to transmit messages. Being tardy to meetings indicates power or having a busy schedule. This behavior sends several messages, including forgetfulness, lack of interest, lack of involvement, or the reaffirmation of the high status of a person to subordinates. Effective use of time indicates efficiency, preparation, commitment, and organization.

Written Communication

Many of the rules that apply to spoken communication apply to written communication as well. Written communication can be formal or informal. For assistant principals in most situations, writing style should remain simple, emphasizing clarity and conciseness. Effective written messages should be clearly stated and presented so that the reader knows what action or response is needed. If the message is for information purposes, then only relevant, fact-based information should be provided. Written communication that requires a response should state the type of response desired, the medium for conveying the response, and when the response is due.

Hughes and Hooper (2000) note that language used in written communication should be understandable and noninflammatory. They state that lessons can be learned from newspaper reportage. Newspaper language is direct and simple, sentences and words are short, and writing is jargon-free. Hughes and Hooper present a "Fog Index" for judging the simplicity and directness of written messages. The formula provides an estimation of the number of years of schooling an individual needs to read the message with ease and understanding. The following steps can be taken to compute the Fog Index:

1. Determine the average number of words in a sentence in the message.
2. Count the number of words with three or more syllables.
3. Add the results of steps one and two and then multiply by 0.4. (The resulting number roughly corresponds to the years of schooling a person needs to read the message with ease and understanding.)

For assistant principals writing to parents, teachers, students, and community members, this index can be invaluable.

A standard rule of thumb for written communication to teachers is the "5 × 3 method." That is, if a message takes longer than 5 minutes to write or 3 minutes to read, it will probably be circular-filed. For teachers, messages should be short and concise; contain standard vocabulary; tell how the message *directly relates* to the teacher; and be presented in a line-item format, when possible.

All written communication should be carefully edited for grammar, spelling, and content by a third party. Neatness and professional presentation are essential because messages represent an impression statement from the assistant principal. Personal notes that thank teachers for assistance or acknowledge achievement serve to increase teacher morale and maintain positive interpersonal relations. Memos, although less formal than letters, should, like letters, be on the school's letterhead, free of jargon, and concise. Negative statements or "threat words" should be avoided because written messages have an emotional effect that cannot be clarified by immediate feedback or body language. Threat words and phrases include "again, I must call your attention to," "lack of caring," and "this behavior cannot be excused."

The following is recommended when writing to teachers, parents, or community members (Hughes & Hooper, 2000).

1. Be concise.
2. Keep sentences and paragraphs short, state your purpose clearly, and use correct grammar.
3. Get straight to the point and avoid abstractions.
4. Write to be understood, not to impress.
5. Use the active voice and put action in your verbs.
6. Use nouns and verbs that are meaningful to the senses.
7. Check all facts and avoid ambiguity.
8. Keep the message short so it can be read it quickly and easily.

Crisis Management and Communication Plan

Daily, schools are confronted with crisis situations. Often chaos or panic results from the lack of a well-planned crisis management and communications system. Crisis is the result of unanticipated events that require immediate attention from administrators to maintain the effective operations of the school and ensure the safety of students, teachers, community members, or others. To maximize the probability of satisfactory outcomes from crisis situations, school administrators must (a) develop a crisis management plan, (b) make employees aware of the plan, and (c) periodically *rehearse* the plan. With a crisis management plan as part of the organization's overall communications system, administrators can have greater control over unforeseeable events and increase the probability of satisfactory outcomes. In many schools, the assistant principal is the administrator designated to develop a crisis management plan.

Fink (1986) notes that the worst time to plan for crisis management is in a time of crisis. At this time, panic reactions are common, and rational thought is in short supply. Conducting "damage control" in times of panic or chaos often compounds a bad situation. Every crisis management plan should address three broad objectives:

1. To provide general direction on how to respond to crisis regardless of the crisis situation
2. To train teachers and staff on how to deal with crisis situations and define the roles of teachers and administrators
3. To resolve the crisis in the most appropriate manner with regard to the safety of students and school personnel

Developing a Crisis Management Plan

No single crisis management plan is best for all schools, and no single set of crisis management procedures will best address the variety of crises that confront school administrators. But there are some common denominators that provide direction for developing a generic crisis management plan.

1. Decide on a signal system to alert teachers and students of crisis situations in progress. An example is as follows: *Code 1* is door lockdown, meaning a weapon is in the school, and classroom doors should be locked; *code 2* is personal crisis, including suicide, heart attacks, strokes, or serious accidents; and *code 3* indicates bomb threat, hurricane, or tornado evacuation.

2. Detailed instructions of what to do for each code should be contained in student and teacher handbooks and periodically circulated. Periodic drills should be held for each code.

3. Copies of school maps and telephone numbers of key people and organizations to be contacted (such as the fire department) should be widely distributed and readily available, and specific people should be designated to contact these emergency sources.

4. Designate an area as a crisis center with an assigned director (an assistant principal) who acts as spokesperson and coordinates information flow and crisis operations.

5. Designate certain teachers and counselors as members of the crisis intervention team specifically trained to work with students and adults in high-stress situations.

Bagin and Gallagher (2001) present a list of essential steps administrators should take during the first 10 minutes of crisis:

1. Activate the code appropriate for the situation through a schoolwide announcement.

2. Report the incident to the proper authorities and to the central office.

3. Activate the crisis control center procedures.

4. Decide whether to lock or evacuate the school.

5. Provide first aid until rescue units arrive. Verify through facts what has happened.

6. Start keeping a record of the time sequence of events and log all calls made and received.

7. Have runners deliver any additional instructions to classrooms and bring back student and teacher status information.

8. Direct parents and media to a designated area with assistance and information from a designated crisis team member.

Communicating With Community Groups

Communicating with formal and informal community groups is essential to fostering community support of a school. American communities are made up of groups of people organized around special interests. Some of these groups sponsor programs that parallel those of the school while others seek to use the school to foster their own interests or philosophical positions. Assistant principals need to be aware of both formal and informal groups in their communities and familiar with these groups' philosophies as they relate to the goals and mission of public education. Moreover, assistant principals need to be in contact with members of these groups or have sources familiar with these groups to advise them of their goals and objectives as they relate to the schools.

Formal Groups

Many formal groups and organizations are national in scope, have local chapters, and are devoted to fostering American values and ideals. These groups support public education and have programs that coincide with those offered in the schools. For example, civic groups such as Rotary, Kiwanis, and Optimist clubs concern themselves with problems of education, social welfare, and government. Economic and patriotic groups such as chambers of commerce and Veterans of Foreign Wars embrace the teaching of government, civic responsibilities, improvement of social conditions, and patriotism. Many business and industrial leaders enter "Adopt-a-School" programs to help schools better educate students and provide resources otherwise unavailable. With few exceptions, these groups work closely with public schools, support the goals of public education, and come to the assistance of public schools in times of conflict.

Informal Groups

Informal groups, often referred to as special interest groups (SIGs), are often political in nature and have their own agendas to promote. Some of these groups concern themselves with the impact school board policy has on the community and its cost to taxpayers. Other SIGs focus on school programs that run counter to their philosophies and attempt to pressure schools to accept their philosophical positions and alter their programs or curriculum. Some seek to censor textbooks and library books, and some SIGs are created to stop school boards from taking specific actions that they feel run counter to the group aims.

Special interest groups, relates Dolan (1996), generally result from citizen dissatisfaction with school policy or programs, and they organize to criticize and confront the schools on specific issues. Usually, the word *concerned* is part of the organization's name, and such groups focus on attracting media attention to their cause. They rely on "facts" as they know them to criticize schools, amass public support, and gain acceptance for their desired outcomes. Tactics used by these SIGs include using a recognized formal group or organization to raise a concern or issue and get immediate, widespread attention; influencing public officials to comment or make inquires about their concern or issue; and "flooding" the media with position papers, calls for town meetings, and charges exaggerated to receive attention.

Evaluating the Legitimacy of Critics

Citizens have the right to have "honest differences" with public agencies. Sometimes leaders of public agencies overstep their authority or have misplaced priorities. When public concern arises over policy or issues, leaders must address these concerns immediately. Dolan (1996) points out that citizen concerns are best addressed by providing a clear *rationale* for a decision with *facts* that substantiate the decision. Holding a series of open forums allows for the discussion of opposing views, provides a venue where all sides can be heard, and allows for the presentation of facts and rationale.

Who Are Legitimate Critics?

There is no single accepted "acid test" to determine legitimate criticism, but Hughes and Hooper (2000) provide guidelines to gauge legitimate critics and criticism:

1. Do the critics present the correct facts or do they slant the facts in their favor?
2. Are the critics willing to meet without the media present?
3. Are the critics willing to listen to information that challenges or refutes their position?
4. Are the critics emotional rather than rational in their arguments, and do their arguments relate to a specific credo?
5. Are the critics willing to accept demonstrated facts?
6. Are the critics honest in discussing the reasons for their concerns?

If critics fail to meet the above criteria for legitimacy, one may well question their legitimacy and prepare for conflict. It is essential that documentation exists that supports efforts to resolve the critics' concerns. There should also be documentation detailing the critics' responses to conflict resolution efforts. Tape recordings are the best means of documentation.

Dealing With Critics

Meeting with critics should and can be viewed as a positive way to improve the school and gain information about community sentiment. Valid criticism, when acted on, can strengthen school programs and the bonds of trust and respect between the school and the community. Unfair or unfounded criticism can destroy relationships and weaken confidence in the schools. Criticism should never be overlooked or suppressed, because neglected criticism grows, becomes exaggerated, and gives the impression that the criticism may be true. Finally, some critics tell schools things others hesitate to mention. "Sometimes only the frankness of a critic can motivate further evaluation and action. Instead of avoiding critics, we should realize that their barbs and frankness can add perspective to the management of a school" (Kindred et al., 1990, p. 147).

Conferencing With Critics

Many times, assistant principals are asked to deal with critics of the school. When this is the case, the assistant principal will find it helpful to meet with the critic face to face for an interview on one or more occasions. Gallagher, Bagin, and Kindred (1997) present the following format for meeting with critics for the first time:

1. Listen to the critic and ask questions to get specific details of the complaint.
2. Ask questions that get to the source of the critic's information, provide background to the complaint, and allow the critic to provide examples.
3. Find out if the critic is speaking from a personal perspective or for others.
4. Determine if the complaint is local or systemwide, or a concern about schooling or education in general.
5. Ask questions that elicit specific facts from the critic.
6. Occasionally ask the critic to check his or her understanding of the facts with yours.
7. Ask clarifying questions to make sure you understand what the critic is really trying to communicate.
8. Before you respond, make sure you have heard all the critic wishes to say on the topic.

These questions will help the assistant principal determine if an explanation should be provided to the critic or if a second interview should take place. Most agree that providing immediate answers is desirable and courteous. On the other hand, some information may not be readily available, or the critic may be too emotional to listen. The decision is a judgment call. It is important not to become defensive over the complaint even if the criticism appears unjustified. Defensiveness implies some degree of guilt, and it may cloud judgment and objectivity.

Should a second interview be necessary, the following format should be followed:

1. At the conclusion of the first interview, set specific goals for the second interview, set a time limit for discussion, and delineate the responsibility of each party.

2. Ask the critic to gather facts and supporting information for his or her side of the complaint, and explain that you will gather relevant information as well.

3. If other parties are to attend, reach an agreement on who will attend and the importance of their presence. Insist that there be no surprise visitors or it may be necessary to terminate and reschedule the conference, depending on the situation and the purpose of the visitors' presence.

4. At the second interview, the critic should first be given an opportunity to revise his or her complaint or state a new conclusion. Time and new information often provide the critic with a different perspective, and it may be that the critic has resolved the issue or complaint with the information you provided at the first interview.

5. If the critic wishes to continue, remind him or her of the time limit and allow the critic to proceed based on facts and documented information, not on emotion or hearsay.

6. Then present to the critic your facts and documented information, free of emotion and hearsay.

7. Reach a resolution with the critic based on facts and on an objective assessment of the points presented. If the critic has made valid points or pointed out inequities, take measures to incorporate these points in the complaint, and always thank the critic for his or her interest, time, and concern.

Key Communicator Programs

Knowledgeable school leaders often use well-known and respected community members to set up a *key communicator program* to send and receive important information. Key communicators are high-profile people in the community who interact with large numbers of people and are trusted and respected by community members. Key communicators may or may not be power agents; their high profiles in the community as business leaders, government officials, or church officials ensure their influence over a wide array of people, nevertheless.

Key communicators have three primary functions: (a) to interact with community power agents about issues affecting the schools, keep them informed about school happenings, and relay their inclinations to educators; (b) to advertise the positive and successful aspects of the schools or diminish the impact of adverse or negative feelings regarding the schools; and (c) to get the pulse of the community through quick phone calls about rumors, the community's feelings about issues impacting the school, and local government decisions that could change attendance lines, influence the tax base, or impact plans for school consolidation. The key communicator program allows school administrators to receive and send timely, accurate information.

As Gallagher et al. (1997) relate, a major benefit of key communicator programs is their ability to "squelch rumors." Rumors about such matters as drugs, racial problems, and violence spread quickly but can usually be halted in their early stages through the use of key communicators. Key communicators have contacts with the local media, and their access to information can positively impact media coverage of school issues.

Initiating a Key Communicator Program

Assistant principals can initiate a key communicator program by soliciting names from teachers, staff members, parents, and personal contacts throughout the community. References from the local chamber of commerce, names of prominent people appearing in newspapers, and recommendations from members of civic organizations such as the Rotary are additional sources of names for a key communicator program.

A personal telephone call or letter can serve as an administrator's initial contact with the community member, asking that person to serve as a key communicator. The purpose of the program (to improve and support the schools through better communication) should be explained and a time should be set for an orientation session. The orientation meeting should delineate the goals of the program and allow for questions and discussion from the participants. Usually, a good time for the meeting is at a breakfast or lunch to show appreciation for their participation. The number of key communicators varies, but 5 to 10 are usually sufficient for a school. Meetings should be scheduled on an as-needed basis, with an annual meeting designed to show appreciation for their work. A nice way to show this appreciation is with a dinner during which recognition plaques are awarded to the key communicators. Such an event is also a good time to provide key communicators with information on the status of the school.

Communicating Using Meetings That Work

It has been said that meetings comprise "a group of the unprepared, appointed by the unwilling, to do the unnecessary." Why do we have meetings? Effective meetings—meetings that work—are used to communicate. Thompson (1992) relates that meetings are necessary for the following *specific* reasons:

1. Give or exchange information
2. Create new ideas
3. Decide on goals or issues
4. Delegate authority or work
5. Share work responsibilities
6. Persuade or inspire
7. Establish or maintain relations

The assistant principal who masters the art of effective meetings will have mastered many of the essentials of effective communication. One of the first rules to follow for effective meetings is this: Don't mix reasons for meeting. When meetings are called for one purpose—say, to give or exchange information—the chair should never move into a new meeting mode. Each meeting purpose has its own set of dynamics and its own requirements for success, and its participants have preconditioned mind-sets preparing them to focus on the business at hand.

Traditional meetings are mostly counterproductive because they have one important element in common: the quest for *individual dominance*. That is, each participant wants to outdo the others by being more vocal, providing more "fresh" ideas, and attaining more recognition. These participants have agendas to advance, and others often react with boredom or cynicism. Helping participants move away from the quest for dominance to the more productive "communal mind" requires the development of synergy, where each participant respects the others as competent professionals and each participant is valued for his or her unique knowledge and skills. Each participant makes contributions, not to outdo one another, but to build on or enhance another contribution. In this way, a communal mind is developed that creates an end product representing the maximum use of the participants' collective knowledge (Thompson, 1992). An assistant principal can help participants develop this communal mind through the modeling of expected behaviors and through occasional discussions with participants about effective meeting behavior.

What Time and Day Are Best for Meetings?

Some would facetiously say, "No time or day is best for a meeting," but Thompson (1992) reports that timing is crucial to the success of any meeting. Morning meetings are more productive than afternoon meetings, with midmorning starting times preferred over the 8 a.m. starting time. The midmorning starting time gives individuals an opportunity to psychologically prepare for the meeting and time to take care of those last-minute glitches.

Tuesday is the day most often mentioned as preferable for meetings. Monday and Friday are least preferred, and Wednesday is preferred to Thursday. Reasons offered for these preferences include time being needed to prepare for a meeting after a weekend, and Tuesday being early enough in the week to capture work enthusiasm and commitment.

Conducting Effective Meetings

Meetings, when they take place, should be truly necessary. The person calling the meeting should follow some basic guidelines to ensure that the desired outcomes from the meeting are achieved:

1. State the specific reason for calling the meeting in a letter or agenda to all participants well in advance of the meeting. State the meeting time and location.
2. State what participants will be required to do—for example, they should read the distributed materials and critique their content—for resolving the issue at hand.
3. State the expected outcomes of the meeting.
4. Provide a list of planned visitors, experts, or consultants, with a brief description of their credentials and the specific reason for their participation.
5. Provide a draft of the meeting agenda with a call for additional agenda items and a deadline for item submission.

Responsibilities of the Chairperson

Good leadership begins with a well-planned meeting, and meetings should be planned in relation to their objectives. Morrison (1994) provides the following essential responsibilities of committee chairpersons:

1. Plan the meeting carefully. Use *who, what, when, where, why,* and *how* as a planning guide.
2. Solicit agenda items and prepare and disseminate the agenda well in advance.

3. In the agenda, communicate the date, time, place, and purpose of the meeting; agenda items should have times allotted for presentation.

4. Arrive early; arrange the meeting room; and have copies of agenda, minutes, and handouts at the door for late arrivals.

5. Start on time. Don't reward lateness by delaying the meeting and punishing those who arrived on time.

6. Open the meeting by communicating the purpose for the meeting and the anticipated outcome(s) from the group. Clarify goals, briefly go over the agenda, and clarify points of confusion.

7. Approve the previous meeting's minutes.

8. Conduct the meeting according to the agenda and procedural rules.

9. Close the meeting on time and on a positive note. That is, review accomplishments, committee assignments, and target dates for accomplishing tasks.

10. Set a date, time, and plan for the next meeting. Solicit items for the next agenda.

Many meetings are viewed as time wasters and, as Imundo (1993) points out, are ineffective for the following reasons:

- *Lack of Purpose:* Some meetings have become ritualistic and institutionalized. When all else fails, these are meetings to decide on a purpose to meet.

- *Sparring Sessions:* Some meetings serve as forums for disputes, gripes, and complaints; participants may come for entertainment and wager on the results of the fight(s).

- *Too Casual:* Some meetings are like an open house. Participants come late and leave early. Friendship and social conversation predominate and confusion abounds.

- *No Focus:* Some meetings have no agenda. Side or fun issues are discussed, and substantive issues are avoided. Many issues are tabled or assigned to subcommittees. Closure is seldom reached.

- *Process Oriented:* Some meetings are conducted with more emphasis on process than on results. Procedures for voting, making motions, and so on, suffocate meaningful debate.

- *Game Playing:* Some meetings are dominated by gamesmanship, political motives, or show-and-tell sessions. Many enjoy feeding their egos while others seek to foster their own agendas. Some see if they can outdo the others, and some "play games of beating their breast by telling how hard they suffer for the organization." (p. 107)

What are the characteristics of those people who, when taken together, form a group in which meetings are most productive? McEwan (1997) provides a list of ideal characteristics that people should display in meetings:

- *Trust:* People can freely and openly state their views and differences without fear of ridicule and retaliation.

- *Support:* People receive reinforcement from others and provide the same to others without concern for hidden agendas.

- *Meeting Objectives:* With objective or agenda items, people work through their differences until resolution is reached and commitment is gained.

- *Conflict Resolution:* People do not suppress conflict or pretend conflict does not exist. Conflict is resolved through conflict management techniques.

- *Use of Members:* People's knowledge and skills are fully utilized.

- *Control:* People accept responsibility for their behavior, keep communication flowing and relevant, and work to gain timely closure on substantive issues.

- *Climate:* The meeting atmosphere is one of openness, respectfulness, and tolerance for individual differences. Professional and ethical behavior are the norm for conduct.

Using an Agenda to Conduct Effective Meetings

Agendas can be used to ensure the efficiency and effectiveness of meetings. The following practices are recommended:

1. Call for agenda topics well in advance of the meeting.
2. Prepare a draft copy of the agenda, circulate it several days prior to the meeting, and ask for feedback or additional agenda items. Include copies of documents to be discussed and expect attendees to have read the documents prior to the meeting.
3. Follow the agenda. Items on the agenda should have set time periods for discussion. No new topics should be discussed during the meeting, but items can be placed on the agenda for subsequent meetings.
4. Introduce each agenda item and have those who requested that the item be placed on the agenda provide background on why the item is being discussed.
5. Discuss each topic, use visual aids if applicable, have a timekeeper indicate when topic discussion is over, and call for a vote.
6. Refer to the documents disseminated before each topic is discussed. Briefly summarize the document(s) under consideration and allow for general discussion or comments.

Let's Review

Good communications skills bring people together; facilitate problem solving; and promote credibility, morale, and confidence in leadership. Effective communication is a process that requires careful planning. Good listening skills are essential to effective communication and developing them requires practice and concentration. Lack of good communication and listening skills can promote rumor and speculation and cause rework, waste, and overall organizational inefficiency. Effective leaders rely more on influence and persuasion than on their positional authority to achieve their goals. Cultivating subordinates' trust in leadership is essential to the influence and persuasion process.

Effective leadership requires one to be prepared for crisis situations and to have a well-developed plan to handle a variety of natural and man-made emergencies.

Schools have their vocal critics, and dealing effectively with them is essential in maintaining a good relationship with the community to ensure its continuing trust and support. Essential to good school-community relations is a key communicator program. *Key communicators* are people in the community who are highly respected, influence popular opinion, and "take the pulse" of the general community's feelings. In times of crisis and conflict, these community influentials help schools defend their programs and practices against unwarranted attacks by those seeking to further their own agendas.

Exercises

Exercise 1: Change Model

Think of a current situation in which you are being asked to make a change (any kind of change) or think of a current situation in which you will ask or are asking another to change. Refer to Loinberger's five-stage model (1960) and apply it to the selected situation. If you are being asked to change, ask the person requesting the change to explain the personal benefit(s) to you, and answer the following questions: (a) Can the benefit(s) be explained to your satisfaction? (b) Are the benefits personally appealing? Why or why not? (c) Do these personal benefits make *change* more appealing to you?

When asking another to change, experiment with the five-stage model. That is, apply the Loinberger model in a situation where you are attempting to initiate change among subordinates. Ask those subordinates the three questions listed above. Then ask them, what personal benefit(s) would be most appealing? Then ask yourself, can you provide these benefits? Why or why not?

Exercise 2: Psychological Type and Communication

Refer to the section in the chapter discussing the application of Carl Jung's theory of psychological type. Identify four people among faculty members or peers with the characteristics of the four cognitive styles. Select a mode of communication, oral or written, and tailor your communication to the style most preferred by each of the four individuals. Do this for a period of time—say, 4 or 5 weeks. Do you notice a difference in their responses over time? How are they different? Next try this exercise with your superior, spouse, or relatives. Do you notice any response differences? How are the responses different?

Exercise 3: Avoiding Foggy Messages

Refer to the "Fog Index" presented in this chapter. Examine copies of your prior communications to subordinates, parents, students, or peers. Try to recall any misunderstandings that resulted from these messages. After writing down the misunderstandings, begin to write your current messages using the Fog Index. Keep a log recording any comments about the new message form and any misunderstandings resulting from your messages. Is there a difference? What differences are there? Does the Fog Index work?

Exercise 4: Crisis Management Plan

In small groups, develop a *comprehensive* crisis management plan for a school. Use the information in the chapter as an outline for your comprehensive plan. Consider the following: Who should be involved in developing the program (representatives from the fire department, etc.)? How are you going to conduct different drills for different codes? What roles will parents and teachers play in each drill? How are you going to handle questions from representatives from the media? Who will manage the crisis center, who will serve as runners, and who will serve as contacts for information? What will you do once the crisis is controlled? How will you evaluate the effectiveness of your program?

Case Study: The New Student Newsletter

Mr. Telal, the new principal of Happy High School, made a pledge to the school board when he was hired: "I will allow students a forum to express their opinions," he told the board, "and I'll have the forum supervised by an assistant principal."

It seems that Mr. Telal's last job was filled with controversy and he resigned primarily because he did not believe students were mature enough to express themselves through printed media such as a school paper.

As the school year began, he appointed Ms. Claire as the advisor to the student newsletter. A first-year assistant principal, Ms. Claire wanted to do everything right. She was a perfectionist; she was caught up in her newly acquired "power"; and, above all, she wanted to please Mr. Telal. She knew that doing a good job and pleasing her boss were the keys to a principalship in her time frame of 5 years. She had taken a course in school law in her master's program, was quick to point out that she had received an A, and just knew that she could stay on top of things despite her numerous other responsibilities. "Ms. Claire," she told herself, "you are not in a position to say no."

The newsletter was published bimonthly, consisted of four to five pages, and was run by four seniors who excelled in Journalism Club activities. All four had A averages and indicated they wanted a career in journalism.

Harry Goslip, editor of the paper, was looking for a story to fill the last page of the newsletter. The press had to roll in 8 hours, and he wanted a piece that had wide appeal, but he was at a loss for an idea.

He entered Ms. Claire's office for advice but she wasn't there. Harry noticed the results of the graduation test and a letter from the state department of education on her desk. He read a sentence circled in red ink: "Over one-fourth of the seniors at Happy High School failed two or more sections of the graduation test." Harry made a copy of the test results and the letter and went to the newsletter office. Examining the letter from the state department of education, Harry noted that the majority of the seniors outperformed the rest of the seniors in the state. What a story!

Next afternoon, as Ms. Claire turned to the last page of the newsletter she read the headline of the article: "One-Fourth of Students Are a Disgrace to Their Top Performing Peers." Names and test scores were reported for all seniors, and the names of those students who failed one or more sections of the test appeared in bold print. As Ms. Claire was about to go and look for Harry, she was confronted by three irate parents demanding to know why their children were being ridiculed in public and labeled as a disgrace to their peers. Just then, Mr. Scheister, a local lawyer, broke into the conversation and handed Ms. Claire a letter. He said, "The letter states that I am representing a group of parents whose children failed the graduation test and a few parents whose children did well on the test but who are sympathetic to the cause of the other parents. I would advise you to read it carefully. You are negligent and in violation of privacy statutes." At this time, one of the parents began yelling "Lawsuit, lawsuit," and four newly arrived parents joined the chant. Meanwhile, Mr. Telal entered the building with five irate parents demanding an explanation. He had just returned from a meeting with the superintendent where he had assured her that this academic year was one marked by peace and progress.

As Mr. Telal was about to enter the school, his cell phone rang. It was the superintendent. "Mr. Telal, right now you will (a) place Ms. Claire on administrative leave, (b) suspend the entire newsletter staff, (c) get to the bottom of this by 5 p.m. today, and (d) report to my office by 8 a.m. tomorrow, where you will fill me in on this fiasco and have your annual evaluation. It doesn't look good at all. Might want to job-hunt, Buster."

1. If you were Mr. Telal, what is the first thing you would do? What are the second and third things you would do (taking the correct sequential steps is important in successfully managing criticism)?

2. Be specific in stating what you would say to Ms. Claire and who would be involved in this conversation.

3. Be specific in stating what you would say to Harry Goslip and the newsletter staff.

4. Be specific in stating what you would say to Mr. Scheister and the parents.

5. What would you tell the superintendent at your 8 a.m. meeting?

6

Leadership for
Instructional Improvement

In This Chapter

This chapter explores the concept of instructional leadership, the core characteristics of effective instructional leaders, and the essential variables associated with leadership for instructional effectiveness. The significance of leadership in curriculum development is presented along with curriculum development models found in effective schools. Models are also presented for building an instructional climate, conducting action research, preparing teacher-made tests with validity and reliability, and assessing teacher performance.

What Is Instructional Leadership?

In quality-oriented schools, principals and their assistants, working as a team, are the key individuals for providing instructional leadership to facilitate teacher awareness and develop effective instructional practices. DuFour and Eaker (1992) define instructional leadership by the following specific behaviors:

- With staff members, developing a school's vision and defining a mission and goals that emphasize academics and learning
- Modeling behaviors that demonstrate that learning and academics are the most important reasons for schools to exist
- Modeling the belief that all students can learn
- Making classroom learning time a top priority

- Monitoring student learning and using it as a basis for school improvement

- Applying research to achieve school excellence and enhance academic programs

- Observing classrooms regularly and recognizing the academic achievements of teachers and students

- Helping teachers become more effective through supervisory practices; staff development programs; and other programs that enhance instructional performance, such as coaching and mentoring

Research and Instructional Leadership

Research by Ogden and Germinario (1994) found that effective schools are led by principals and assistant principals who believe that all students *can* and *will* learn, who are continuously dissatisfied with the school's outcomes and seek new and better ways to improve schooling, and who instill in their teachers the motivation to provide the best instruction possible so that all students can reach their full potential. Instructional leaders, Ogden and Germinario maintain, are highly visible motivators, facilitators, and mentors with high expectations for themselves and their teachers. They do not accept average performance from themselves, their teachers, or their schools. Principals and assistant principals model the behavior expected of others and unite their faculties through the development of joint vision, mission, and goals, which they then use as daily achievement targets by which all can measure their performance.

How can assistant principals ensure that they are developing the skills needed for instructional leadership? They should focus on the following: spend a maximum amount of their daily time with teachers and department heads on instructional and curricular matters; communicate daily with teachers and students about the vision of the school and the importance of student learning; practice management-by-walking-around to diagnose problems impeding effective instruction and take immediate steps to correct identified impediments; and continually investigate new and better ways to improve the teaching-learning process (Weller, 1999). Principals and their assistants in "high-performing" schools are avid consumers of research who hold bimonthly seminars with preassigned topics as a focus for investigation and discussion (Weller & Weller, 2000). These discussions then become the foundation for strategic planning, staff development programs, and instructional improvement activities. Henson (1996) found that instructional leadership is demonstrated by the priorities and the decisions principals and their assistants make. Those, for example, who are primarily concerned with the budget, the daily operations of the school, bureaucratic details, and teacher and student behavior are not instructional leaders. Rather, they are allowing their time to be consumed by what is called the "3 Bs" in education: *beans, busses,* and *butts.*

Lunenburg and Ornstein (1996) relate that instructional leaders emphasize the development of a school climate and culture that foster a unified spirit and promote collegiality through teams and teamwork. *Climate,* part of a school's culture, is rooted in psychology. It is the "feel" one gets from the greetings one receives and the demeanor of the people one encounters when one walks into a school. Climate allows one to say, "Gee, what a great place to work!" or "No way would I work here!" Lunenburg and Ornstein present the following descriptions of school climate: *"open, warm, easy going, informal, cold, impersonal, rigid,* and *closed"* (p. 74).

Creating an effective school climate, according to Johnson (1985), is the key to promoting effective instructional outcomes. Four basic areas of school climate must be developed if effective schooling outcomes are to be achieved:

- *Physical Climate:* Schools are clean, safe, and orderly. Teachers have good working conditions and well-equipped classrooms.

- *Academic Climate:* Teachers and students talk about academics, and academics form the basis for leisure activities. Expectations for success are high for both teachers and students, but they are not unreasonable. Academic achievements are rewarded and widely recognized and achievement is highly prized and respected.

- *Organizational Climate:* Schools have few rules, but those they do have are reasonable, clear, and widely communicated. Teachers play a large part in making decisions concerning school policy, instruction, and curriculum. Teachers are viewed as experts and are respected by the administration.

- *Socioeconomic Climate:* The school is a welcoming and enjoyable place to visit. There is an aura of respect and trust that permeates the school, and the school feels safe to be in.

The *culture* of a school represents the shared beliefs, norms, values, assumptions, and attitudes of what the organization stands for. Culture is rooted in sociology, history, and anthropology, and represents the sum total of what the school's inhabitants truly believe, value, and expect. Culture reflects the natural behavior of people as they engage in their daily activities to achieve both personal and organizational goals. To a large extent, according to Deal (1993), culture contributes to the school's effectiveness or ineffectiveness and is a product of the school's leadership. Culture sets the standards and guides the daily actions of administrators, teachers, and students alike. Cunningham and Gresso (1994) found that leadership behaviors in effective schools with "healthy" cultures are those most often associated with the democratic leadership behaviors of teamwork and democratic decision making. In these schools, achieving academic excellence is a top priority, school administrators and teachers are vision focused, and improving instruction and student learning are the two most salient goals of the school. A report of the Northwest Regional Education Laboratory (1990) identified several research-based characteristics of this type of leader:

- Emphasizes academics, with learning being the primary reason for students being in school
- Models the belief that all students can learn and has high expectations that all students will master basic skills and learn the curriculum content
- Keeps teachers focused on the mission of the school and provides the necessary *time, moral support,* and *resources* for teachers to promote effective classroom teaching and learning
- Maintains a safe and orderly environment that is conducive to teaching and learning
- Is actively and consistently involved in all phases of the school's instructional program
- Consumes and applies new research to improve instruction
- Maintains good home-school relations programs that involve parents in student learning
- Involves teachers in planning and making decisions about programs to improve instruction and curriculum
- Rewards and praises student and teacher successes and informs parents and the community of these achievements

The common core behaviors of effective instructional leaders that emerge from the literature are the following:

- Developing schoolwide vision, mission, and goals
- Instilling and modeling the belief that all students can and will learn
- Monitoring student learning and using results for school improvement, and rewarding and recognizing student and teacher accomplishments
- Consuming and applying research findings on effective schools and on teaching and learning methods that affect student progress

- Developing a school culture and climate in which administrators, teachers, and students value academics and where student learning is the school's only purpose for existing

- Establishing strong parent-teacher support programs

Leadership in the Area of Instruction

Effective school principals and assistant principals lead by inspiration, not manipulation. They inspire teachers to excel at their work; they promote risk taking; they allow teachers the flexibility and freedom to make independent decisions about the teaching-learning process; and they motivate their staff members by practicing good human relations and communication skills (Chubb & Moe, 1990; Weller, 1999). Effective principals and their assistants practice "controlled direction" over the school, the curriculum, and the instructional program by continuously modeling and reminding others of the mission and goals of the school (Weller, 1999).

Assertive leadership is based on courage, conviction, and consistency. Leaders with these characteristics have high standards and expectations for success, the courage to implement their convictions, and the resolution to stand firm over time in their beliefs. Lunenburg and Ornstein (1996) state, "A powerful and long-term commitment is required to bring about substantial, widespread, and enduring gains in the [academic] performance of students" (p. 348). Assertiveness also means having to make tough unpopular decisions; placing instructional programs as top priorities; and keeping teachers focused on their sole reason for being teachers, which is to provide students the best classroom instruction possible (Weller, 1999). Assertive leaders are risk takers. They take calculated risks based on research findings or practices proven successful, and they refrain from making changes or decisions based on intuition or experience alone.

Effective school leaders know that lasting change comes from within, not from external mandates. Teacher participation in change efforts and school governance provide the needed variables of intrinsic motivation and sense of ownership that are essential for school effectiveness. Effective school leaders freely praise and reward teachers and students for academic progress and success, and they are frequent participants in team meetings, where they work to unite and energize teachers to work toward instructional improvement in the curriculum and the classroom (Weller & Weller, 2000). Sagar (1992) relates that instructional leaders use teacher teams to strengthen teacher commitment to the goals of school effectiveness and enhance the overall instructional program. Through teacher teams, leaders ensure that knowledge and requisite skills have *meaning* to students and are *matched* to the instructional goals of the school with appropriate learning materials and that delivery systems are incorporated in the instructional program. This provides continuity across grade levels and ensures content coverage, basic skills development, and the use of appropriate student assessment techniques.

Principals and their assistants who characterize themselves as instructional leaders model expected behaviors for teachers, visit classrooms regularly, assert their convictions and beliefs, and are research oriented. Action research is a common practice in high-achieving, quality-oriented schools as leaders seek new and better ways to improve instruction and increase student learning (Weller, 1996). Principals and their assistants in quality-oriented schools practice "bonding," as defined by Etzioni (1988), which creates a common commitment in a workforce to achieve constancy of purpose (Weller, 1999). Bonding is achieved by jointly identifying salient personal and organizational goals and then bringing them into alignment. Goal alignment fosters teacher motivation, job satisfaction, and commitment. Instructional leaders jointly develop with teachers a vision and mission statement that focus on attaining excellence in instruction and student learning (Weller & Weller, 1997). Through team planning, problem solving, and decision making, the improvement of instruction remains the constant top priority for these quality-oriented schools.

Assistant principals can actively facilitate improvement in the school's instruction and curriculum in the following ways:

- Scheduling daily blocks of time for teacher teams to plan instructional activities together that are consistent with the school's curriculum

- Providing essential fiscal and technical resources for teachers to achieve their instructional goals

- Freeing teachers from unnecessary assignments and responsibilities so they can concentrate on being effective classroom teachers, including using parent and community volunteers to monitor lunchrooms and parking lots and to serve as teacher aides

- Modeling behaviors consistent with the school's vision and mission

A sound knowledge of effective school practices is essential to effective instructional leadership. Understanding teaching and learning theories is essential to helping teachers become more effective in classroom performance. Assistant principals serve as mentors, coaches, and resource persons to assist "marginal" teachers in becoming strong, effective teachers. As facilitators, assistant principals provide necessary assistance that falls outside their areas of expertise by bringing in consultants or having teachers observe peers who can serve as mentors or coaches.

Planning and providing staff development programs is another instructional leadership function. When staff development programs are *personalized* they are more effective, professionally meaningful, and personally satisfying to teachers (Weller, 1999). Personalized programs allow teachers to choose topics of need and interest and can be scheduled at times that allow for teacher application and evaluation of learned knowledge and skills. Preplanning is an ideal occasion for conducting these programs, because it does not interfere with teacher instructional time and allows teachers the opportunity to apply and evaluate learned material. All too often, staff development topics are selected by school leaders who deem the topics important, although they are of little interest to teachers. Such programs are often received with apathy or disdain.

Mentoring programs for new or veteran teachers promote school effectiveness. DuFour and Eaker (1992) found that mentoring programs help new teachers understand the school's culture, vision, and goals, and encourage an immediate feeling of belonging and acceptance. Peer coaching allows teachers to gain new knowledge and skills or refine existing skills with peers of their choice (Weller & Weller, 2000). This approach to instructional improvement promotes collegiality among teachers and makes classroom evaluations less threatening.

Practicing good management skills is essential to promoting an effective school. Good management skills complement effective instructional leadership skills, and include handling routine tasks with speed and efficiency; being well organized and paying attention to detail; making efficient and effective use of personnel, resources, and facilities through planning and budgeting procedures; and practicing management-by-walking-around, troubleshooting, and anticipating and attending to problems that may distract teachers from instructional tasks.

Part of school management is enforcing district policy, but relaxing certain rules and regulations that impede effective instruction may be important to promoting school effectiveness. Policy is made and therefore policy can be unmade. Effective leaders work within the system to have their school boards "unmake" policies deemed detrimental to effective schooling outcomes. Strother (1983) points out that effective school managers look for opportunities to ward off potential problems that may cause undue teacher frustration. Leaders, acting in the role of managers, look for problem areas daily as opportunities for school improvement planning and staff development.

Effective school leaders model effective classroom teaching practices. These leaders have a thorough knowledge of the teaching-learning process, visit classrooms on a regular basis, and find ways to assist teachers in becoming more effective in instruction. Their ability to work closely with teachers in their classrooms is essential to creating effective schools, report Ogden and Germinario (1994). Examples of effective instructional improvement practices include the following:

- Modeling effective teaching methods by team-teaching lessons with classroom teachers

- Videotaping teachers and assisting teachers in critiquing their instructional practices

- Establishing coaching or peer support networks to help teachers learn new skills or strengthen areas of weakness

- Creating self-improvement seminars where teachers read research on improving instruction and discuss and plan for the application of these research findings in their classrooms

- Providing substitutes frequently for teachers to observe other teachers and attend professional conferences and workshops

Assistant Principals as Instructional Leaders

The effectiveness of assistant principals as instructional leaders is situation specific and depends on (a) the leadership philosophy of the principal, (b) the priority the principal sets on improving instruction, and (c) the degree of authority the principal is willing to delegate to the assistant principal. The more likely the principal is to practice a democratic leadership style and focus on academics as the sole reason for schooling, the more effective that principal will be as an instructional leader.

Assistant principals with little principal-granted authority can practice instructional leadership by applying the following characteristics of instructional leadership:

- Develop a mind-set that instructional leadership is the most salient role an administrator can perform and make improving instruction a primary goal

- Model the belief that academics are the reason for schooling and that academic achievement, teamwork, and teaching are top priorities

- Have high expectations for teacher and student success and inspire and motivate students and teachers to excel

- Consult teachers for preferences when developing class schedules and for needed resources when developing the budget

- Plan and conduct staff development programs based on teacher needs and interests

- Foster good parent-teacher relationships by meeting with parents and stressing the importance of their support in promoting student learning

- Recognize and reward academic achievement for both students and teachers

- Consume and apply the latest research findings and help teachers conduct action research to improve instruction and the curriculum

- Free teachers from unnecessary responsibilities to allow them time to focus on being an effective classroom teacher

Curriculum Development

A *curriculum* is a *planned* and *taught* program developed by a state, system, school, or department, with goals and objectives for student mastery. A curriculum includes learning activities, experiences, and materials for the learners that are appropriate for their grade level and abilities. *Instruction* includes the various teaching strategies and methods used to implement the curriculum. Clark and Starr (1991) define *what* teachers teach as curriculum and *how* teachers teach as instruction. Good teacher planning delineates the *what* and *how* of teaching. Instruction is specific to situations and individuals. That is, there is no one best way to teach all students. Good instruction means developing a repertoire of teaching strategies and learning activities to meet the needs of individual learners.

The curriculum is impacted by state standards; the goals of the school; and the values, norms, beliefs, and assumptions of those developing the curriculum. Central to curriculum development are three major processes: *planning, implementing,* and *evaluating.* Planning requires a needs assessment, the setting of priorities, a committee with broad-based representation, a timeline for completion, guidelines for staff development, and specifications of the learning materials and activities to be included in the curriculum. Evaluating the curriculum requires knowledge of evaluation processes and techniques and a specific outline of how the evaluation process will occur.

Two common approaches to curriculum development are presented below.

1. *Behavioral Approach.* Perhaps one of the oldest and most popular approaches to curriculum development, the behavioral approach was developed by Taylor (1949). This approach emphasizes goals as the foundation for curriculum development. Goals are identified by subject matter, needs and interests of the learner, and contemporary life issues. A needs assessment of educators, parents, students, and community members identifies the goals and instructional objectives, which are then developed into a curriculum by a curriculum committee.

Taylor's model (1949) stresses the selection of *learning experiences* to achieve the identified goals and objectives. Learning experiences must be appropriate for the age, ability, background, and environment of the learner. Vertical organization (recurring subject matter) and horizontal organization (integration of different subjects) occur at the same grade level. Evaluation is used to determine if the instructional objectives are met and if the learning experiences have resulted in the desired behaviors.

2. *Humanistic Approach.* The humanistic approach is a curriculum model of the "affect." Developed by Weinstein and Fantini (1970), the model emphasizes *relevant* as opposed to *traditional* content, and is group oriented as opposed to individual oriented. Knowledge of the common characteristics and interests of learners is the primary source for determining curriculum content. Instructional strategies are developed by identifying learner needs and assessing the *reasons* for those needs. Affective needs include improved self-concept, self-image, and human interaction skills.

Learner needs are grouped and become themes or topics centered around life experiences and the social environment of the learner. Learner-appropriate affective and cognitive skills and values are interwoven in theme content, and teaching strategies and materials are selected to match content and student learning styles. Evaluation focuses on changes in student behaviors in the cognitive and affective domains. Evertson and Wade (1989) found the humanistic model most appropriate for students who are highly independent learners, prefer low-structure situations, and have a high degree of self-control. Learning objectives in the humanistic model stress cooperative learning, independent learning, small group learning, and values.

Regardless of the curriculum model chosen, curriculum development must focus on content, learning activities, and the interrelatedness of the two. When both content and activities are presented in ways that are appropriate for the learner's ability level and stimulate learner interest with relevant knowledge and skills, the primary goals of humanistic curriculum development are achieved.

A Curriculum Development Model

Presented below is a seven-step model that blends the behavioral and humanistic approaches to curriculum development for a model appropriate for contemporary curriculum development.

1. A committee of administrators, teachers, parents, students, and community members synthesize the vision, mission, and goals of the school with data collected from student surveys and interviews to develop interdisciplinary themes by grade level.

2. The committee focuses on student interest and relevance of content in both the traditional curriculum and student survey and interview results. These data are then compared to federal and state requirements, and the criteria for curriculum content are established.

3. The committee then selects the *essential* knowledge and skills for content coverage and addresses Taylor's (1949) question, "What knowledge is of the most worth?"

4. The committee identifies themes by assessing the *interrelationships* between the needs and interests of the learner and the essential knowledge and skills to be taught.

5. The committee identifies learning activities, experiences, and material for each theme. Content teachers play a crucial role in examining essential knowledge and skills, identifying learning activities and materials, and ensuring smooth transition activities for students as they proceed from one theme to another.

6. Teachers then develop units within each theme and sequence the units in order of presentation. Unit objectives are identified, and learning activities, experiences, and materials are correlated to each objective within each unit and theme.

7. Pilot-testing the thematic units is the final step. The results are examined for learning effectiveness, and the curriculum committee modifies the curriculum as needed.

Building an Instructional Climate

Building an instructional climate is essential to promoting effective schooling. Instructional climate is a frame of mind, a collective attitude and set of values and beliefs concerning the importance of academics and the purpose of instruction. Ubban and Hughes (1987) state that in effective schools, the instructional climate has four traits in common: (a) High expectations for achievement are held for all students, (b) students are recognized and rewarded for academic success, (c) time-on-task is emphasized and learning is viewed as a no-nonsense business, and (d) parental support reinforces the goals of the school.

High Expectations for Students

Research on effective schools, as synthesized by Scheerens and Bosker (1997), finds that high expectations for student success are central to effective schooling outcomes. The following are key behaviors for holding high learner expectations:

- Teachers and administrators make frequent and explicit statements to students and parents regarding high achievement expectations and mastery of work.

- Teachers and administrators communicate to students that they expect them to achieve the highest possible scores on standardized achievement tests.
- Teachers firmly believe that their teaching will promote student success.
- Teachers emphasize that student performance can always be improved.
- Teachers constantly recognize and reward good student performance and achievement.
- Teachers continually challenge the abilities of their students through homework, group work, classwork, and teacher-made tests.
- Teachers set minimum competencies above recognized or generally accepted standards.

Student Recognition and Rewards

Recognizing and rewarding students for their achievements, contributions, and citizenship is an essential component of effective schools. The following are ways effective schools recognize and reward students:

- Praise students for their achievements and behavior both in private and in public
- Reward students through certificates and the like for their achievements, using public forums such as school assemblies or awards banquets
- Recognize students for their accomplishments through the local media, such as newspaper, radio, and television
- Display student work in areas where parents, community members, and students can see their accomplishments
- Appoint students to committees or councils based on their talents and abilities

No-Nonsense Learning Environment

The amount of time-on-task that students spend impacts achievement positively. Time-on-task, or *learning time,* is defined as that time in which students are actively engaged in an academic learning experience. *Instructional time* is defined as the amount of time teachers engage students in providing instruction. Student learning time is free from interruptions that distract student concentration, including announcements, programs that "pull out" students, or extracurricular projects that cause students to miss classwork (Squires, Huitt, & Segars, 1984).

Socializing with students, taking roll, and other administrative responsibilities that take up instructional time should be kept to a minimum. Classes should start and end on time, the learning environment should be structured and orderly, lessons should be well planned, students should be constantly engaged in learning activities, and enrichment activities should be provided to those who complete work early or excel above the norm (Squires et al., 1984).

Parent Support

Parent support and participation in school programs are other essential components in promoting school effectiveness. Jones (1991) relates that when parents feel welcome and are viewed as part of the school's "instructional team," they become more actively involved in school events and are more willing to support the goals of the school. When parents and teachers work together and parents reinforce the school's goals at home, students have a more positive attitude toward school. Increases in student achievement result.

Too often, parents are viewed as intruders who visit the school to complain and criticize rather than to provide support and assistance. When parents have personally satisfying ways to make contributions and feel their assistance is valued, their attitude toward teachers and administrators becomes more positive and they seek ways to make a constructive impact (Weller, 1999). Parents can be guest lecturers, instructional aides, and school committee members. Parent programs are more likely to succeed when parents are asked *how* they want to be involved, when involvement in school-parent programs is *personally satisfying*, and when they are *recognized* for their efforts and contributions.

Some parents choose not to participate in school programs. One reason may be that their own school experiences were personally unrewarding or unpleasant and being involved in the school reminds them of failure or unfriendly teachers. Second, some schools are perceived as unfriendly places. When parents perceive they are not welcome at the school or in the classroom or they have been treated discourteously, they feel their presence and assistance are not wanted. Third, minority parents speaking English as a second language often feel uncomfortable in school situations and avoid public meetings that could cause them embarrassment. The use of interpreters and materials printed in their language of preference increases parent participation. Finally, single-parent families may have work schedules that conflict with parent programs, and others may lack transportation or child care.

Parent Surveys. Parent surveys are starting points for building successful home-school programs and increasing parental support. Surveys should assess family needs, parent personal needs, and interest areas. Survey results can then become the foundation for planning programs that address the specific needs and interests of parents. Ogden and Germinario (1994) note that effective parent programs are data driven and provide the information and assistance most valuable to parents. Jenkins and Jenkins (1995) found successful parental programs to be structured, assisting parents with home educational activities and meeting the needs of parents. Parents who are active in school and home programs rate teachers' interpersonal skills higher and have greater appreciation for classroom problems. This close parent-teacher relationship fosters better student conduct in the classroom, increases student achievement and attendance, improves student self-concept, and lowers dropout rates.

Programs for Parent Support. Effective parent programs begin with an ongoing comprehensive communication effort to inform parents about the nature and variety of parent involvement programs and the importance and benefits of parental involvement in school activities. Programs can be designed around a series of workshops, seminars, and focus groups and should be arranged to accommodate varying work schedules of parents. Following is a list of parent programs found in effective schools:

- *Parents-as-learning-partners programs* provide information on how to assist the school by reinforcing its goals and objectives at home, on the importance of structured time to complete homework, and on the importance of parents being actively engaged and interested in their children's work.

- *Communication and study skills programs* emphasize good communication skills, the importance of open and honest conversations between parent and child, conflict management skills, the nature of the teaching and learning process, and study and memory skills.

- *Homework hotline and parent-student study session programs* provide structured times where teachers are available to work with parents and students on homework assignments on the telephone or in the cafeteria or library, where teacher volunteers circulate among parents and their children.

- *Adult refresher programs* are designed to assist parents in becoming more competent in helping their children in core academic areas with such things as research papers and book reviews. In these programs, parents learn to become more effective home teachers.

- *General learning programs* provide information and lists of books, journals, and videos for parents to explore various topics of their own interest and those that will help them reinforce school goals. Seminars and focus groups on topics of interest to parents are ways to meet specific needs of parents. (Weller, 1999)

Effective Classroom Instruction and Teaching Strategies

Much research has been conducted on effective teaching and learning strategies. Two excellent resources on this topic are the works of Paul D. Eggen and Donald P. Kauchak (1988) *Strategies for Teachers: Teaching Content and Thinking Skills* and Donald P. Kauchak and Paul D. Eggen (1989) *Learning and Teaching*. Howard Gardner's work on multiple intelligences has gained wide recognition and credibility. Gardner's book *Frames of Mind: The Theory of Multiple Intelligences* (1993) presents the theory of intelligences existing beyond the confines of the IQ score. And Robert J. Steinberg's book *Thinking Styles* (1997) presents 13 different styles and explores their process of development and their application to thinking and learning in the classroom.

Other sources essential for effective classroom teaching are the taxonomies of learning which move from the basic to the complex or abstract. Sources are Bloom, Engelhart, Furst, Hill, and Krathwohl's *Taxonomy of Educational Objectives: Handbook I: The Cognitive Domain* (1956) and Krathwohl, Bloom, and Masia's *Taxonomy of Educational Objectives: Handbook II: The Affective Domain* (1964).

Teacher-Directed Strategies

Teaching strategies are activities performed by the teacher during the teaching-learning process. Content covered can be characterized as either *declarative* knowledge (facts, concepts, and generalizations) or *procedural* knowledge (learning of skills or how to do something). These knowledge areas are not independent of each other and often interact. Teaching strategies are based on which of these two knowledge areas is to be taught. Teacher-directed strategies are used to direct student learning, and require little active student involvement. These strategies have advantages and disadvantages: both are effective. These strategies include the following:

- *Lecture:* Formal lectures are direct presentations of facts and concepts and can convey vast amounts of information in short time periods. Informal lectures call for student questions and are most effective when teachers ask questions using the Socratic method. Here higher-order cognitive development is promoted through comprehension, analysis, synthesis, and evaluation.

- *Explicit Teaching:* Explicit, or direct, teaching is where teachers allow for student participation, the use of small group work, class time to work on the content or skills being taught, and evaluation of student learning.

- *Demonstration:* Demonstration is the use of models or experiments to provide students with auditory and visual learning experiences.

- *Recitation:* Recitation is a type of questioning process (of which there are many) that requires individual student interaction with the teacher. Probing questions form the basis of this interaction, which is used to test the student's knowledge of facts, theories, and concepts.

- *Discovery Learning:* Discovery, or problem-solving, learning is designed to show students *how* to learn rather than *what* to learn. Activities that are structured or guided by the teacher allow students to acquire learning skills that are essential for all disciplines.

- *Brainstorming:* Brainstorming is used to stimulate creative thinking and problem solving. Teachers pose problems and ask probing questions as students generate ideas and solutions.

Learner-Directed Strategies

Learner-directed strategies are designed to involve students in the learning process and to stimulate self-learning. Learners apply these strategies to understand the more complex concepts and abstract ideas presented through teacher-directed learning strategies. Learner-directed strategies include the following:

- *Independent Study:* Self-directed learning that allows students an opportunity to identify problems of interest and seek solutions on their own. Teachers act as resource persons and support students by providing avenues for research and personal motivation.

- *Debates and Small Group Discussion Panels:* Self-directed learning strategies whereby students choose areas of investigation and interact with teacher input. Teachers serve as resource persons while students gather research, organize material, and align arguments as they debate the merits of issues or attempt to find solutions to problems.

- *Role Playing:* A highly effective strategy whereby students act the part or assume the role of another and examine different perspectives, emotions, and values. Research is required and students can express their feelings, acquire and practice interpersonal skills, and relieve their frustrations.

Effective instruction requires the careful planning, integration, and use of both teacher-directed and learner-directed strategies. The key to their effectiveness lies in the appropriate selection of a strategy for the intended instructional outcome.

Multiple Intelligences Theory

Multiple intelligences theory has direct implications for student learning style theory and teaching strategies theory. Students' learning styles are what Gardner (1993) calls "proclivities" or inclinations in specific intelligences exhibited at an early age. Students' preferred way of learning (use of their preferred intelligences) at school age challenges teachers to diagnose students' preferred learning styles and then tailor instructional activities to maximize student learning. Gardner notes that all students can learn through each of the intelligences and care must be taken to nurture those intelligences that are least preferred. This theory opens the door to innovative approaches to teaching and makes diagnosing for individualized instruction easier. Gardner's multiple intelligences are linguistic, logical-mathematical, spatial, bodily-kinesthetic, musical, interpersonal, intrapersonal, and naturalistic.

Action Research

Action research, states McMillan (1996), is a type of applied research designed to solve specific school problems, improve local practice, or enhance classroom instruction. Action research is like true experimental research but with two exceptions. First, action research does not require random sampling, and, second, it lacks tight control group design to control for variance within independent variables. These constraints pose no major problem for action researchers because the results are not used for generalizing the findings to other populations but to solve local problems.

Action research is a powerful tool for assistant principals who seek to help teachers improve classroom instruction and promote student learning. Action research provides teachers with *functional* knowledge that can be immediately applied to their classroom. There are three types of action research: (a) *independent* research where the teacher is the sole investigator; (b) *collaborative* research where two or more researchers investigate a mutual problem; and (c) *schoolwide research* where multiple researchers, across grade levels or departments, investigate schoolwide problems such as student discipline, student dropout, or teacher morale. As powerful as action research is in improving all aspects of schooling, its application to school problems is limited. Despite the success of action research in school situations, many administrators remain unfamiliar with the practice, have little or no interest in it, and lack the training to conduct action research in their schools (Weller, 1998). Moreover, few if any incentives or rewards exist for teachers to either learn about or conduct action research in their own classrooms.

Regardless of which of the three types of action research is conducted, the process consists of six basic steps:

1. Review the related literature on the topic or problem to gain information on research design, resources needed, and data analysis techniques.

2. Research the present problem by compiling all available fact-based data from all relevant sources. Interviews, observations, records, and questionnaires serve as the basis for gathering data.

3. Develop one or more problem statements or hypotheses, which are guesses about what the outcomes of the research will be.

4. Develop a research design to test the problem statements or hypotheses. The design is a "roadmap" that provides direction for conducting the study.

5. Select the appropriate data-gathering techniques (interviews, questionnaires, etc.), collect the data, and then analyze the data.

6. Make a decision based on the research findings. Sometimes another study may be needed to verify initial study results or additional data may be needed that was not originally anticipated. (Weller, 1993)

Assessment and Evaluation of Student and Teacher Performance

Effective schools have adopted the philosophy that students and teachers can *continuously improve,* and these schools are never satisfied with either student or teacher performance. Central to enhancing student performance is evaluating student progress and mastery of content. Leaders of high-achieving, quality-oriented schools provide adequate planning time for teachers and teacher teams to (a) assess student needs, (b) prepare tests and other evaluation instruments, (c) read and discuss research about effective teaching and student evaluation practices, and (d) carefully examine student homework, projects, and test data (Lezotte & Jacoby, 1992). In effective school districts, the written, taught, and tested curriculum are aligned, and when student evaluation measures accurately reflect what is taught, an accurate measure of mastery can result.

Evaluation of teacher performance is a legal responsibility that represents judgments about individual performance on objective criteria that accurately reflect the requirements of the job and the overall goals and objectives of the school. "The primary purpose of teacher evaluation is to improve the teaching-learning phenomena to maximize student achievement" (Weller & Weller, 2000, p. 219).

Teacher evaluations should be both formative and summative in scope, and diagnostic in nature. Assessment instruments must be valid and reliable and should serve as the basis for remediation and staff development programs, employment status, and salary increases.

Assessing Student Performance

Effective schools assess student performance through both formal and informal assessment techniques. *Formal* assessment is accomplished through standardized achievement tests designed to assess mastery of basic skills and compare student progress both between and within schools. Squires et al. (1984) note that if schools are not successful in teaching basic skills, they are probably not considered successful by parents, the school board, or the community. Mastery of basic skills is essential to future success in schools, and gains or deficits in standardized test scores tend to have a cumulative effect over time.

The emphasis placed on standardized test results has given rise to the debate on how much help teachers should provide students in preparing for standardized achievement tests. Short of teaching the test (telling students the actual questions on the test), teachers in effective schools do everything they can to prepare students to do well (Weller & Weller, 1997). This includes using the same kinds of examples in their classroom instruction as are found in questions on the test. For example, if pie charts or histograms are used to test understanding of percents and fractions, teachers use these graphs in their own classroom instruction. Some effective schools also teach test-taking skills, thereby providing their students with another competitive edge.

Informal assessment measures are those constructed by teachers. Informal assessments should be valid and reliable, accurately reflecting what is taught in the classroom. Content assessment takes place *before, during,* and *after* instruction. This ensures continuous monitoring of student progress. Pretests should be administered prior to instruction so that teachers know what students know before instruction begins. Pretests are diagnostic tools that allow teachers to assess student readiness and determine what additional instruction needs to take place beyond what was originally planned. Pretests can also be used to individualize instruction and to group students for learning activities.

Content should reflect the goals and objectives of the curriculum and should be appropriate for the maturity level of the learner. Content that is assessed but not taught or vice versa yields lower gains in student achievement and reveals nothing about student progress or learning.

There should be at least 7 to 10 days of instruction between pre- and posttesting. Other forms of student assessment should be administered while instruction is in progress. This usually includes quizzes and individual or group exercises. Following are some typical informal assessment techniques.

Homework in effective schools is not busywork but purposeful work with two major goals: (a) It is used to monitor student understanding of class content; and (b) it extends academic time on task, which correlates strongly with student achievement. Homework is most effective when it allows practice of classroom learning, challenges students to go beyond what was covered in the classroom, and is used to provide immediate feedback to students about their progress.

Portfolio assessment is a collection of student work. Teacher-collected portfolios are those containing samples of student work that provide teachers with an overview of the development of each student's abilities. Student-collected portfolios contain work students select themselves that reflects their best efforts in accordance with criteria set by teacher or student.

Teacher-made tests, the most common informal assessment techniques, should be valid and reliable. *Valid* means the test is an accurate assessment of what is taught or of what it purports to measure. *Reliable* means that the test yields consistent, noncontradictory results. That is, the test is a consistent measure of what it is supposed to measure.

Content validity of tests should be of primary concern to classroom teachers. It is acquired through questions that are truly representative of the content being tested, and that appear on the test in a balanced way. Content validity is assessed by an objective comparison of test items with content covered in the classroom. Content validity is developed by doing the following:

1. Write test questions that correlate to content covered in the classroom. Test items should come from the textbook and any supplementary material used for instruction. Reference each test item with page number, paragraph, and sentence of content material on a separate worksheet. Check for balance of content coverage on test items.

2. Submit the test to a panel of "judges," peer teachers who are well acquainted with the content. Two or more teachers or administrators may serve as judges. The judges assess the test items and indicate whether the items measure predetermined criteria, objectives, and content.

3. Revise test items based on the judges' recommendations and resubmit them for a second review for content validity. The goal is greater than 90% agreement between test items and content.

The same procedure can be used for *essay questions*. In essay questions, the domain needs to be specified (cognitive or affective), as do the specific objectives in each domain hierarchy. The essay questions should be submitted to judges with a copy of the material covered in the classroom. The material should be referenced to the essay questions and to the specific objectives in the domain hierarchy being assessed. A sample exemplary answer to each question should accompany the material presented to the panel of judges. Revisions to essay questions should be made in accordance with the judges' recommendations and a second review process should then follow.

Reliability, a determination of whether a test measures what it purports to measure over time, is essential to good classroom tests. The major consideration for writing test items is that they be domain referenced. For example, if a test item is to assess knowledge of facts, it should not be written to assess the ability to problem-solve.

Unlike validity, reliability is assessed through a correlation coefficient. Reliability coefficients for tests vary between zero and ±1.00, with 1.00 or –1.00 indicating perfect reliability. The closer a test's reliability score is to ±1.00, the more the test is free of error variance, such as unclear test wording, confusing directions, inadequate number of items to measure an attribute, or human conditions such as student motivation, fatigue, and anxiety.

There are several ways to compute test reliability for classroom use. Borg (1987) notes that higher reliability coefficients can be found in single test administrations than in test-retest or split-half testing situations, which are more prone to human error factors. Teachers wanting to assess test reliability can apply the Kuder-Richardson Formula 21 (KR-21) to their classroom tests. The KR-21 formula can be found in any educational research methods textbook. Correlation coefficients of .90 or higher indicate high test reliability.

Determining reliability for essay questions focuses on preparation and scoring. When preparing an essay test, the following procedures should be used to enhance test reliability:

- Do not write a test question hastily or distractedly.
- Write the essay question in accordance with the procedures used to ensure test validity discussed above.
- Questions should be free of grammatical errors; terms should be used that students understand; and students should know what the evaluator is looking for in the essay. Never just say "discuss" the topic.
- Ask several short-answer essay questions. Shorter questions allow for more comprehensive content coverage and can better assess higher-order thinking skills.
- A panel of judges should evaluate the scoring of key, or "ideal," answers and point distribution for essay questions.

Reliability for essay tests can be increased by using the following scoring procedures:

- Read the responses of all students to a single question, grade the question, and repeat the process with subsequent questions.

- Use codes devised by students in place of names on the test. The code sheet is withheld from the scorer until the grades are given.

- An ideal answer should be prepared and used as the grading key. A specific number of points should be assigned for each component of the ideal answer.

Assessing Teacher Performance

The primary goal of assessing teacher performance is to improve teaching and maximize student achievement. Teacher assessment instruments should be valid and reliable; they should be both formative and summative in scope; and they should be based on job-related objectives. Meaningful and individualized remediation programs, based on appraisal results, should be provided to teachers who fail to meet acceptable performance criteria levels.

A Positive Approach to Teacher Assessment. Because enhancement of job performance is the overarching goal of teacher assessment, teacher assessment should be viewed as a nonthreatening process designed to improve classroom performance and assist teachers to develop personally and professionally. Assistant principals can create positive attitudes toward performance assessment by emphasizing the positive aspects of evaluation for both teachers and students.

Positive teacher attitudes toward performance assessment begin with the type of relationship assistant principals have with teachers and the way in which the performance appraisal is conducted. When teachers view assistant principals as having their best interests at heart, they tend to see performance assessment in a positive light. Teachers are more likely to take recommendations for improvement more seriously and have greater commitment to improve when teacher evaluators have teachers' respect (Duke & Stiggins, 1993). Moreover, there is a positive correlation between teacher evaluation results and teacher improvement when good interpersonal relations exist between teacher and evaluator, and when performance appraisal results are considered fair and accurate. When teachers view evaluation results as unfair, inaccurate, or invalid, they feel resentful, are less open to improvement, and are more prone to low morale.

Teachers view performance appraisal more positively when they know the results will be used for staff development programs, individual improvement plans, and recognition of achievement. When assessment is viewed as a vehicle that allows the teacher to continuously improve as a professional, evaluations are less threatening and more satisfying.

Teacher Assessment Instruments. Teacher evaluation instruments are prescribed by the state or the local board of education. Sometimes training and evaluation certification are required, especially on state-mandated instruments. Two questions concerning teacher performance are usually included in all teacher evaluation instruments: (a) "Is the teacher able to demonstrate satisfactory performance on the assessment criteria?" and (b) "Does the teacher demonstrate and apply the required knowledge and skills in an appropriate manner?" The first question requires the evaluator to assess the overall knowledge and ability levels of the teacher, and the second question requires judgment decisions on the appropriate application of essential knowledge and skills. For teacher evaluations to be valid and reliable, the following must happen:

1. Teachers must be familiar with the assessment criteria and the formal process designed to conduct teacher evaluations. Assistant principals should conduct periodic seminars for all certified and new teachers on the teacher appraisal process.
2. Evaluators must know the goals and objectives of the lessons being observed and the types of students being taught.
3. Evaluators must have training on scoring the assessment instrument.

Most state-mandated assessment instruments are non-criterion-referenced assessments. Criterion-referenced tests use local standards as the basis for performance assessment and take into account the actual job responsibilities and expectations for each local school system. Norm-referenced instruments use teacher performance criteria of groups of teachers to determine "acceptable" teaching performance. Ideally, criterion-referenced assessment instruments are used to assess the desired competencies deemed essential for each local school system.

Many evaluation models provide guidance for developing a fair process. The generic five-step model presented below is a structured, professional, non-threatening approach assistant principals can use in the teacher appraisal process.

1. Conduct an orientation session at the beginning of the school year for all teachers. Discuss the purpose of evaluation, share your philosophy of teacher evaluation, and provide teachers with copies of the assessment instrument.
2. One week prior to classroom observations, meet individually with teachers and obtain a copy of their weekly lesson plans. Review the assessment criteria with each teacher, discuss any personal or student-related problems, and decide on a specific time or span of time in which the observations will occur.

3. Carefully read the lesson plan and evaluate the teacher on the agreed-on criteria and procedures. Be on time and *do not* deviate from the procedures discussed in the preobservation conference. Meet with the teacher within 2 days of the observation and discuss the observation results using the scored evaluation instrument to focus discussion.

4. Within 2 days of the postobservation conference, the teacher should be provided a written record of conference results. If an improvement plan is needed, it should be mutually agreed on during the conference, and a copy of the plan should be provided to the teacher. The written results of the postobservation conference and the remediation plan should be signed by both of you. Any remediation plan must include adequate *time, support,* and *resources.*

5. For a teacher working under an improvement plan, follow the plan as it was agreed on. Any deviation from the plan or failure to provide resources or support will necessitate a new improvement plan, or an adjustment in the existing plan, that is mutually agreed on. New or adjusted improvement plans must be in writing and signed by both parties.

Although classroom observations can be part of an improvement plan, periodic conferences should be held to assess a teacher's progress and identify difficulties encountered by the teacher. Peer coaching, attendance at conferences, videos and books, and any other support resources must be made available to the teacher.

Supplemental Evaluation Material. Supplemental evaluation material can be used in conjunction with mandated performance evaluation instruments to provide a more comprehensive view of teachers' knowledge and skills. Supplemental material should be jointly agreed on by teachers and evaluators, and a joint decision should be made regarding their weight. The most common forms of supplemental material used for teacher evaluations are as follows:

- *Lesson Plans:* Lesson plans are performance criteria that can be objectively evaluated according to local goals, standards, and expectations.

- *Self-Evaluation:* Teachers have important information about themselves to share with others that is valuable to the overall performance appraisal profile. Self-evaluations provide administrators with a more complete picture of the variables impacting teaching performance. Self-evaluations, when completed objectively, can provide a balance to the "halo effect" that may result from classroom observations. Examples of self-evaluations include logs, self-rating scales, and portfolios with documented student and parent comments and recognition and rewards and for achievement.

- *Peer Appraisals:* Peer evaluations can be valuable as an additional piece of information in a holistic assessment package. Peer or master teacher evaluations provide "expert judgment." Also, when mentoring or coaching programs are in place, mentors are natural choices for evaluation responsibilities.

- *Teacher Portfolios:* Use of portfolios to evaluate performance is another way to assess teachers. Portfolios, which are document focused, are assembled by teachers, have objective criteria, and allow teachers more control over what is being assessed. The task is time consuming and requires organized record keeping. Information included in portfolios are videotapes of classroom teaching, lesson plans, tests, handouts, grade distributions, parent comments, student evaluations, workshops and staff development sessions attended, peer or mentor evaluations, and professional improvement plans and documented progress toward meeting objectives. Evaluators and teachers decide what should be included in the portfolio, the criteria for evaluating the work, and the weight assigned to these documents.

- *Student Achievement Test Scores:* Use of student achievement scores to evaluate teacher effectiveness is under much debate. Some hold that test scores should be used to evaluate teachers because the bottom line for assessing teacher effectiveness is increased student test scores. This is the view held by most parents, community members, business leaders, and government officials (Weller, 1999). But a heavy reliance on achievement test scores lends too much credibility to instruments with inherent limitations that lay people fail to realize. Major weaknesses of standardized tests include the possibility of cultural bias, a mismatch between teaching and testing, the "high generalizability" test makers build into tests for marketing purposes, and inadequate or low validity or reliability.

When teachers establish content validity and reliability on their own tests, they can use this data to support their findings to others (Weller, 1999). In this case, teacher-made tests are the best and most practical way to assess teacher performance. When teacher-made tests are used in conjunction with other teacher assessment data (portfolios, etc.), a more comprehensive profile is possible.

Developing a Model for Teacher Appraisal. Teacher evaluation is a situation-specific activity that must take into account a variety of locally impacting variables if an accurate picture of performance is to result. The following variables should be considered when developing a situation-specific, school-based model for teacher appraisal.

1. Local school board standards and expectations must provide the foundation for the teacher assessment model. State standards, if they apply, must be incorporated in the model. Teacher job descriptions, the overall goals and objectives of the school system, and information in the school system's curriculum guides should be included in the design of an instrument or teacher assessment process.

2. The school's student ethnic demographics, its distribution of student socioeconomic status, the IQ range of students, and other student-associated variables unique to the school must be taken into consideration.

3. Specific abilities of students in each classroom being observed regarding IQ range, student knowledge and skill levels in relation to peers in other classrooms, and resources available for teachers to teach the lessons observed must be considered.

4. Test measures for students must have validity and reliability.

5. Teacher evaluation measures must be made known to teachers, and teachers must be assessed on realistic criteria that are made known to them.

6. Teacher performance should be based on a variety of assessment measures to provide a complete and comprehensive profile of teacher performance.

Let's Review

Assistant principals are instructional leaders and catalysts for improving classroom instruction and the curriculum and creating an instructional climate that promotes effective teaching and student learning. Assistant principals can play a key role in building parent support programs, assisting teachers in developing effective classroom teaching strategies, assisting teachers in conducting action research, and making teacher performance assessment a personally and professionally rewarding experience.

Exercises

Exercise 1: Evaluating Teacher Performance

Several teachers in your school have expressed concern over the years about the unfairness of the teacher evaluation system. They feel one or two classroom observations on a standardized instrument is inadequate to assess their "true" performance levels and their impact on students. They seek your assistance in initiating a more comprehensive teacher evaluation process. How would you go about addressing the concerns of these teachers? How would you suggest they pursue their desired outcomes? What suggestions would you have on alternative assessment methods? (Be creative in your answer and provide the positive and negative aspects of each alternative assessment method you list. Some answers to the above questions lie in other chapters in this text.)

Exercise 2: Improving Teacher Performance

As assistant principal for curriculum and instruction, you have decided to improve teacher performance in your school. You know that creating a positive attitude toward teacher evaluation is needed to make performance assessments more beneficial and less threatening. Develop a plan that will both improve classroom performance *and* create a positive attitude toward teacher evaluation. Be specific on how you will implement each step in your plan.

Exercise 3: Using Parent and Student Evaluations

Evaluating teacher performance is like walking in a minefield. One false step and you trigger conflict or litigation or both. Many teachers favor parent or student evaluations, but others clearly do not. Make a list of all the possible advantages and disadvantages of both parent and student evaluations in gaining a more comprehensive overview of teacher performance, then share your results with your peers and see if they can add to your list. When the list is complete, ask the following questions: (a) Would you favor parent or student evaluations if increases in your annual salary were to be directly linked to these evaluation results? (b) Would you favor parent or student evaluations if the granting of tenure were directly linked to these results? Are you surprised at the answers? Why?

7

Effective Leadership Through Effective Staff Development

In This Chapter

A major goal of effective schools is to maximize human potential. The best way to achieve this goal is through a personalized, structured, and systematic staff development process designed to develop individual skills and knowledge. This chapter discusses the importance of a comprehensive staff development program as a leadership competency that is responsive to the personal and professional needs of teachers. Assistant principals in high-performing schools play a central part in developing and maintaining programs that promote educational excellence, help teachers improve, and establish a synergistic relationship between teachers and administrators.

What Is Staff Development?

Staff development has many definitions. Terms such as *inservice education, human resources development,* and *professional* or *continuing staff development* are frequently used. Each implies a common goal: to change teacher behavior. Duke (1987) relates that effective staff development programs allow for an "ongoing socialization process" in a school whereby values, key expectations, and norms governing behavior are reinforced or changed. When staff development is linked with the goals and culture of the school, the programs become the keystones for educational excellence. Duke (1990) defines staff development as programs or activities targeted to improve school systems, schools, and teachers, to help them achieve their respective goals and strengthen their task performance. Staff development is a planned, structured process in which activities are delivered to improve classroom performance, increase professional competency, and satisfy personal growth needs (Weller, 1999). To meet these all-inclusive requirements, teachers must have autonomy in identifying their own needs, designing their own programs, and determining which activities best promote learning. Effective programs are conducted in accordance with adult learning theory and take the form of focus groups, seminars, and traditional whole-group instruction (Weller, 1999). Teacher-led programs are viewed by other teachers in a positive light and have a significant impact on teacher morale, motivation, and self-image.

Planning Staff Development Programs

Traditional staff development programs are usually planned by central office personnel or the principal, and topic selection is usually the result of "random thinking" or "what's in vogue today." Programs are of the "one size fits all" type, usually mandatory, and designed as a "one shot and done" remedy. These programs are grounded in the belief that "more of the same" is best. These unilaterally planned programs selected by others prescribe what teachers need to *know*, what they will *learn*, and *how* they will learn the material. But Schmoker and Wilson (1993) found that traditional staff development programs result in "deficit thinking." Deficit thinking, one of the most common effects of resistance to change, is a result of defense mechanisms triggered by innuendo or implications of incompetence. An unwillingness to change springs up before the advantages of the change can be objectively presented.

Traditional staff development programs have been criticized for their lack of adequate resources and for "preaching to the choir." The topics, according to DuBrin (1995), are mostly designed to maintain the status quo and send the message that although administrators are dissatisfied with teacher performance, they are at a loss for coming up with a better alternative. Teachers view staff development as "regulatory." Programs do not meet their personal or professional needs, and there is little if any follow-up support or evaluation. All of these factors make any top-down type of staff development program ineffective.

Process Management and Staff Development

Assistant principals can take leadership initiative by designing staff development programs through the *process management* model. Highly effective in the business world, process management is used to promote efficiency and effectiveness in change initiatives. Process management is a systems-thinking approach to improvement that calls for synergistic efforts between management and labor in planning, coordinating, and evaluating programs (Swift, Ross, & Omachonu, 1998). Table 7.1 presents a five-step process management model.

As shown in the figure, process design begins with the leader's personal commitment to make improvements *with* representatives of the work force. As a team, the process is then designed through mutually targeted improvements, and a step-by-step plan is developed that clearly delineates the roles and responsibilities of each party. Coordinating the improvement process requires shared responsibility and authority. Employees assume primary responsibility for program implementation, with management being responsible for providing resources and moral support.

Program evaluation is both formative and summative in nature. Formative evaluation is used to adjust for inadequacies in the process design and delivery system. Summative evaluation methods provide an overall assessment of the impact of the change variable. The end result is more effective and efficient change through teams, empowered employees, a plan for improvement based on process design, and evaluation processes that allow for midcourse corrections and the assessment of overall impact.

Process management replaces "randomized prescription" (anything labeled as innovative and somewhat successful) and "volume thinking" (the idea that more is better). Volume thinking supplies more of the same, and randomized presciption ignores the need for a personalized approach to problem solving. Each school is different by nature of its faculty, staff, students, administrators, and parents, and for successful outcomes to take place, the specific needs and expectations of the school must be addressed.

The learning outcomes model described by West-Burnham (1993) is a process management model with six core components. Each component is essential for promoting an effective learning outcomes staff development program:

1. Have those undergoing change plan the program for change.
2. Use learning strategies appropriate for the target audience and vary the learning activities and instructional delivery methods frequently.
3. Vary time requirements for learning, but make sure learning is sequential and comprehensive, not fragmented in scope.
4. Actively involve learners in the learning process.
5. Base instruction on previous knowledge and skills. Pretesting allows for the introduction of new knowledge and keeps learner interest high.
6. Conduct formative and summative assessments to redirect and enrich learning and instruction.

Table 7.1 Five-Step Process Management Model: A Systems Approach to
　　　　　Effective Outcomes

1. Personal Commitment	Leader makes a personal commitment to make improvements through leader and member participation.
2. Process Design	Process improvement plan is developed with clearly defined goals and activities, and roles and responsibilities are clearly delineated.
3. Process Coordination	Members primarily responsible for program completion share responsibilities and authority.
4. Evaluation	Formative and summative evaluation methods are used to adjust program activities and assess overall impact.
5. Effective and Efficient Outcomes	

In this model, the program is tailored to the needs of teachers and not to administrator convenience or preferences. As adult learners, teachers need the practical, not the theoretical; they want hands-on examples and information they can apply immediately in their classrooms. Programs that do not provide these essential components or that fail to convince teachers that new practices are superior to existing ones will fail to change teacher behavior.

Three other components are equally essential to making staff development programs effective for teachers (Weller & Weller, 2000). First, those doing the training must have *credibility* with teachers. Having "teachers train teachers" is not a novel idea, but it is one that is rarely practiced. Respected peers carry more credibility with teachers than do consultants, regardless of their academic credentials, theoretical knowledge, or reputation. Second, there must be a *rewards* system for improvement after staff development. Teachers are in the best position to develop a rewards and recognition system that is meaningful to them. Moreover, teachers are the ones who should evaluate peer performance and designate who should be rewarded. Third, teachers must have the *autonomy* to plan and implement the staff development they deem necessary. When teachers have the authority to determine what is needed, staff development is meaningful and intrinsically rewarding.

Staff Development and Change: Survey Results

We asked 100 assistant principals what if any responsibilities they had for planning teacher staff development programs. Of the 94% responding to the question, over 80% indicated they had little if any responsibility. Those with some responsibility for planning staff development programs noted they were on a committee or team responsible for staff development. This usually consisted of representation on a school's site-based council or committee designated for planning staff development programs or other teacher-related matters. Approximately 13% responded that they had total responsibility for planning teacher staff development programs.

Comments from those assistant principals with some involvement in planning programs varied, but generally indicated that program topics came from central office personnel, usually a director for staff development, or from the principal. Rarely was teacher input mentioned as a source for program topics.

Assessing Teacher Staff Development Needs

Although a variety of techniques exist for assessing the staff development needs of teachers, the three most common techniques are classroom observations, the voluntary exchange of ideas with peers and assistant principals, and needs assessment inventories. Identifying needs precedes planning for any type of staff development program. Two types of needs should be assessed: operational and individual needs. *Operational needs* focus on the needs of teams, work groups, or other configurations requiring the involvement of more than one teacher. *Individual needs* are specific needs held by individuals. Operational and individual needs can, on occasion, be synonymous, and programs can be designed to meet both types of needs. Individual needs must first be satisfied, however, so teachers can concentrate on operational needs. For example, a staff development program could be organized first around "clusters" of individual teacher needs with multiple sessions running concurrently. These daylong sessions could take the form of focus groups or seminars and address specific individual needs. Day 2 could then be devoted to meeting operational needs through large group sessions. Follow-up

Assistant Principals on Staff Development for Teachers

"Our staff development is arranged by the staff development coordinator in the central office or by the principal. To be honest, I know what teachers say they need and I know there is a better way to deliver it."

"My principal plans it. She keeps up on all the latest things being offered, gets all excited, and plans what the teachers will receive."

"I think most staff development programs waste teachers' time. At our school, the leadership team decides on which topics are needed. There are three teachers, four administrators, and three department heads making the decisions. The teachers are outnumbered."

SOURCE: 2000 Survey of 100 Practicing Assistant Principals From Urban, Rural, and Suburban Schools

or "break-out" sessions could then be conducted to help teachers apply newly learned knowledge or skills to their unique situations.

Developing a Needs Assessment

Assistant principals can take the lead in developing needs assessment instruments from information gained through teacher conversations, classroom observations, or individual teacher requests. Needs assessments should be anonymous to allow for candid responses. Needs should be identified as personal or professional, and operational or individual. Table 7.2 presents a sample needs assessment inventory of staff development topics for identifying operational and individual needs. As shown in Table 7.2, this assessment can be placed on a Likert-type scale with appropriate high to low descriptors for the stem items (topics). Rating scales should have an *even*-number response range to ensure respondents a "forced choice." Odd-numbered response scales, say 1 to 5, allow for a midpoint, a "neutral" response. People have opinions, mild or strong, and even-numbered response scales, such as 1 to 6, require them to come down on one side of the scale or the other.

Analyzing needs assessment results through frequency count and percentage allows for rank ordering of topics for program planning. The results will indicate clusters of needs or interests expressed by teachers and the number of teachers most likely to attend each session. Those topics of high interest or need should be presented on two separate occasions to allow for teacher choice. This format usually attracts some teachers who originally expressed neither need nor interest.

Assistant Principals on Individual Improvement Plans

How familiar are assistant principals with the literature on effective staff development?
- 50% said they were "somewhat familiar."
- 20% said they were "familiar."
- 30% said they were "unfamiliar."

How much knowledge do assistant principals have on adult learning theory?
- 78% said they had little or no specific knowledge of adult learning theory.

Do assistant principals have the knowledge they need to develop improvement plans for teachers needing remediation or assistance in implementing newly learned staff development skills?
- 69% said they had some specific knowledge of how to develop teacher improvement plans. Less than 20% said that they actually developed such plans.

SOURCE: 2000 Survey of 100 Practicing Assistant Principals From Urban, Rural, and Suburban Schools

Support for Staff Development Training

Teachers need prompt, accurate feedback and administrator support if change in behavior is to be effective. Joyce and Showers (1988) found that teachers who receive frequent feedback and moral support from administrators are more effective in applying new knowledge and skills than teachers with administrators who are critical or indifferent to newly learned behaviors. Administrators who establish peer coaching networks or teacher support groups promote *retention* of newly learned behaviors and increase teacher *satisfaction* with the changes in their behavior.

Contributing to the success of peer coaching networks is a structured process that includes a review of lesson plans, classroom observations, and mutually agreed on improvement plans that specify areas needing improvement and activities designed to facilitate improvement. Effective coaching outcomes also depend on the willingness of the teacher to be coached, the degree of trust and openness between the teacher and the coach, and the degree to which the targeted change in behavior is valued by the teacher.

Table 7.2 Needs Assessment Inventory for Operational and Individual Staff
　　　　　　Development Needs

Directions: Listed below are staff development topics proposed by teachers. The
inventory is divided into two sections with topics placed between the two sections.
Read each topic and then respond first to Section I, Operational Needs, by circling the
number on the interest scale that corresponds to your need for staff development on
the topic. Next, read the topic and then circle the number on the interest scale that
corresponds to your need for staff development under Section II, Individual Needs.
Responses will be anonymous.

Section I Operational Needs				Topics	Section II Individual Needs			
Low	Moderate	High	Very High		Low	Moderate	High	Very High
1	2	3	4	1. Time management	1	2	3	4
1	2	3	4	2. Stress management	1	2	3	4
1	2	3	4	3. Conducting effective meetings	1	2	3	4
1	2	3	4	4. Conducting effective parent-teacher conferences	1	2	3	4
1	2	3	4	5. Building validity and reliability into teacher-made tests	1	2	3	4
1	2	3	4	6. Saying "no" to accepting additional assignments when work agenda is full	1	2	3	4
1	2	3	4	7. Applying the Myers-Briggs Personality Type Indicator to classroom instruction	1	2	3	4
1	2	3	4	8. Conflict management techniques	1	2	3	4
1	2	3	4	9. Classroom management techniques	1	2	3	4
1	2	3	4	10. Applying the critical thinking concept to classroom instruction	1	2	3	4
1	2	3	4	11. Other(s) 1. _____ 2. _____ 3. _____	1	2	3	4

Ineffective Staff Development Programs

Characteristics of ineffective staff development programs are as follows:

- Lack of a comprehensive plan with a clear focus and sequence of delivery
- Lack of sufficient resources, administrative support, and follow-up activities such as peer coaching networks
- Lack of practical applications and hands-on activities for immediate use for participants
- Lack of relevance or importance to participants regarding implications for improving student learning
- Lack of a theoretical base to support new programs and practices
- Lack of teacher input in planning and implementing learning activities (Smylie & Carson, 1991)

Additional factors have been identified as contributing to ineffective staff development programs. Teachers have a more positive attitude toward staff development when programs are conducted on "school time" rather than on "personal time" (Weller & Hartley, 1994). Teachers resent infringements on time not included under contract and lose respect for administrators who expect or require teachers to "work without pay." This includes programs scheduled before and after regular school hours and on days prior to the opening of school. Joyce and Showers (1988) note the importance of a school's culture for effective staff development programs. Teachers at schools lacking a culture where personal and professional development are valued view staff development as just another mandated, waste-of-time exercise. Moreover, when creativity or innovation is discouraged or unrewarded in schools, teachers see little value in taking the initiative or going beyond the status quo.

How Adults Learn

Traditional staff development programs, despite their potential for contributing to effective teaching and student learning, do not take into consideration how adults learn best, nor are the activities built around adult learning theory. Adult learners, for example, are more self-disciplined and less dependent than children. Adult learners enjoy shaping their own learning experiences and find risk taking challenging. Adults are more self-motivated when they deem the learning to be either personally or professionally important and when they can see an immediate and direct application of learned material to their classroom. When these criteria are met, learning becomes fun and satisfying (Levinson, 1978; Sheehy, 1976).

For adults, the learning environment needs to be informal and action oriented. Adults learn quickly, and rapid pacing stimulates interest. Lectures and long periods of noninvolvement create lack of interest, whereas demonstrations and case studies trigger interest and attention. Direct and immediate feedback regarding learning mastery is essential, and any redirection in learning should be done quickly with a variety of activities.

Adult Development Stages

Adult development stages also influence adult learning. Cross (1981) notes that those 18 to 22 years of age focus on adventure, and autonomy is a major concern. Adults between 23 and 28 years of age look for new friendships, are more mature, begin to contemplate marriage, and begin to explore different careers or contemplate career goals. From 29 through 34 years of age, job stability is desired, mentors are sought for guidance, singles often marry, separation and divorce occur, and long-range security becomes important. Being successful takes on major importance, and teachers may experience conflict between leaving the profession and job security. Between 39 and 42 years of age, promotion becomes very important and mortality becomes an issue. Dependent ties with the boss and spouse are reduced as reassessment of personal priorities and values take place. The time to change is running out. Between ages 43 and 55, careers peak, and adults begin to serve as mentors to others. Community involvement is high as children leave home. New hobbies and interests emerge, and self-satisfaction and lifestyle enjoyment begins. This is the age for the greatest job productivity for teachers and administrators remaining in their career fields. From ages 56 to 63, retirement preparation is a major concern. Spouses and friendships become important and goals to be fulfilled consume effort and time.

Career teachers in particular, those age 40 and older, have their time and priorities well planned; they do not want to waste time in meetings; they are not highly receptive to new ideas or innovations; and they seek satisfaction from professional achievements. Teachers in this age bracket are good, dedicated teachers who seek to do what is best for their students. Therefore new programs or new practices must have both personal and professional appeal before these teachers will be willing to commit the time and effort required to change their behavior (Krupp, 1983).

A summary of the findings regarding characteristics about adult learners is presented below.

1. *Motivation:* Internal, not external, motivators promote adult learning. Forced training may cause animosity.

2. *Self-Learning:* Adults are self-directed learners and gain satisfaction from choosing how and what they learn. Learning for learning's sake is secondary to job enrichment learning.

3. *Immediate Gratification:* Adults want to apply new knowledge and skills immediately and enjoy success in their own work environments.

4. *Experience:* Adults have had many life experiences, and their values and beliefs are firm. Change is slow, and to promote it in adults, the change variable *must* represent "something better" than that which exists and it must coincide with "reality" as they know it.

Teams and Staff Development

In some quality-oriented, high-performing schools, teacher teams plan and conduct their own staff development programs. In these schools, teams engage in a four-step planning model to address curriculum changes, acquire new knowledge and skills, and improve teaching and learning practices (Weller, 1999):

1. Teachers brainstorm and use other problem-solving techniques to identify knowledge and skills that are essential to classroom effectiveness, and then they determine how this knowledge can be best learned and taught. Goals and measurable, behavioral objectives are subsequently developed to guide the learning process.

2. Enabling objectives—learning activities essential to fulfilling the behavioral objectives—are then developed. A list of needed resource materials is compiled and carefully matched to each behavioral objective.

3. A detailed, sequential plan is developed that lists the learning objectives, the learning materials, and the facilitators needed to accomplish each behavioral objective. Timelines and alternative learning methods are included to ensure proper pacing and content mastery.

4. Evaluation methods, both formative and summative, are identified to assess program effectiveness. Evaluation data may include student tests, teacher diagnostic logs, parent feedback, and teacher self-assessment inventories.

Planning for Effective Staff Development: The Continuous Improvement Model

Aristotle said, "We are what we repeatedly do. Excellence, then, is not an act, but a habit." Habits leading to excellence begin with working smarter, not harder; being open to new ideas and perceptions of others; and adopting the continuous improvement model as a way of work life. Deming (1986) included continuous improvement as one of his 14 points for implementing quality management practices. Deming maintains that by nature people want to do their best, take pride in their work, and be actively involved in the workplace. It is the job of management to help them do so by improving the system in which they work. In schools practicing the principles of quality management, student achievement on standardized tests increased, student absenteeism and dropout rates decreased, and teachers' job satisfaction and morale increased (Weller & Hartley, 1994). Central to promoting these positive outcomes are principals and assistant principals who place high value on administrator-teacher collaboration, teamwork, research, and data-based decision making. Continuous improvement becomes a daily goal of teachers and administrators whose mission is to produce quality in everything they do. Quality in these schools is a conscious commitment to excel.

The infrastructure of continuous improvement is a research-centered, data-driven model, the Plan, Do, Check, Act (PDCA) cycle, which has proven successful for school, department, and classroom improvement. The PDCA cycle is not new to education. This improvement cycle describes what good classroom instruction calls for and what effective teachers do daily. That is, they plan their lessons (plan), they teach their lessons (do), they evaluate the impact of their teaching (check), and they decide whether to reteach the lesson or go on to the next lesson based on the effectiveness of their teaching (act). Whether they reteach or go forward, they begin the PDCA cycle again by planning for instruction.

The PDCA cycle encompasses the following:

1. *Plan:* Identifying opportunities to improve or to solve problems requires an analysis of the problems or areas needing improvement. When this is accomplished, a plan is developed on how to *solve* the problem or *improve* the situation. Two or three plans may be developed at once and rank-ordered. If the first plan is ineffective, the second plan may be implemented, and so on. One way a team can approach planning is to apply the Delimiting Factors Model. Planning should begin with the following questions:

"Where are we?"
"Where do we want to be?"
"What is keeping us from getting there?"
"How can we best get there?"
"How will we know when we get there?"

2. *Do:* Implement the plan as developed. Pilot-testing is recommended when implementing new programs or methods. Part of the Do cycle is using formative evaluation techniques that provide feedback as the project unfolds so that modifications can be made.

3. *Check:* Evaluate the effects of the implemented plan. Summative evaluation measures are used to assess the overall impact of the program when activities are concluded.

4. *Act:* Adopt the program if evaluation results yield the desired outcome. If results are unsatisfactory, implement a contingency plan by returning to the Do and Check phases of the PDCA cycle.

Assistant principals can apply the PDCA cycle to solve school and department problems, and teachers can apply the model to solve classroom or team problems. Teachers and teacher teams are more willing to apply the PDCA cycle when formal training is provided and training examples include current problems (Weller & Hartley, 1994).

Goals and Goal Setting

Goal setting is essential to achieving effective and efficient outcomes. Goals are "global" statements identifying a desirable end state and are used as the source of program evaluation. Goals, clearly stated, can be transformed into measurable behavioral objectives. When the behavioral objectives are met, the goals are achieved. When the goals are achieved, the plan is successful.

In shared governance schools, where teacher teams are empowered to make decisions, staff development activities become more meaningful because teachers themselves plan staff development programs around their own needs and interests. Schmuck and Runkel (1994) list six essential factors teams must address to achieve program goals:

1. Goals must be few in number, realistic, challenging, and attainable.
2. Tasks to achieve goals must be personally challenging and professionally rewarding.
3. Individuals must have the necessary skills to problem-solve and resolve conflict.
4. Individuals must see a personal or professional benefit in achieving goals.
5. Individuals must have the knowledge and skills to meet goals.
6. Goals must be important to the leaders and to the organization to receive the necessary resources and support.

According to Blanchard (1995), "Goal setting is only effective when leaders *prepare* their people to set goals and then set up situations where they can perform well enough to achieve them" (p. 19). This requires training, commitment of resources, adequate time to meet the goals, and a work environment that rewards goal setting and goal completion. Leaders who are not committed to these criteria are neither serious nor dedicated to achieving excellence.

Classification of Goals

Goals have three classifications: (a) program goals, (b) staff goals, and (c) learner goals. *Program goals* provide clear direction for school programs. *Staff goals* focus on improving members in a department or work unit. *Learner goals* are those that focus on specific, expected outcomes for students (Ubban & Hughes, 1987).

Assistant principals, as instructional leaders, can facilitate the school's and departments' collective efforts to develop program, staff, and learner goals. With the participation of the school's faculty, program and staff goals should be developed, prioritized, and reviewed annually. Learner goals are the primary responsibility of teachers, who develop behavioral or instructional objectives to achieve them.

Objectives to Achieve Goals

Depending on the goals to be achieved, one of two basic types of objectives is recommended. *Improvement objectives* are most appropriate for program and staff goals because they identify how the goals will be achieved, but they may or may not specify the expected behavioral outcome. An example of an improvement objective is, "Teachers will attend a one-day staff development session on how to infuse multiple intelligences theory into their classroom teaching practices." The intent of the objective is to tell *who* will do *what* and *how,* not to describe what teacher behavior will be after the session.

Instructional or *behavioral objectives* are appropriate for learner goals because they guide the instructional process by providing specific measurable or observable outcomes. Specific conditions under which measurement will occur and the criteria for learner success or mastery are key components of behavioral objectives. An example of such an objective is, "After students read a short passage, they will be able to correctly identify 98% of the nouns, verbs, and adjectives contained in the passage."

Setting Personal Goals

Personal goal setting is a cognitive process that can be used to increase motivation and job satisfaction. Personal goals are choices individuals make about available options or desired end states, and they have four key components. These components are goal *importance,* which determines the amount of energy one will put forth to achieve the goal; goal *content,* which is the desired outcome; goal *commitment,* which determines how dedicated one is to meeting the goal; and goal *intention,* which is the basic motivating force needed to reach the goal. Specific goals are more likely to be achieved than general goals. Difficult goals require greater commitment and intention than do easier goals, but they may be more satisfying. When those seeking to improve participate in goal setting, commitment to the goal increases. Periodic feedback from superiors is essential to goal achievement (Lock & Latham, 1995).

For assistant principals, goal-setting theory has particular value in that it provides a vehicle to facilitate teacher motivation. Lock and Latham (1995) present five conditions to be met if administrators are to help teachers develop individual goals for self or organizational improvement:

1. Goals must be set devoid of emotional influences or situations, and the personal benefits must be appealing and clearly stated.

2. Goals must be prioritized and teachers must understand that difficult goals have higher risk but provide greater satisfaction.

3. Goals must be specific, perceived as attainable, and worth the effort expended.

4. Frequent, specific feedback is essential to sustain motivation and to increase the probability the goal will be attained.

5. New goals are more likely to be developed when goal completion is personally satisfying, when rewards meet expectations, and when one is satisfied that the effort expended was worth the reward.

It is most important that the assistant principal make clear the personal benefits to teachers when helping them set goals. Self-interest must be aroused, the rewards must be personally appealing, and teachers must deem the goal attainable. If there is a choice among multiple goals, choice will be based on value judgments. Goals deemed more personally valuable will then be targeted for completion. There is no substitute, however, for the assistant principal's knowing the teachers on a personal basis for individual goal setting to be successful. To know what teachers personally value requires a knowledge of their personal needs and professional aspirations. Attending team meetings, engaging in chit-chat, and conducting teacher self-improvement seminars are ways assistant principals can come to personally know their teachers.

The Clinical Supervision Model

The clinical supervision model is an effective approach assistant principals can use to help teachers set realistic, challenging, and achievable goals. The five-step model presented below presupposes that the assistant principal has a close working relationship with teachers.

1. Individual conferences are held to clarify and prioritize personal and professional needs. Personal and professional needs are closely linked, and in work settings the achievement of professional needs will often also meet a teacher's personal needs.

2. Focusing the conference on self-improvement and emphasizing the importance of identifying goals allows for professional and personal development. Some teachers may view goal setting as a self-disclosure of weaknesses or deficiencies and may hesitate to be candid. Unless mutual trust and respect exist, open and honest dialogue cannot take place.

3. Knowing the teacher's ability is central to identifying realistic, challenging, and attainable goals. Regardless of the teacher's ability level, the assistant principal should help the teacher set short-term, easily attainable goals first so immediate success and satisfaction can result. Early success builds confidence and increases the likelihood that additional goal setting will take place.

4. A jointly developed action plan follows the goal identification process. Action plans include objectives to meet the goals, a list of needed resources to meet each objective, and an evaluation design and timeline to assess progress toward goal achievement.

5. When the goals are met, the process is repeated with additional and more challenging goals.

When several teachers or departments have similar needs or goals, assistant principals can use this opportunity to plan staff development programs. In this way, staff development becomes personalized, individualized, and professionally rewarding.

Evaluation Techniques for Staff Development Programs

Evaluation is a process designed to assess the worth or *effectiveness* of something. Many different types of evaluation techniques exist to assess the effectiveness of staff development programs, and each technique has a specific purpose. Presented below are five different evaluative techniques assistant principals can use to assess the effectiveness of staff development activities: (a) the pre- and posttest design, (b) the postprogram questionnaire, (c) the self-report instrument, (d) the classroom observation checklist, and (e) the portfolio.

Pre- and posttests are designed to assess the degree to which program activities changed participant behavior. Comparing the results of the pretest, a survey administered prior to training activities, to those of the posttest, the same survey administered at the conclusion of the training, gives one a more accurate measure of program effectiveness than results from a posttest-only survey.

If a pretest is not administered prior to the training activity, the data can still be captured by designing an ex post facto survey like the one presented in Table 7.3. Here the survey questions are placed in the middle of the instrument and the pre- and posttest rating scales are at either side of the questions. Some argue that the pretest ratings may not be as reliable when teachers are asked to recall their knowledge or skill levels prior to the training, but others argue that any index that serves as a pretreatment measure is better than no measure at all. We agree with the latter argument because most participants can make reasonable judgments about their prior knowledge levels.

As shown in Table 7.3, the pre- and posttest assessment method is presented in a before-and-after format. Assistant principals can get an overall measure of workshop effectiveness by comparing the means (average scores) on each question and then using this same information to determine which participants need additional assistance on one or more activities. Numbers will dictate the means of assistance to be provided. For example, two or three teachers needing assistance can be handled individually or through peer coaching, whereas five or more teachers needing assistance may require a seminar or focus group. Larger numbers may call for whole-group instruction in which a scaled-down version of the original program is presented.

The next evaluative instrument, the *postprogram questionnaire,* is the most common type of survey instrument used to assess program effectiveness. This after-the-fact assessment or posttest-only format is used to assess participant perception of the impact of the program. This type of evaluation fails to capture measurable data to assess the degree to which participant behavior changed, however. The postprogram questionnaire lists the survey questions on the left side of the page and a Likert-type scale on the right side of the page. Results are analyzed by frequency count and percentage, and mean scores are computed for each survey question.

Self-report instruments are questionnaires designed to assess teachers' perception of program effectiveness *after* they have had time (3 or more days) to reflect on or apply newly learned behaviors. Castetter (1996) notes that self-report instru-

Table 7.3 Ex Post Facto Survey for Time Management Workshop

Directions: This ex post facto survey is designed to assess your perception of your knowledge and skills about time management *before* workshop activities begin and then *after* workshop activities are conducted. Statements are presented in the middle of the survey and rating scales for your knowledge and skill levels in relation to the statements are presented on both sides of the statements. On the *before workshop* scale rate your knowledge and skill levels prior to workshop activities. Then rate your knowledge and skill levels on the *after workshop* scale when workshop activities are concluded.

Before Workshop				Questions	After Workshop			
Never	Seldom	Frequently	Always		Never	Seldom	Frequently	Always
1	2	3	4	1. I set daily goals.	1	2	3	4
1	2	3	4	2. I set daily work priorities.	1	2	3	4
1	2	3	4	3. I procrastinate over unpleasant tasks.	1	2	3	4
1	2	3	4	4. I complete the toughest assignment when I am "fresh" and motivated.	1	2	3	4
1	2	3	4	5. I delegate tasks of lesser importance to others.	1	2	3	4
1	2	3	4	6. I say "no" to accepting additional assignments when my work agenda is full.	1	2	3	4
1	2	3	4	7. I limit my "socializing" time with others to my lunch break.	1	2	3	4
1	2	3	4	8. I always take work with me so I don't waste time.	1	2	3	4
1	2	3	4	9. I assess how my time is spent every day and plan to make more efficient use of time the next day.	1	2	3	4
1	2	3	4	10. I work on hard or complicated tasks a piece at a time.	1	2	3	4
1	2	3	4	11. I tell others when I do not want to be distracted.	1	2	3	4
1	2	3	4	12. I set deadlines for myself regardless of deadlines imposed by others.	1	2	3	4

Table 7.4 Self-Report Instrument for Assessing Knowledge and Skills for Team Building

Directions: This self-reporting instrument is designed to help you improve your application of team-building knowledge and skills. After a time period of 3 or more days after the staff development, and after reflecting on and applying the newly learned behaviors, rate your perceived performance level on each of the knowledge/skill area statements presented below. You may use the reverse side to make additional comments concerning any assistance needed in strengthening your performance.

Questions	Response Scale			
	Low	Moderate	High	Very High
1. My understanding that team members must share their social norms with other team members is	1	2	3	4
2. My understanding that team members must take mutual responsibility for failure and success is	1	2	3	4
3. My understanding that team members should always feel free to express their honest opinion is	1	2	3	4
4. My understanding that teams should be able to discuss issues openly and listen to all points of view before making a decision is	1	2	3	4
5. My understanding that team members must recognize and utilize the talents of each team member is	1	2	3	4
6. My understanding that team members must be skilled in conflict management techniques is	1	2	3	4
7. My understanding that team members must take turns in assuming leadership roles is	1	2	3	4
8. My understanding that team members must raise controversial issues in team meetings rather than in private "gripe sessions" is	1	2	3	4
9. My understanding that team members must share equally in resolving issues that keep the team from achieving its goal is	1	2	3	4
10. Comments regarding additional assistance needed:				

_____   _____

_____   _____

_____   _____

ments are a highly valuable source of information because they allow teachers to disclose important information about themselves after having had time to reflect on or apply new knowledge or skills. Koehler (1990) found that self-report instruments have positive psychological effects on teachers because the instruments are perceived as a nonthreatening approach to performance improvement and they allow teachers time to "self-test" newly acquired behaviors. Further, teachers are more receptive to improvement suggestions after they know their limitations from actual classroom application. Table 7.4 presents an example of a self-report instrument designed to assess a participant's ability to implement team-building skills after staff development training. On this type of instrument, results are tallied by frequency count and percentage and are used to provide individual or group assistance. Comments from participants on this type of instrument are most important to address. Frequently, comments represent the exact kind of assistance teachers need to effectively apply newly learned behaviors.

Observation checklists are instruments used to assess the degree to which knowledge or skills are actually applied in the classroom. The observations are like those used to assess teachers' performance for contract renewal or tenure, where observers rate the observed behaviors of teachers on established performance criteria. On observation checklists, teachers' behaviors are observed by others and then recorded relative to the frequency and degree to which the behaviors were actually applied in the classroom. Table 7.5 presents an observation checklist designed to assess the degree and frequency with which first-year teachers apply nine basic teaching principles after staff development training.

As shown in Table 7.5, the observation checklist assesses the number of times (frequency) a teacher displays one or more of the nine teaching behaviors, over a 25-minute time period, using 5-minute time segments as observation windows. Some behaviors may not be observed due to the content being taught or the structure of the lesson. Preobservation and postobservation conferences should be held, with the postobservation conference being diagnostic, used to identify ways to strengthen teacher competency.

Portfolios are a recent approach to evaluating teacher performance that allow teachers more control over what they deem important to be assessed. Portfolios are especially valuable in assessing teacher classroom performance given the wide distribution of student ability levels. Portfolios are document focused, assembled by the teacher, and jointly evaluated through jointly established criteria. Videotapes, copies of lesson plans, samples of students' work, and self-report instruments are examples of documents for portfolios. Wolf (1991) notes that portfolios allow administrators to actually see teaching and learning "as they unfold and extend over time" (p. 136), thus providing an accurate and authentic assessment of classroom performance. Wolf notes that the success of portfolio evaluation depends on the mutual agreement between teacher and administrator about

Table 7.5 Observation Checklist for Assessing First-Year Teachers on Effective
        Teaching Practices

Directions: This observation checklist is designed to assess the *frequency* and *degree* to which first-year teachers implement nine effective teaching strategies. The nine strategies are presented in Section I; the frequency of observed occurrences of each strategy in 5-minute time modules is presented in Section II; and the degree to which each strategy is implemented within each of the time modules is presented in Section III. The observer will identify which of the nine teaching behaviors were displayed during each of the 5-minute time modules, over a 25-minute time period, and then record the frequency of the behavior and the degree to which it was implemented.

Section I *Strategies*	Section II *Frequency of Occurrence in 5-Minute Modules*	Section III *Degree of Implementation*			
		0 None	1 Somewhat	2 Moderately	3 Frequently
1. Classroom rules and procedures are enforced and student behavior is continuously monitored.		0	1	2	3
2. High expectations for student success are maintained for all students in all activities.		0	1	2	3
3. Inappropriate behavior of students is handled promptly.		0	1	2	3
4. Student work is checked and prompt feedback is provided (this includes homework, seatwork, and questioning procedures).		0	1	2	3
5. Interactive teaching takes place (this includes presenting and explaining new material, discussions, question sessions, checking for student understanding, and reteaching).		0	1	2	3
6. Academic instruction is observed (this includes time spent on direct instruction and management of student work).		0	1	2	3

Table 7.5 Continued

Section I	Section II	Section III			
Strategies	*Frequency of Occurrence in 5-Minute Modules*	*Degree of Implementation*			
		0	1	2	3
		None	Somewhat	Moderately	Frequently
7. Pacing of information is appropriate for students' ability to comprehend.	_____ _____ _____ _____	0	1	2	3
8. Transitions from one learning activity to another are made smoothly and without confusion.	_____ _____ _____ _____	0	1	2	3
9. Lessons are presented clearly, logically, and sequentially, and illustrations and instructional objectives are provided.	_____ _____ _____ _____	0	1	2	3

document content. Portfolio documents should be listed and copies retained by both parties for future reference. No effort to score the documents should be made because of the diversity of the documents found in portfolios. If scoring is deemed essential, teachers and administrators should jointly agree on the criteria and method of scoring, and both criteria and scoring method should be applied evenly across the board.

Managing Change for School Improvement

Staff development means change, and assistant principals must be knowledgeable about change theory and change practices to effectively maximize teacher potential. Bringing about effective change is one of the most important, and one of the most difficult, tasks confronting leaders. Presented below are four key factors that promote effective change.

1. Leaders must personally believe in and have a strong commitment to the change variable. Modeling expected behaviors is the single most important behavior a leader can exhibit to demonstrate both belief and commitment.

2. Leaders must have access to adequate fiscal and material resources before the change initiative begins.

3. Leaders must include all of those involved in the change initiative in planning, implementing, and evaluating the change effort. Plans must include goals and objectives, clearly defined activities to prepare teachers for change, and both formative and summative evaluation procedures.

4. Leaders must be able to specify the personal and professional benefits of change to teachers. When teachers are aware of direct, personal benefits, they view change more positively. (Weller & Weller, 2000)

Pointing out the personal or professional benefits of change is not always an easy task. Benefits may be short or long range in nature and may have either direct or indirect effects on individual teachers or teacher groups. Some teachers will immediately see the benefits of change and others will not. It is this latter group of teachers that will require individual attention and that will call for creativity on the part of the leader to explain the positive effects of change for each teacher. Without recognizing a personal benefit to change, teachers will actively or passively resist change.

Resistors to Change

Understanding the more common resistors to change allows leaders to be more successful when planning for change. Connor (1995) presents these common resistors:

1. *Lack of Trust:* Distrust in those who propose change will cause resistance and magnify the effects of other resistors. Even when there is no personal threat from change, people will suppose that hidden agendas exist and that these agendas will become obvious only after the change takes place. When leaders lack trust in subordinates, only selective reasons for change are made known. This serves to compound the lack of trust among subordinates.

2. *Change Is Unnecessary:* When an obvious need for change is not evident, change will be resisted. People who are not currently experiencing problems or who are successful under existing conditions will resist change, and leaders who exaggerate how well the organization functions under existing conditions will find it difficult to convince people of the need for change.

3. *Change Is Not Feasible:* When past change efforts have failed, regardless of the cause of the failure, people will greet a new change initiative with cynicism and doubt and look for reasons to resist it. Moreover, when change appears to be radically different from existing conditions, the change process will be viewed as too difficult to attempt and too likely to fail.

4. *Economic Threats:* If change threatens a decrease or loss of income, benefits, or job security, change will be strongly resisted regardless of how good it is for the organization.

5. *Cost of Change:* Any change is costly, and when sufficient fiscal and material resources are not available to complete the change effort, failure results. Failure promotes negative attitudes in subordinates about change and leadership competency.

6. *Fear of Personal Failure:* Change frequently requires learning new knowledge and skills or performing traditional tasks differently. People who are unwilling to learn or believe they cannot adapt their behavior will resist change. People will more likely accept change if job security is assured, if adequate training is provided, and if they have input in planning the training process.

7. *Loss of Status and Power:* All people have status or power in their work unit or the organization itself. Any change that they perceive as lessening their status, power, or job security will be strongly resisted. On the other hand, those who see an opportunity to increase their status or power will strongly favor change.

8. *Threats to Values and Ideals:* When personal values and ideals are threatened, change is resisted. Any replacement will have to be viewed as good, personally desirable, and better than what is replaced. When new cultures replace existing ones, subordinates must be involved in planning and implementing training that promotes the new values, norms, and behaviors that will replace existing ones.

9. *Threats of the Unknown:* People fear the unknown. Discontented as some are with their work, when change is mentioned, fear of an uncertain future suddenly transforms the current situation into one that is much desired. Known factors and the reliable behaviors of others provide psychological security—an individual security blanket. Change often threatens one's security and triggers many possible outcomes deemed less desirable than existing circumstances. When psychological security is threatened, change is resisted.

The Politics of Change

Implementing change requires an understanding of politics and subcultures in the organization. In all organizations, there are subcultures or informal groups that have their own power structures and political interactions. Each group member has status, power, and a role to play in the group's membership. When change threatens the group's power and status structure, resistance to change will take place through overt or covert activity. Certain guidelines exist, however, to minimize political activity. Kotter (1996), Weller (1999), and Connor (1995) suggest several precautions change agents should take when implementing change:

1. Identify leaders of subcultures or informal groups and discuss change initiatives. Be honest. Present the pros and cons of change and listen to their inclinations and seek their support. Know who is for and against change. When

the majority of these power agents view change favorably, include them in the planning, implementation, and evaluation stages of the change process.

2. Let everyone know the specific reasons why change is needed and that the leadership is fully committed to change. Provide data, testimonials, and other evidence that the change will yield positive personal and organizational outcomes. Verify that the needed resources exist to complete the change process and provide an estimate of time for completing the change initiative.

3. Act quickly. This sends the message that you are serious about change. Initiate planning by establishing an overall planning committee and several committees with specific tasks related to the planning function. Have each committee chaired by power agents, whether they support change or not, because their influence is wide and they are respected by their peers. Their visible moral support is essential from the beginning.

4. Create a sense of urgency about the need for change. Most people want to change on their own timetable and most are unlikely to understand the need for immediate action, even despite available comprehensive information. Emphasize the positive aspects of change and send the message that the sooner change takes place, the sooner all will reap the benefits.

5. Prepare people to adjust to change. Provide comprehensive training sessions where new knowledge and skills can be learned, and allow time for the practice of newly learned behaviors. Without adequate training, the change initiative will fail.

6. Begin implementing the change initiative on a small scale. Pilot-testing is most desirable because it allows for identification of problems that can be adequately and quickly addressed. Whereas failure on a large scale negatively impacts morale and confidence in leadership, success stimulates enthusiasm for change throughout the organization, regardless of the size or amount of the change.

7. Demonstrate continuous commitment to the change initiative. Reward and praise effort and success, and keep people continuously informed about the process of change through team or committee meetings, newsletters, and whole-group meetings. Make sure the rewards are meaningful to subordinates and not just rewards that you value or think they should value.

8. Evaluate the change process through formative and summative evaluation methods. Use formative evaluation to modify, redesign, or remediate. Formative evaluation helps ensure success and a more effective and efficient end product.

9. Become knowledgeable about the staff development process and change by becoming an active consumer of the research and literature on these topics. The box on page 190 provides suggested readings to begin to develop such a foundation of knowledge.

Let's Review

This chapter provided ways that assistant principals can step into a leadership role in the area of teacher staff development. Guidance for assistant principals in planning, implementing, supporting, and evaluating staff development programs was included, as well as information for further skill and knowledge development in the area of the political ramifications for assistant principals who initiate change.

Exercises

Exercise 1: Understanding the Staff Development Process

In small groups, develop a comprehensive staff development program for a hypothetical school with a faculty of 50 teachers. Carefully outline the specific steps you would take to ensure you have the most effective staff development program possible. Be sure to include the following:

1. Needs assessments and other data-gathering instruments
2. How the data from these survey instruments will be used in planning and implementing your staff development program
3. How you will evaluate the effectiveness of your staff development program
4. How you will use teacher evaluation results to ensure mastery of learned behaviors

Exercise 2: Curriculum Improvement

You are a new assistant principal, and one of your assigned duties is to coordinate staff development in your school. Your principal is concerned that teachers "really learn" the recently state-mandated curriculum for English and social studies. She says, "No hit-or-miss activities or anything else for this show. I want these adults to learn the material cold! You figure it out and you do it."

How would you go about constructing a staff development program that would ensure maximum content mastery from teachers? Be specific in your answer.

Exercise 3: Setting Up Challenges

As an assistant principal, you have visited with at least seven faculty members who have expressed a need for "more of a challenge" in their work. This does

---

Readings on Staff Development

- *Clinical supervision,* by R. Goldhammer (1969). New York: Holt, Rinehart, & Winston.
- *Training in Organizations: Needs Assessments, Development, and Evaluation* (2nd ed.), by I. L. Goldstein (1996). Monterey, CA: Brooks/Cole.
- *Supervisory Leadership,* by A. Ghatthorn (1990). Glenview, IL: Scott, Foresman.
- *Student Achievement Through Staff Development,* by B. Joyce and B. Showers (1988). New York: Longman.
- "Instructional Improvement Through Personnel Evaluation," by J. R. Thorson (1987), in *Educational Leadership, 44,* 52-54.
- *Quality Human Resources Leadership: A Principal's Handbook,* by L. D. Weller and S. Weller (2000). Lanham, MD: Scarecrow.

---

not mean more work, but the ability to more fully use their creativity, talents, and skills on the job. How would you go about making their job more challenging? Be specific in your answer.

Case Study: Here We Go Around the Bush

Mr. Heighton Hopper, known as "Hi" for short, thought Dale Hill, his assistant principal, to be very capable, very bright, and highly aggressive. "Energetic" is how Hi describes Dale. The superintendent has just informed Hi that his school has been selected as a pilot-study school for implementing shared governance. As Hi states, "Dale, the super is nuts. He said he wants teachers to be empowered to make decisions, solve problems, and help run the school. On another topic, he wants me to attend a Las Vegas convention with him. I want you to begin the staff development training while I'm gone." Hi looks Dale in the eye and then says, "You can do it. Nothing to it. Herd 'em up and move 'em out into the real world of grief, turmoil, and indigestion—that's administration. While I'm gone, you run the school. Just don't let it fall to pieces on me. I think I'm going to be the next assistant superintendent for finance when old Caddimus Lopper retires in June. Bless his heart."

Dale knows just what to do to get this shared governance "stuff" going. "Why," he says, "these teachers just love to be on committees, love to talk, love to waste time, and to make BIG D-E-C-I-S-I-O-N-S." He tells Hi, "I'll have everything in perfect order when the old Hi Hopper comes hopping back from Vegas. Hi, count on me to make sure teachers love this empowerment stuff."

Dale's first morning in command begins with an announcement over the intercom prior to the beginning of the first class period: "All teachers must report to a called faculty meeting this afternoon at 3:30 sharp! No excuses for missing the meeting will be accepted. None! No makeup meeting will be conducted. Names must appear on the attendance sheet and the sheet will be picked up, by me, at 3:40, sharp! Enjoy your day."

At 3:30 sharp Dale circulates the attendance sheet and at 3:40 picks up the sheet with several teachers still entering the auditorium. Dale takes the microphone and begins his prepared motivational speech.

"Do I have a surprise for you! You are all going to be empowered to make decisions, solve problems, and help me and the Hi Hopper run this school. Now, the Hopper is in Vegas. When he comes back, we are going to show him how industrious we are as a group, our little family. Aren't we having fun? Well, anyway, I'm going to plan your change program for you. Teach you to be real effective leaders. I'm going to set up committees, assign you to them, and make sure you all work hard at being successful. Now, with power comes responsibility. You know that, I think. Command is lonely, and you and you alone are held responsible for your actions. So when you get this training I'm going to prescribe, then you are going to be responsible, totally responsible, for any foul-ups you or your committees or teams or whatever you call 'em commit. You foul up with parents, you solve the problem you create. See, you're empowered. You foul up with students, same story. You are big boys and girls now. Don't you just love being empowered?

"Let's start in and make the old Hi Hopper real proud. I'll call once for volunteers for committees. Hearing none, I'll do that random assignment thing that's so popular. Well, on second thought, I'll circulate a sign-up sheet for the required duty you must perform. Remember, each of the nine committees must have at least five people. I like even numbers. Keeps things tidy. And by the way, I have lined up that super-duper consultant that you all call 'Freddie the Con Man' for your listening pleasure. I think he's a real motivator. Just what this faculty needs. A fire! A real fire! Well, now I want all you 'laters,' you know, all you who came in late, to stand. That's it. Come on up here so we can all see you, and I'll have a real special committee assignment for you as a group. Now, you are all dismissed. Oh! Have a good evening."

Next morning at 8 a.m., the chair of the board of education calls Dale. She introduces herself as Mrs. Jim Nasium and says she is concerned about the morale of the some 20 teachers who called her last evening. She thinks empowerment is a very good idea and is behind the superintendent's recommendations for shared governance, but she says she wants to meet with Dale that afternoon in her office, at her law firm, to discuss teacher concerns.

As Dale ends the call, Ms. Steady, the secretary, comes to Dale's door all flustered and in tears. It seems that over 20 teachers called in sick and 10 took personal leave days. There is no way classes can be covered, and students are already rowdy and roaming the halls. Dale quickly gets on the intercom and demands that all teacher aides and teachers having a planning period report to the office. Just then, Ms. Steady hands a cell phone to Dale. It is Hi Hopper calling to see if everything is OK. Dale takes the phone and begins the conversation with, "Hello Hi! Having a great time, are you? Big winner at craps, are you? Well, let me fill you in on what these teachers really think about shared governance. Why . . . "

1. What do you think Dale told Mr. Hopper about his first day in command?

2. If you were Dale's best friend and he asked you for advice about how he could have handled things differently, what would you tell him? Start from the beginning of the case study and carefully identify each of Dale's mistakes, and then be specific about the corrective advice you would give him.

3. Are there any early indications that Dale's approach to initiating change may be "unorthodox"? Be specific. If you were the Hi Hopper, what would you see in Dale that would give you confidence that Dale would be successful in implementing this change?

Appendix

This appendix contains a sampling of checklists and forms that can be used by assistant principals to help them move from managers to leaders. The samples provide assistant principals a means of stepping back and seeing "the big picture" in various arenas of leadership rather than continuing with their heads down, concentrating solely on the managerial tasks at hand.

Administrator's Checklist for the Beginning of the School Year

This is not a complete list of things to do. However, it may help you prepare.

Policies

_____ 1. Review student, personnel, and instructional policies in Board Of Education manual.

_____ 2. Check all new or updated policies and share with faculty.

_____ 3. Prepare faculty handbook.

_____ 4. Prepare student handbook.

_____ 5. Post required notices, including the following: No Tobacco, No Weapons, Drug-Free School, Nondiscrimination, Workers' Compensation, Pesticides Used, Emergency Exit Lights, Disabled Parking, Disabled Restrooms.

_____ 6. Hold a meeting for review of Code of Ethics with all staff.

_____ 7. Review discipline policies and procedures with all staff members.

_____ 8. Hold a meeting on procedures for recognizing and reporting child abuse with all staff.

_____ 9. Review special education requirements and changes with teachers.

Personnel

_____ 1. Ensure that all positions are filled by qualified people.

_____ 2. Send welcome letter to all staff members.

_____ 3. Ensure that the personnel records of new hires are in order.

_____ 4. Complete the master schedule.

_____ 5. Plan a teacher orientation. Assign mentor teachers for each new teacher, where possible. If there are no trained mentor teachers available, assign best possible "buddy teacher."

_____ 6. Complete committee assignments (or procedure for choosing committees). At a minimum, each school needs (a) leadership team, (b) hospitality/ sunshine committee, (c) curriculum committee, (d) public relations committee, (e) safety committee.

_____ 7. Plan duty rosters/special assignments (bus duty, restroom & hall monitor, etc.).

_____ 8. Prepare preplanning time schedule.

_____ 9. Plan faculty meeting agendas.

_____ 10. Complete special assignments for the first day of school (assist bus or car drop-off/pickup, volunteer assistance in office, etc.).

_____ 11. Review office personnel assignments.

_____ 12. Plan and hold meetings with custodians, food service personnel, and bus drivers before the first day of school. Discuss schedules, work rules, school procedures.

Students

_____ 1. Set registration times and procedures (written requirements and forms available).

_____ 2. Ensure student information is entered *correctly* in computer system.

_____ 3. Assign students homerooms.

_____ 4. Plan orientation/open house activities.

_____ 5. Prepare schedules for students.

_____ 6. Ensure that student records are in good order and available for teacher review.

_____ 7. Select student volunteers to help in orientation, touring, etc.

_____ 8. Prepare forms for lunch, insurance, etc. for distribution.

School Study for Attendance Action Plan

Data to Gather

✓	Your school's Spring Performance Report
✓	Other attendance data
✓	Report on attendance for specific groups, collated by a school staff member

Attendance Trends for All Students

Year	Rate
1997-98	
1998-99	
1999-00	
2000-01	

2000-01 Results for Specific Groups

Groups	Rate
Male	
Female	
White	
African American	
Hispanic	
Asian	
Other Ethnicity	
Low Socio-Economic Status	

Enter data here from report collated by a school staff member. Then make notes on thoughts and concerns.

Student Questionnaire Data (Optional)

Look through those results for information that may bear on attendance issues.

Question	Notes on Positive Implications for Student Achievement	Notes on Negative Implications for Student Achievement

Attendance Rate: A Deeper Look

Use your school's attendance data and any other relevant data here.

Issue	Trend Shown in the Data	Thoughts and Concerns
Patterns of absences (excused, unexcused, days of the week, etc.)		
Patterns of tardies (excused, unexcused, days of the week, etc.)		
Kinds of learning activities that could enhance attendance (different learning styles, real-life situations, etc.)		

Key Points

From all the data above, identify the Key Points you want to contribute to the School Study Overview.

School Study for Safety and Discipline Action Plan

Data to Gather

✓	School Safety Report
✓	Surveys of parents, teachers, and students
✓	Any information available from local law enforcement

Discipline and Discipline Referral Trends

Factor	Trends in the Data	Thoughts and Concerns
Categories of discipline and discipline referrals showing a steady increase		
Patterns by grade		
Patterns by day or time		
Other patterns you identify		
Comparison by gender		
Comparison by ethnicity		
Comparison by family income level		
Comparison of regular and special education		

Specific Challenges

Issue	What Evidence Do We Have on the Presence or Absence of This Problem?	What Strategies Do We Have to Prevent This Problem, and Do They Reach All Grades?	What Professional Development Are We Providing for Our Staff?	Thoughts and Concerns
Drug involvement				
Gangs				
Sexual harassment				
Racial, ethnic, or religious harassment				
Bullying and teasing				
Early identification of problem behavior				
Equitable and consistent discipline				
Follow-up to ensure consequences are applied				
Up-to-date crisis response plan				

Title IV: Safe and Drug-Free Schools and Communities

Issue to Consider	Information We Acquired	Thoughts and Concerns
Main things this program is doing to improve student performance		
Main barriers to this program's efforts to improve student performance		

Key Points

From all the data above, identify the Key Points you want to contribute to the School Study Overview.

Introductory Administrative Meeting With Students
at the Beginning of the School Year

Introductions
Welcome
School Pride
       Academics
       Athletics
       Attendance
       Character
Mission
       Learning/High Expectations
Agenda Book/Handbook
Bus Discipline
Discipline
       In-School Suspension
       Out-of-School Suspension
       Alternative School
Harassment
Bullying
Threats
Fighting
Inappropriate School Behavior
Dress Code
Reporting Incidents, Items, & Behavior
Self-Reporting
School Resource Officer

Bus Discipline Evaluation

Bus drivers: Please return this information to the assistant principal in charge of bus discipline. Your name is not required.

Please rate the following items using a scale from 1 to 4.

```
1 = Strongly Disagree
2 = Disagree
3 = Agree
4 = Strongly Agree
DNA = Does not apply to my situation
```

_____ 1.   My bus discipline referrals were handled promptly.

_____ 2.   Bus discipline referrals were handled according to the discipline code.

_____ 3.   I feel supported by the outcome of the majority of my bus referrals.

_____ 4.   The assistant principal was available/accessible when I required assistance.

_____ 5.   Bus dismissal occurs in an organized/safe manner.

_____ 6.   My copy of the referral was returned in a prompt manner.

_____ 7.   The assistant principal explained bus conduct expectations to my students at the start of the year.

_____ 8.   I feel supported in conferences with parents or students.

_____ 9.   Assigned seats improved the behavior on my bus.

____ 10.   This school has a strong bus discipline program.

My comments/suggestions for improving bus procedures:

_____

_____

_____

Teacher Discipline Evaluation

Teachers: Please return this information to the assistant principal.

Please rate the following items using a scale from 1 to 4.

> 1 = Strongly Disagree
> 2 = Disagree
> 3 = Agree
> 4 = Strongly Agree
> DNA = Does not apply to my situation

_____ 1. The assistant principal for discipline is visible in the hall and classroom.

_____ 2. The assistant principal for discipline educated students regarding the discipline code during the first week of school.

_____ 3. The assistant principal for discipline is accessible when assistance on discipline matters is needed.

_____ 4. The assistant principal for discipline is available for parent conferences.

_____ 5. The assistant principal for discipline consistently enforces the school's discipline plan.

_____ 6. The assistant principal for discipline deals promptly with discipline referrals.

_____ 7. The assistant principal for discipline returns the pink copy of the referral promptly.

_____ 8. The assistant principal for discipline supports teachers in conferences with parents and students.

_____ 9. The assistant principal for discipline creates individual student discipline plans for chronic offenders.

_____ 10. The assistant principal for discipline empowers/supports the staff in the management of classroom discipline.

My comments/suggestions for improving schoolwide grade discipline:

_____

_____

_____

Guidelines for Addressing School Attendance Issues

Absences will be followed up by school personnel in the following order.

After 1 absence

- The homeroom teacher will check for parent excuse (after absence). The homeroom teacher needs to call the parent if no excuse is sent. Document the reason for the absence on an attendance card and give all excuses (written or verbal) to the attendance clerk.
- The teachers will assign students makeup work and set a reasonable date for its return.

After 2 absences

- The homeroom teacher will make a phone contact to the parents.

After 4 absences

- A documented phone call will be made to the parents by the homeroom teacher informing the parents of absences and concerns and requesting a parent conference if grades are affected.

After 6 absences

- A letter will be mailed to parents.
- The counselor will receive a copy of the letter.
- The counselor will share the letter with the school social worker.

Note: It is *essential* that *all* excuses, verbal and written, be reported to the attendance clerk. A referral to the school social worker will be made after 20 absences (excused or unexcused) for all students. Attendance guidelines will be monitored monthly through Student Support Team (SST) meetings.

Teachers Support Specialist (TSS) Action Plan for Madison County High School Beginning Teacher (BT) Checklist

Early August

_____Check with administration about TSS assignment

_____Get name & address of BT

_____Collect information about school & county (teacher handbook, student planner, brochures, phone lists of faculty & subs, pay scales) to share with BT

_____Get BT's room assignment (verify location so you can show BT when you visit school)

_____Get BT's teaching books & material

_____Call BT & make arrangement for lunch and/or school visit

_____Get BT a small gift for room

_____Meet new BT

_____Discuss the general information about school (use collected material)

_____Discuss the handbook (rules, dress code, special meetings the 1st day of school, general info about normal procedures)

_____Visit school with BT—tour the facility & assigned room

_____Invite BT to move in early if interested

_____Begin setting your own classroom in order to have time for the BT when school begins

Preplanning

_____Introduce BT to other teachers, staff, & custodial crew

_____Introduce BT to department members

_____Help move materials/equipment (VCR/overhead) into the room

_____Show BT where everything is located (media center for grade book, supplies, computer lab)

_____Give help in BT's room (if wanted)

_____Show curriculum materials or introduce to person who knows BT's subject matter

_____Go over discipline procedures; review handbook; discuss student insurance forms, lunch forms, & schedule changes

_____Go over lunch duty schedules

_____Discuss extracurricular activities & fund-raising requests

_____Go over equipment/supplies

_____Check periodically during each day to see if any information is needed

_____Invite BT out to lunch with other teachers

_____Discuss copy procedures

_____Discuss check sheets for special ed students

_____Discuss procedures for 1st day activities

_____Give pep talk day before school begins

First Week of School

_____Check in to see how BT made it during the 1st day of school (any problems to discuss or questions?)—celebrate!
_____Check each day to see if there are any problems
_____If possible, invite BT to eat with you in the lunchroom
_____Show BT how lesson plans are recorded and procedures for filing lesson plans
_____Review attendance policies
_____Go over discipline (ISS, lunch detention, Saturday school, alternative school)
_____Suggest & talk about effective discipline techniques/policies

First Month (September)

_____Invite BT to observe your class
_____Conduct postobservation conference
_____Sit with BT at a pep rally and/or invite to home football game
_____Discuss problems BT may be having with specific students or concepts
_____Go over teacher evaluation process
_____Discuss midterm progress reporting procedures (suggest grading setup)
_____Show BT where student permanent records are kept; explain graduation tests
_____Discuss picture day
_____Look at time management techniques
_____Explain various student services, clubs, and/or referral programs
_____Conduct preobservation session #1
_____Conduct scheduled BT observation #1
_____Conduct postobservation conference #1
_____Go over end-of-the-9-weeks grading information
_____Discuss pacing of curriculum—offer resources/suggestions for "best" times to do certain content material

Second Month (October)

_____Show BT how to use the Scantron machine
_____Discuss progress report day
_____Discuss parent/teacher conferences & open house policy
_____Discuss problems BT may be having with specific students or concepts
_____Conduct preobservation session #2
_____Conduct scheduled BT observation #2
_____Conduct postobservation conference #2 (make notes; be specific with suggestions in preparation for 1st classroom observation)
_____Discuss 9th-week exam schedule & procedures

Third Month (November)

_____Give encouraging note to BT

_____Continue to check with BT occasionally about problems/questions

_____Discuss the BT's first observation, which should take place around this time

_____Discuss specific student behavior problems & learning problems that have been identified

_____Suggest ways to keep students motivated

_____Conduct preobservation session #3

_____Conduct scheduled BT observation #3

_____Conduct postobservation conference #3

Fourth Month (December)

_____Discuss holiday traditions as far as school parties, etc.

_____Discuss leave time during holiday and how pay works

_____Discuss snow day procedures

_____Discuss the problems encountered around winter holidays as students become unsettled and unruly

_____Explain that exams are right after winter break (it's a quick 2 weeks!)

_____Do something special for BT

Fifth Month (January)

_____Discuss the end-of-the semester grading procedures

_____Discuss any special grading procedures (end of 1st semester)

_____Discuss semester schedule changes

_____Review lesson plans and procedures in preparation for 2nd observation

_____Conduct preobservation session #4 (in preparation for 2nd observation, if needed)

_____Conduct scheduled BT observation #4

_____Conduct postobservation conference #4

Sixth Month (February)

_____Discuss the procedures normally followed for contracts for coming year

_____Give BT a "pick me up" gift or note

_____Discuss any problems related to observation, students, or the curriculum

Seventh Month (March)

_____Discuss any special problems with BT about students, procedures, etc.
_____Discuss budget requests & priority of needs
_____Conduct preobservation session #5 (if needed)
_____Conduct scheduled BT observation #5
_____Conduct postobservation conference #5
_____Give end-of-3rd-9-weeks information
_____Discuss standardized testing procedures & schedule
_____Discuss 3rd observation

Eighth Month (April)

_____Discuss registration information for students
_____Discuss prom/graduation attendance requirements
_____Conduct preobservation session #6 (if needed)
_____Conduct scheduled BT observation #6
_____Conduct postobservation conference #6

Ninth Month (May)

_____Discuss honors night and voting process for special senior awards
_____Discuss end-of-the-year tasks so BT can begin a few of the tasks early (get a copy of the old checklist if new one is not available)
_____Discuss final exams and procedures for exemptions, etc.
_____Discuss yearbook & senior rec days
_____Review locker checks, book collection, fees owed, student failing list (especially seniors)

Postplanning (June)

_____Remind of graduation attendance & invite BT to come with you
_____Discuss permanent record procedures
_____Discuss how to prepare purchase request for next year
_____Go over checklist with BT & discuss checkout procedures on last day
_____Show how to close up room for summer/store items, etc.
_____Celebrate!!

The Peer-Coaching Process

A. **The Preobservation Conference:** The coach and teacher meet to plan for a classroom observation. The meeting should have several purposes:

1. To identify the focus of the observation and discuss the session plan to be observed (topic, goals, group methods selected, anticipated difficulties, what type of feedback the coach is looking for, etc.)
2. To select a method of gathering data during the observation (checklist, observation forms, anecdotal notes, videotapes, etc.)
3. To gather background information on the class to be observed (students' ability levels, problems that have occurred, and any other special circumstances)
4. To choose a time for the observation

B. **The Classroom Observation:** The coach should do the following:

1. Arrive on time at the beginning of the session and stay until the end
2. Sit in an unobtrusive location where he or she can observe both the teacher and the students
3. Be prepared to take notes unless he or she has been asked not to
4. Gather data based on methods discussed in the preobservation

C. **The Postobservation Conference:** The following points should be considered when meeting to discuss the data gathered by the coach during the observation:

1. Hold the conference as soon as possible after the observation
2. Make sure the teacher sets the agenda and that the environment is comfortable
3. Establish a collegial tone so that the conference is not judgmental or evaluative
4. Limit the feedback to what the teacher can use

Evaluation of Team Performance
Carroll County Schools Problem-Solving Team

	Disagree				Agree
1. This group is a place where people feel comfortable expressing themselves.	1	2	3	4	5
2. I like the members of my group.	1	2	3	4	5
3. I would like to work with members of my group on another similar project.	1	2	3	4	5
4. We are a closely knit group and we are able to create synergy.	1	2	3	4	5
5. I contribute important ideas to the decision-making process.	1	2	3	4	5
6. I have a lot of influence on the group's decision making.	1	2	3	4	5
7. I contribute important information to the group's decision making.	1	2	3	4	5
8. Without my input and suggestions, the group would not be able to make as good a decision.	1	2	3	4	5
9. During group meetings, I participate whenever I want to.	1	2	3	4	5
10. The other members of the group like me.	1	2	3	4	5
11. Other members of the group really listen to what I say.	1	2	3	4	5
12. I am a genuine member of the group.	1	2	3	4	5
13. We approach our task in an organized manner.	1	2	3	4	5
14. This group is able to accomplish its purpose.	1	2	3	4	5
15. Our group works well together.	1	2	3	4	5
16. This group uses effective decision-making techniques.	1	2	3	4	5
17. The group reached the right decision.	1	2	3	4	5
18. We selected the best alternative available.	1	2	3	4	5
19. Our group's decision/solution is appropriate.	1	2	3	4	5
20. I support the final group decision.	1	2	3	4	5
21. I am willing to put my best effort into carrying out the group's final decision.	1	2	3	4	5

References

Allport, G., & Postman, L. (1954). The basic psychology of rumor. In W. Schramm (Ed.), *The process and effects of mass communication.* Urbana: University of Illinois Press.

Bagin, D., & Gallagher, D. R. (2001). *The school and community relations* (8th ed.). Boston: Allyn & Bacon.

Bardwick, J. M. (1991). *Danger in the comfort zone.* New York: AMACOM.

Bass, B. M. (1965). *Organizational psychology.* Boston: Allyn & Bacon.

Bass, B. M. (1985). *Leadership and performance beyond expectations.* New York: Free Press.

Bass, B. M. (1990). *Handbook of leadership: A survey of theory and research.* New York: Free Press.

Bass, B. M., & Stogdill, R. M. (1990). *Bass and Stogdill's handbook of leadership* (3rd ed.). New York: Free Press.

Bennis, W., & Nanus, B. (1985). *Leaders: The strategies for taking charge.* New York: Harper & Row.

Blanchard, K. (1995). Goal setting is overrated. *Quality Digest, 15*(11), 19-20.

Blau, P. M., & Scott, W. R. (1962). *Formal organizations: A comparative approach.* San Francisco: Chandler.

Bloom, B. S., Engelhart, M. D., Furst, E. J., Hill, W. H., & Krathwohl, D. R. (1956). *Taxonomy of educational objectives: Handbook I: The cognitive domain.* New York: David McKay.

Bonner, S. F. (1977). *Education in ancient Rome.* Berkeley: University of California Press.

Borg, W. R. (1987). *Applying educational research: A practitioner's guide for teachers* (2nd ed.). White Plains, NY: Longman.

Borg, W. R., & Gall, M. D. (1983). *Educational research: An introduction* (4th ed.). White Plains, NY: Longman.

Bossert, S. T. (1988). School effects. In N. J. Boyan (Ed.), *Handbook of research on educational administration* (pp. 341-352). New York: Longman.

Boulding, K. E. (1989). *Three faces of power.* Newbury Park, CA: Sage.

Brewer, J. H., Ainsworth, J. M., & Wynne, G. E. (1984). *Power management: A three-step program for successful leadership.* Englewood Cliffs, NJ: Prentice Hall.

Buckner, K. G., & McDowelle, J. O. (2000). Developing teacher leaders: Providing encouragement, opportunities, and support. *National Association for Secondary School Principals Bulletin, 84*(616), 35-41.

Burbules, N. C. (1993). *Dialogue in teaching: Theory and practice.* New York: Teachers College Press.

Burns, J. M. (1978). *Leadership.* New York: Harper & Row.

Carlson, R. V. (1996). *Reframing and reform: Perspectives on organization, leadership, and school change.* White Plains, NY: Longman.

Castetter, W. B. (1996). *The human resource function in educational administration* (6th ed.). Englewood Cliffs, NJ: Prentice Hall.

Chubb, J. E., & Moe, T. M. (1990). *Politics, markets, and America's schools.* Washington, DC: Brookings Institution.

Clampitt, P. G. (1991). Communication tips for school leaders. *High School Magazine, 1,* 12-14.

Clark, L. H., & Starr, I. S. (1991). *Secondary and middle school teaching methods* (6th ed.). New York: Macmillan.

Connor, D. R. (1995). *Managing at the speed of change: How resilient managers succeed and prosper where others fail.* New York: Villard.

Cross, P. (1981). *Adults as learners.* San Francisco: Jossey-Bass.

Cuban, L. (1990). Reforming again, again, and again, *Educational Researcher, 19,* 3-13.

Culbertson, J. A., Jacobson, P. B., & Reller, T. L. (1960). *Administrative relationships: A casebook.* Englewood Cliffs, NJ: Prentice Hall.

Cunningham, W. C., & Gresso, D. W. (1994). *Cultural leadership: The culture of excellence in schools.* Needham Heights, MA: Allyn & Bacon.

Daft, R. L. (1991). *Management* (2nd ed.). New York: Dryden.

Deal, T. E. (1993). The culture of schools. In M. Sashkin & H. J. Walberg (Eds.), *Educational leadership and school culture.* Berkeley, CA: McCutchan.

Deming, W. E. (1986). *Out of the crisis.* Cambridge: MIT Press.

Dilenschneider, R. L. (1994). *On power.* New York: HarperCollins.

Dolan, G. K. (1996). *Communication: A practical guide to school and community relations.* Belmont, CA: Wadsworth.

Drucker, P. (1995). *Managing in a time of great change.* New York: Truman Talley.

DuBrin, A. J. (1995). *Leadership: Research, findings, practice, and skills.* Boston: Houghton Mifflin.

DuFour, R., & Eaker, R. (1992). *Creating the new American school.* Bloomington, IN: National Education Service.

Duke, D. L. (1987). *School leadership and instructional improvement.* New York: Random House.

Duke, D. L. (1990). Setting goals for professional development. *Educational Leadership, 48,* 71-75.

Duke, D. L., & Stiggins, R. (1991). Beyond minimum competency: Evaluation for professional development. In J. Millman & L. Darling-Hammond (Eds.), *The new handbook for teacher evaluation* (pp. 116-132). Newbury Park, CA: Corwin.

Edmonds, R. R. (1982). Programs of school improvement: An overview. *Educational Leadership, 40,* 4-11.

Eggen, P. D., & Kauchak, D. P. (1988). *Strategies for teachers: Teaching content and thinking skills.* Englewood Cliffs, NJ: Prentice Hall.

English, F. W. (1994). *Theory in educational administration.* New York: HarperCollins.

English, F. W. (1995). *Educational administration: The human science.* New York: HarperCollins.

Etzioni, A. (1988). *The moral dimension: Toward a new theory of economics.* New York: Free Press.

Evertson, C. M., & Wade, R. (1989). Classroom management and teaching style. *Elementary School Journal, 89,* 374-393.

Fiedler, F. E. (1967). *A theory of leadership effectiveness.* New York: McGraw-Hill.

Fink, S. (1986). *Crisis management.* New York: American Management Association.

Fisher, B. A. (1980). *Small group decision making* (2nd ed.). New York: McGraw-Hill.

Fitzgerald, C., & Kirby, L. K. (1997). *Developing leaders.* Palo Alto, CA: Davies-Black.

Fleishman, E. A., Harris, E. F., & Burtt, R. D. (1955). *Leadership and supervision in industry.* Columbus, Ohio: State University Press.

Foucault, M. (1972). *The archaeology of knowledge.* New York: Pantheon.

French, J. R., & Raven, B. H. (1968). Bases of social power. In D. Cartwright & A. Zander (Eds.), *Group dynamics: Research and theory* (pp. 259-270). New York: Harper & Row.

Gallagher, D. R., Bagin, D., & Kindred, L. W. (1997). *The school and community relations* (6th ed.). Boston: Allyn & Bacon.

Gardner, H. (1993). *Frames of mind: The theory of multiple intelligences.* New York: Basic Books.

Gardner, J. (1990). *On leadership.* New York: Free Press.

Ghatthorn, A. (1990). *Supervisory leadership.* Glenview, IL: Scott, Foresman.

Goldhammer, R. (1969). *Clinical supervision.* New York: Holt, Rinehart, & Winston.

Goldstein, I. L. (1996). *Training in organizations: Needs assessments, development, and evaluation* (2nd ed.). Monterey, CA: Brooks/Cole.

Golen, S. (1990). A factor analysis to barriers of effective listening. *Journal of Business Communication, 27,* 25-36.

Grady, M. L., Wayson, W. W., & Zirkel, P. A. (1989). *A review of effective schools research as it relates to effective principals.* Tempe, AZ: University Council for Educational Administration.

Hall, E. T. (1980). *The silent language.* Westport, CT: Greenwood.

Hammer, M., & Champy, J. (1993). *Reengineering the cooperation.* New York: HarperCollins.

Harris, T. E. (1993). *Applied organizational communication.* Hillsdale, NJ: Lawrence Erlbaum.

Henderson, J. E., & Hoy, W. K. (1983). Leader authenticity: The development and test of an operational measure. *Educational and Psychological Research, 2,* 123-130.

Henson, E. M. (1996). *Educational administration and organizational behavior* (4th ed.). Boston: Allyn & Bacon.

Hersey, P., & Blanchard, K. H. (1988). *The management of organizational behavior* (5th ed.). Englewood Cliffs, NJ: Prentice Hall.

Hirschman, A. O. (1970). *Exit, voice, and loyalty: Responses to the decline in firms, organizations, and states.* Cambridge, MA: Harvard University Press.

Hoffman, J. D., Sabo, D., Bliss, J., & Hoy, W. K. (1994). Building a culture of trust. *Journal of School Leadership, 3,* 17-23.

Hoy, W.K., & Miskel, C. G. (1996). *Educational administration: Theory, research, and practice* (5th ed.). New York: McGraw-Hill.

Hughes, L. W., & Hooper, D. W. (2000). *Public relations for school leaders.* Boston: Allyn & Bacon.

Imundo, L. V. (1993). *The executive supervisor's handbook.* New York: AMACOM.

Jenkins, K. D., & Jenkins, D. M. (1995). Total Quality Education: Redefining the middle school concept. *Middle School Journal, 27*(2), 3-11.

Johnson, J. H. (1985). *Four climates of effective middle schools* (NASSP schools in the middle: A report on trends and practices). Reston, VA: National Association of Secondary School Principals.

Jones, L. T. (1991). *Strategies for involving parents in their children's education* (Fastback, No. 315). Bloomington, IN: Phi Delta Kappan Educational Foundation.

Joyce, B., & Showers, B. (1988). *Student achievement through staff development.* New York: Longman.

Kaiser, J. S. (1993). *Educational administration* (2nd ed.). Mequon, WI: Stylex.

Kaplan, F. E. (1984). Trade routes: The manager's network of relationships. *Organizational Dynamics, 12,* 37-52.

Kauchak, D. P., & Eggen P. D. (1989). *Learning and teaching: Research-based methods.* Boston: Allyn & Bacon.

Kawalski, T. J. (1996). *Public relations in educational organizations: Practice in an age of information and reform.* Englewood Cliffs, NJ: Prentice Hall.

Keegan, J, (1987). *The mask of command.* New York: Penguin.

Kellerman, B. (1999). *Making the connection between politics and business: Reinventing leadership.* Albany: State University of New York Press.

Kindred, L. W., Bagin, D., & Gallagher, D. R. (1990). *The school and community relations* (4th ed.). Englewood Cliffs, NJ: Prentice Hall.

Knezevich, S. J. (1975). *Administration of public education* (3rd ed.). New York: Harper & Row.

Koehler, M. (1990). Self-assessment in the evaluation process. *National Association of Secondary School Principals Bulletin, 74*(527), 40-44.

Korda, M. (1975). *Power!* New York: Random House.

Kotter, J. P. (1985). *Power and influence: Beyond formal authority.* New York: Free Press.

Kotter, J. P. (1996). *Leading change.* Boston, MA: Harvard Business School Press.

Krathwohl, D. R., Bloom, B. S., & Masia, B. B. (1964). *Taxonomy of educational objectives: Handbook II: The affective domain.* New York: David McKay.

Krupp, J. A. (1983). Sparking an aging staff through increased awareness of adult development changes. *School Administrators Association of New York Journal, 10,* 9-13.

Kudlacek, B. (1989). Special interest groups: Friends or foes? *National Association of Secondary School Principals Bulletin, 73,* 29-32.

Lawrence, G. (1993). *People types and tiger stripes* (3rd ed.). Gainesville, FL: Center for Applications of Psychological Type.

Leavitt, H. J. (1978). *Managerial psychology* (4th ed.). Chicago: University of Chicago Press.

Levine, D. U., & Lezotte, L. W. (1989). *An interpretive review and analysis of research and practice dealing with unusually effective schools.* Okemos, MI: National Center for Effective Schools.

Levinson, D. (1978). *The seasons of a man's life.* New York: Knopf.

Lewin, H., Lippit, R., & White, R. K. (1939). Patterns of aggressive behavior in experimentally created social climates. *Journal of Social Psychology, 10,* 271-299.

Lezotte, L. W., & Jacoby, B. C. (1992). *Sustainable school reform: The district contest for school improvement.* Okemos, MI: Effective Schools Products, Ltd.

Lock, E. A., & Latham, G. P. (1995). *A theory of goal setting and task performance* (2nd ed.). Englewood Cliffs, NJ: Prentice Hall.

Loinberger, H. F. (1960). *Adaption of new ideas and practices.* Ames: Iowa State University Press.

Lunenburg, F. C., & Ornstein, A. C. (1990). *Educational administration: Concepts and practices.* Belmont, CA: Wadsworth.

Lunenburg, F. C., & Ornstein, A. C. (1996). *Educational administration: Concepts and practices* (2nd ed.). Belmont, CA: Wadsworth.

Luthans, F. (1989). *Organizational behavior* (5th ed.). New York: McGraw-Hill.

Luthans, F., & Lockwood, D. L. (1985). *Organizational behavior modification and beyond.* Glenview, IL: Scott, Foresman.

Mansfield, H. C. (1985). *The prince: A new translation.* Chicago: University of Chicago Press.

Manz, C. C. (1991). *Mastering self-leadership: Empowering yourself for personal excellence.* Englewood Cliffs, NJ: Prentice Hall.

McCarty, D., & Ramsey, C. E. (1971). *The school managers: Power and conflict in American public education.* Westport, CT: Greenwood.

McEwan, E. K. (1997). *Leading your team to excellence: How to make quality decisions.* Thousand Oaks, CA: Corwin.

McMillan, J. H. (1996). *Educational research: Fundamentals for the consumer* (2nd ed.). New York: HarperCollins.

Mintzberg, H. (1989a). *Mintzberg on management: Inside our strange world of organizations.* New York: Free Press.

Mintzberg, H. (1989b). *Power in and around organizations.* Englewood Cliffs, NJ: Prentice Hall.

Morrison, E. K. (1994). *Leadership skills: Developing skills for organizational success.* Tucson, AZ: Fisher.

Myers, I. B., & McCaulley, M. H. (1985). *Manual: A guide to the development and use of the Myers-Briggs Type Indicator.* Palo Alto, CA: Consulting Psychologists Press.

Nasca, D. (1994). The impact of cognitive style on communication. *National Association of Secondary School Principals Bulletin, 78,* 13-18.

Newstrom, J. W., & Davis, K. (1977). *Organizational behavior: Human behavior at work.* Boston: McGraw-Hill.

Newstrom, J. W., & Davis, K. (1983). *Organizational behavior: Human behavior at work* (3rd ed.). Boston: McGraw-Hill.

Newstrom, J. W., & Davis, K. (1997). *Organizational behavior: Human behavior at work* (10th ed.). Boston: McGraw-Hill.

Northwest Regional Education Laboratory. (1990). *Effective school practices: A research synthesis 1990 update.* Eugene, OR: Northwest Regional Education Laboratory School Improvement Project.

Norton, S. M., Webb, L. D., Dlugash, L. L., & Sybouts, W. (1996). *The school superintendency: New responsibilities, new leadership.* Boston: Allyn & Bacon.

Ogden, E. H., & Germinario, V. (1994). *The nation's best schools: Blueprints for excellence: Vol. 2: High Schools.* Lancaster, PA: Technomic.

O'Hair, D., & Friedrich, H. G. (1992). *Strategic communication in business and the professions.* Boston: Houghton Mifflin.

Sagar, R. D. (1992). Three principals who made a difference. *Educational Leadership, 49*(5), 13-18.

Scheerens, J., & Bosker, R. (1997). *The foundations of educational effectiveness.* New York: Elsevier Science.

Schermerhorn, J. R., Hunt, J. G., & Osborn, R. N. (1993). *Basic organizational behavior.* New York: John Wiley.

Schermerhorn, J. R., Hunt, J. C., & Osborn, R. N. (1998). *Basic organizational behavior* (2nd ed.). New York: John Wiley.

Schlechty, P. C. (1990). *Schools for the twenty-first century: Leadership imperatives for educational reform.* San Francisco: Jossey-Bass.

Schmoker, M. J., & Wilson, R. B. (1993). *Total Quality Management education: Profiles of schools that demonstrate the power of Deming's management principles.* Bloomington, IN: Phi Delta Kappa.

Schmuck, R. A., & Runkel, P. J. (1994). *The handbook of organizational development in schools and colleges* (4th ed.). Prospect Heights, IL: Waveland.

Seitel, F. P. (1992). *The practice of public relations.* New York: Macmillan.

Sheehy, G. (1976). *Passages: Predictable crises of adult life.* New York: Dutton.

Smylie, M., & Carson, J. (1991). Changing the conceptions of teacher influence: The future of staff development. *Journal of Staff Development, 12,* 12-16.

Solomon, C. M. (1992). The loyalty factor. *Personnel Journal, 23,* 52-62.

Squires, D. A., Huitt, W. G., & Segars, J. K. (1984). *Effective schools and classrooms: A research-based perspective.* Alexandria, VA: Association for Supervision and Curriculum Development.

Stedman, S. C. (1987). It's time we changed the effective schools formula. *Phi Delta Kappan, 43,* 215-224.

Steinberg, R. J. (1997). *Thinking styles.* New York: Cambridge University Press.

Stevenson, K. R. (1995) Special interest groups: How to use them to your advantage. *School Business Affairs, 17,* 3-8.

Stewart, R. (1982). *Choices for managers: A guide to understanding managerial work.* Englewood Cliffs, NJ: Prentice Hall.

Stogdill, R. M. (1948). Personal factors associated with leadership: A survey of the literature. *Journal of Psychology, 25,* 35-71.

Strother, D. B. (1983). The many roles of the effective principal. *Phi Delta Kappan, 65*(4), 291-294.

Swift, J. A., Ross, J. E., & Omachonu, V. K. (1998). *Principles of total quality* (2nd ed.). Boca Raton, FL: St. Lucie Press.

Taylor, R. W. (1949). *Basic principles of curriculum and instruction.* Chicago: University of Chicago Press.

Thompson, C. (1992). *What a great idea: Key steps creative people take.* New York: HarperCollins.

Thorson, J. R. (1987). Instructional improvement through personnel evaluation. *Educational Leadership, 44,* 52-54.

Ubban, G. C., & Hughes, L. W. (1987). *The principal: Creative leadership for effective schools.* Boston: Allyn & Bacon.

Vecchio, R. P. (1988). *Organizational behavior.* Chicago: Dryden.

Vecchio, R. P. (1991). *Organizational behavior* (2nd ed.) New York: Dryden.

Wang, M. C., Haertel, G. D., & Walberg, H. J. (1993). Toward a knowledge base for school learning. *Review of Educational Research, 63,* 249-304.

Weinstein, G., & Fantini, M. D. (1970). *Toward human education.* New York: Preager.

Weller, L. D. (1993). *Total Quality Management: A conceptual overview and applications for education.* Athens, GA: College of Education, University of Georgia.

Weller, L. D. (1996). The next generation of school reform. *Quality Progress, 29*(10), 65-74.

Weller, L. D. (1998). Unlocking the culture for quality schools: Reengineering. *International Journal of Educational Management, 12*(6), 250-259.

Weller, L. D. (1999). *Quality middle school leadership: Eleven central skill areas.* Lancaster, PA: Technomic.

Weller, L. D., & Hartley, S. H. (1994). Why are educators stonewalling Total Quality Management? *The TQM Magazine, 6*(3), 23-28.

Weller, L. D., Hartley, S. H., & Brown, C. L. (1994). Principals and TQM: Developing vision. *Clearing House, 67*(5), 298-301.

Weller, L. D., & Weller, S. J. (1997). Quality learning organizations and continuous improvement. *National Association of Secondary School Principals Bulletin, 81*(591), 62-70.

Weller, L. D., & Weller, S. J. (2000). *Quality human resources leadership: A principal's handbook.* Landham, MD: Scarecrow Press.

West-Burnham, J. (1993). *Managing quality schools: A TQM approach.* Harlow, UK: Langman Group U.K. Ltd.

Wilson, M. (1993). The search for teacher leaders. *Educational Leadership, 50*(6), 24-27.

Wirt, F. M., & Kirst, W. M. (1992). *The politics of education: Schools in conflict.* Berkeley, CA: McCutchan.

Wolf, K. (1991). The school teacher's portfolio: Issues in design, implementation, and evaluation. *Phi Delta Kappan, 73,* 129-136.

Yukl, G. (1994). *Leadership in organizations* (3rd ed.). Englewood Cliffs, NJ: Prentice Hall.

Yukl, G. (1998). *Leadership in organizations* (4th ed.). Englewood Cliffs, NJ: Prentice Hall.

Yukl, G., & Tracy, B. (1992). Consequences of influence tactics used with subordinates, peers, and the boss. *Journal of Applied Psychology, 77,* 525-535.

Name Index

Subject Index

CORWIN
PRESS

The Corwin Press logo—a raven striding across an open book—represents the
happy union of courage and learning. We are a professional-level publisher of books
and journals for K–12 educators, and we are committed to creating and providing
resources that embody these qualities. Corwin's motto is "Success for All Learners."